PHILOSOPHY, POLITICS AND SOCI

FIFTH SERIES

Philosophy, Politics and Society

FIFTH SERIES

A collection edited by
Peter Laslett and James Fishkin

BASIL BLACKWELL · OXFORD 1979

© in this collection
   Basil Blackwell 1979
All rights reserved. No part of this publication may be
reproduced, stored in a retrieval system, or transmitted, in any
form or by any means, electronic, mechanical, photocopying,
recording or otherwise, without the prior permission of Basil
Blackwell Publisher Ltd.

British Library Cataloguing in Publication Data

Philosophy, politics and society.
   5th series
   1. Social sciences
   I. Laslett, Peter   II. Fishkin, James
   300′.8   H35

   ISBN 0–631–10111–X

Filmset in Great Britain by
Northumberland Press Ltd, Gateshead, Tyne & Wear
Printed in Great Britain by Billing and Sons Ltd.,
London, Guildford and Worcester.
Typography by Douglas Merritt MSIA

Contents

Introduction

'No commanding work of political theory has appeared in the 20th century.' So said Isaiah Berlin, writing in 1962 in the second volume of *Philosophy, Politics and Society,* in answer to the question *Does political theory still exist?* He was taking up a point made six years earlier in the introduction to the first volume. The outstanding difference now, in 1978, is that Berlin's assertion is no longer true.

It ceased to be so in 1971, when *A Theory of Justice* by John Rawls of Harvard was published in Cambridge, Mass.[1] Quite some part of the pursuit of political philosophy in the English-speaking world since that time has been taken up with the discussion of this Olympian work. *Philosophy and Public Affairs,* an American journal, began its career at exactly the same time and has had an important impact too. In its columns, as in those of other journals including *Political Theory* (1973 on, also American) a new descriptive adjective has been coined, *Rawlsian,* a word which will be found to be accepted currency in the collection we now present.

The most influential book to come out during what should perhaps be called the post-Rawlsian era, *Anarchy, State and Utopia*[2] by Robert Nozick, also of Harvard, appeared in 1974. It is regarded by many as a work of stature in its own right, probably as important as any other whose appearance we have recorded in earlier introductions in this series. Its author may perhaps have reason to regret that euphony has prevented his name, as it prevented the name of Montesquieu, from developing an adjectival form.

These most welcome happenings are recorded with enthusiasm here. They make the writing of this little introductory survey and assessment very much easier than it has been these twenty years or more. An English editor may be allowed a twinge of regret that none of this has occurred in his own country, and it is evident from our list of authors how heavily the balance has now come down on the Western side of the Atlantic. But we can have no sensation other than delight to be relieved of the necessity of asking anxious questions about political philosophy and the present quality

[1] Harvard University Press. British edition, Oxford University Press, 1972, during the course of publication of the previous volume of *Philosophy, Politics and Society.*
[2] Basic Books, New York; Basil Blackwell, Oxford.

of its life. It obviously flourishes, all over the English-speaking world and outside it too, and for numerous reasons other than the birth of a contemporary classic in the field. We are conscious that we may have been able to cover these other developments rather less effectively. And we rather wonder if the growing company of political theorists have properly met the challenge of the times even now.

Both Rawls and Nozick appeared earlier in the series, and the discussion of their positions is very evident in the present collection: the studies by Rae, by Fishkin and by Barry are particularly directed towards them. Scarcely any of the others fail to cite their names or to confront the Rawlsian theory, veil of ignorance contractarianism as one of us has ventured to call it. Part of our difficulty has been to prevent this theory from dominating the volume, for much recent work has already been devoted to it.[3] In making our selection we have had in mind a formidable array of issues in philosophy, politics and society which have come to the fore in the middle and later 1970s. Some have close connections with the Rawlsian debate, or are involved within it. But others stand some intellectual distance away, and all have independent origins and areas of importance. We may lay these sets of issues out under three heads.

First, those to do with the growth of human populations and with the effect on the environment, and so upon futurity, of our own relentlessly expansive activities.

Second, those to do with what might be called arithmetic humanity in relation to politics, especially the correct boundaries which should surround any human collection so that a proper political society may appear.

Third, those to do with the obligations owed to their polity by the subjects of contemporary authoritarian states.

We may begin with the third set of issues, which, though in the last few years it has come to face us with a surprising

[3] See, for example: Norman Daniels, ed., *Reading Rawls: Critical Studies of A Theory of Justice* (New York: Basic Books, 1974); Brian Barry, *The Liberal Theory of Justice* (Oxford: Oxford University Press, 1973); Robert Paul Wolff, *Understanding Rawls* (Princeton, N.J.: Princeton University Press, 1977); and the symposium in the *American Political Science Review*, vol. 69, no. 2 (June 1975).

urgency, is most easily fitted into a traditional framework of political philosophy. Those whom Western journalists call the dissidents and especially the Russians amongst them—the writers in what we all know as *Samizdat*—persistently, and in our view justifiably, protest against the failure of Western academic intellectuals to rescue them from the propaganda machines of government and the military. They insist on their incontrovertible right to be taken seriously in the *république des lettres*.

No writer from the authoritarian socialist world, or from under the domination of dictatorships of other kinds, or any who takes part in the conduct of thought in Western European Communist parties, makes an appearance here. Nor do our contributors refer directly to the situation in which these thinkers and authors find themselves, though Robert Lane comes closest perhaps in his reflections on capitalist and socialist personality. Nevertheless we hope that our readers, when they address themselves to *A Well-Ordered Society,* to *Relativism and Tolerance,* or to the theory of democracy in the sophisticated form they find it being discussed here, will do so remembering these other writers and their completely different sets of conditions: their entirely different vocabulary as well, in which democracy might be called a blocked word. The debate in which Carole Pateman engages with Hannah Pitkin[4] bears rather more directly on such problems than at first sight might be supposed.

Perhaps the reader may think that the complexities of democratic theory as elaborated by our contributors are too refined: the message scarcely plain enough for the political world as it actually is, especially where authoritarianism is in possession. But this is not the first time in the history of thought when moral perplexity has given rise to refined distinctions and the intricate manipulations of exact definitions.

The issues to do with arithmetic humanity are continuous with those to do with democratic theory, and two-fold in their character. They are geographical, as when Peter Singer talks so urgently about our duties to distant yet contemporary humans in times of famine, and temporal when Peter Laslett

---

[4] For Pitkin's study, see *Philosophy, Politics and Society IV*.

addresses the problems of generations past and generations yet to come. They are intermediate between the two when we consider the consequences of the ageing of high industrial society, where a huge company of the economically inactive now share the time space with those who have conventionally been supposed to constitute effectively the whole of society. As for the geography of political and moral association, Robert Dahl, and to some extent Robert Lane and Brian Barry too, take up this crucial yet neglected theme when they find themselves asking who has to be included in a body politic to give it moral authenticity. This inevitably raises questions which go to the bottom of our assumptions about society, state, individual and the democratic process. It does so in a way which is particularly important when micro-nationalism, small scale political societies clamouring for an identity of their own, is almost as urgent as the challenge which comes from considering humanity as a whole.

As for the first set of issues, the present position may be set down in little space. Rawl's theory is addressed to certain classical questions of justice—the distribution of income and property, rights and liberties, the 'basic structure' of a just society. There are many other pressing questions which it leaves unanswered. *A Theory of Justice* is not sufficient, and was not intended to be sufficient, to meet the intellectual demands made upon us by environment, population and futurity. An entirely new moral perspective may accordingly have to be worked out now, an effort on a Kantian scale, at the problems of all humans considered over time. Kant is perhaps not the writer to call to mind after all: better the Stoics to whom appeal was made in 1956,[5] a philosophy of all mankind for the latest decades of the 20th century. Nevertheless, scripturalism, as is said on p. 43 of the present book, is decidedly not enough. The collection we publish in 1978 may be taken to show forth, even in its insufficiencies, the still present danger of preoccupation with a small traditional agenda of classical 'problems' in political philosophy and of too much reliance on respected names from the past.

There have been intellectual events, eddies of opinion, bursts of speculation, during the last few years which might perhaps have engaged our attention here. One has been the

[5] *Philosophy, Politics and Society I,* Introduction, p. xiv.

sudden prominence of *Sociobiology,* a huge book with that title by Edward O. Wilson appearing at Harvard in 1975, and giving rise to an intense controversy of a kind which has to be described as philosophical. A shorter, sharper essay in the British mode by Richard Dawkins came out at Oxford in the following year, *The Selfish Gene.* The relationship of what has been called Scientism to ethical and political philosophy in our generation continues to be an uneasy one, and we should have liked to have had it represented here.

Of the other books, controversies, and so on, which have marked the upswell of political and social theorizing and speculation in the 1970s, we may simply say that no collection of this kind could possibly touch upon them all, any more than this brief essay could effectively have introduced all the subjects which do appear in the volume we have put together. It will perhaps be thought that a series of this kind, which is ecumenical in its attempted coverage, has by now outlived its usefulness. But that there could still be occasion for a sixth volume of *Philosophy, Politics and Society* may be gathered from the tone of the few remarks we have ventured to make about the contents of the fifth in relation to the position—intellectual, political and social—which its exponents and would-be exponents have to recognize as theirs.

1 A Well-Ordered Society[1]

John Rawls

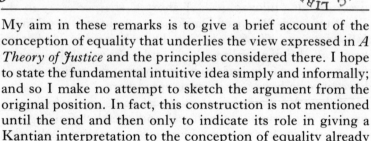

My aim in these remarks is to give a brief account of the conception of equality that underlies the view expressed in *A Theory of Justice* and the principles considered there. I hope to state the fundamental intuitive idea simply and informally; and so I make no attempt to sketch the argument from the original position. In fact, this construction is not mentioned until the end and then only to indicate its role in giving a Kantian interpretation to the conception of equality already presented.

I

When fully articulated, any conception of justice expresses a conception of the person, of the relations between persons, and of the general structure and ends of social co-operation. To accept the principles that represent a conception of justice is at the same time to accept an ideal of the person; and in acting from these principles we realize such an ideal. Let us begin, then, by trying to describe the kind of person we might want to be and the form of society we might wish to live in and to shape our interests and character. In this way we arrive at the notion of a well-ordered society. I shall first describe this notion and then use it to explain a Kantian conception of equality.

First of all, a well-ordered society is effectively regulated by a public conception of justice. That is, it is a society all of whose members accept, and know that the others accept, the same principles (the same conception) of justice. It is also the

[1] Reprinted with permission from *The Cambridge Review* (February 1975), pp. 94–9. The original title was 'A Kantian Conception of Equality.' Sections I, III and IV of this discussion draw upon sections I and III of 'Reply to Alexander and Musgrave,' *Quarterly Journal of Economics*, November 1974. Sections II, V and VI of that paper take up some questions about the argument from the original position.

case that basic social institutions and their arrangement into one scheme (the basic structure) actually satisfy, and are on good grounds believed by everyone to satisfy, these principles. Finally, publicity also implies that the public conception is founded on reasonable beliefs that have been established by generally accepted methods of inquiry; and the same is true of the application of its principles to basic social arrangements. This last aspect of publicity does not mean that everyone holds the same religious, moral, and theoretical beliefs; on the contrary, there are assumed to be sharp and indeed irreconcilable differences on such questions. But at the same time there is a shared understanding that the principles of justice, and their application to the basic structure of society, should be determined by considerations and evidence that are supported by rational procedures commonly recognized.

Secondly, I suppose that the members of a well-ordered society are, and view themselves as, free and equal moral persons. They are moral persons in that, once they have reached the age of reason, each has, and views the others as having, a realized sense of justice; and this sentiment informs their conduct for the most part. That they are equal is expressed by the supposition that they each have, and view themselves as having, a right to equal respect and consideration in determining the principles by which the basic arrangements of their society are to be regulated. Finally, we express their being free by stipulating that they each have, and view themselves as having, fundamental aims and higher-order interests (a conception of their good) in the name of which it is legitimate to make claims on one another in the design of their institutions. At the same time, as free persons they do not think of themselves as inevitably bound to, or as identical with, the pursuit of any particular array of fundamental interests that they may have at any given time; instead, they conceive of themselves as capable of revising and altering these final ends and they give priority to preserving their liberty in this regard.

In addition, I assume that a well-ordered society is stable relative to its conception of justice. This means that social institutions generate an effective supporting sense of justice. Regarding society as a going concern, its members acquire as they grow up an allegiance to the public conception and this allegiance usually overcomes the temptations and strains of social life.

Now we are here concerned with a conception of justice and the idea of equality that belongs to it. Thus, let us suppose that a well-ordered society exists under circumstances of justice. These necessitate some conception of justice and give point to its special role. First, moderate scarcity obtains. This means that although social co-operation is productive and mutually advantageous (one person's or group's gain need not be another's loss), natural resources and the state of technology are such that the fruits of joint efforts fall short of the claims that people make. And second, persons and associations have contrary conceptions of the good that lead them to make conflicting claims on one another; and they also hold opposing religious, philosophical, and moral convictions (on matters the public conception leaves open) as well as different ways of evaluating arguments and evidence in many important cases. Given these circumstances, the members of a well-ordered society are not indifferent as to how the benefits produced by their co-operation are distributed. A set of principles is required to judge between social arrangements that shape this division of advantages. Thus the role of the principles of justice is to assign rights and duties in the basic structure of society and to specify the manner in which institutions are to influence the overall distribution of the returns from social co-operation. The basic structure is the primary subject of justice and that to which the principles of justice in the first instance apply.

It is perhaps useful to observe that the notion of a well-ordered society is an extension of the idea of religious toleration. Consider a pluralistic society, divided along religious, ethnic, or cultural lines in which the various groups have reached a firm understanding on the scheme of principles to regulate their fundamental institutions. While they have deep differences about other things, there is public agreement on this framework of principles and citizens are attached to it. A well-ordered society has not attained social harmony in all things, if indeed that would be desirable; but it has achieved a large measure of justice and established a basis for civic friendship, which makes people's secure association together possible.

II

The notion of a well-ordered society assumes that the basic structure, the fundamental social institutions and their arrangement into one scheme, is the primary subject of justice. What is the reason for this assumption? First of all, any discussion of social justice must take the nature of the basic structure into account. Suppose we begin with the initially attractive idea that the social process should be allowed to develop over time as free agreements fairly arrived at and fully honoured require. Straightaway we need an account of when agreements are free and the conditions under which they are reached are fair. In addition, while these conditions may be satisfied at an earlier time, the accumulated results of agreements in conjunction with social and historical contingencies are likely to change institutions and opportunities so that the conditions for free and fair agreements no longer hold. The basic structure specifies the background conditions against which the actions of individuals, groups, and associations take place. Unless this structure is regulated and corrected so as to be just over time, the social process with its procedures and outcomes is no longer just, however free and fair particular transactions may look to us when viewed by themselves. We recognize this principle when we say that the distribution resulting from voluntary market transactions will not in general be fair unless the antecedent distribution of income and wealth and the structure of the market is fair. Thus we seem forced to start with an account of a just basic structure. It's as if the most important agreement is that which establishes the principles to govern this structure. Moreover, these principles must be acknowledged ahead of time, as it were. To agree to them now, when everyone knows their present situation, would enable some to take unfair advantage of social and natural contingencies, and of the results of historical accidents and accumulations.

Other considerations also support taking the basic structure as the primary subject of justice. It has always been recognized that the social system shapes the desires and aspirations of its members; it determines in large part the kind of persons they want to be as well as the kind of persons they are. Thus an economic system is not only an institutional device for satisfying existing wants and desires but a way of fashioning wants and desires in the future. By what principles are we to regulate a scheme of institutions that has such fundamental consequences for our view of ourselves and for our interests and aims? This question becomes all the more crucial when we consider that the basic structure contains social and economic inequalities. I assume that these are necessary, or highly advantageous, for various reasons: they are required to maintain and to run social arrangements, or to serve as incentives; or perhaps they are a way to put resources in the hands of those who can make the best social use of them; and so on. In any case, given these inequalities, individuals' life-prospects are bound to be importantly affected by their family and class origins, by their natural endowments and the chance contingencies of their (particular early) development, and by other accidents over the course of their lives. The social structure, therefore, limits people's ambitions and hopes in different ways, for they will with reason view themselves in part according to their place in it and take into account the means and opportunities they can realistically expect.

The justice of the basic structure is, then, of predominant importance. The first problem of justice is to determine the principles to regulate inequalities and to adjust the profound and long-lasting effects of social, natural, and historical contingencies, particularly since these contingencies combined with inequalities generate tendencies that, when left to themselves, are sharply at odds with the freedom and equality appropriate for a well-ordered society. In view of the special role of the basic structure, we cannot assume that the principles suitable to it are natural applications, or even extensions, of the familiar principles governing the actions of individuals and associations in everyday life which take place within its framework. Most likely we shall have to loosen ourselves from our ordinary perspective and take a more comprehensive viewpoint.

III

I shall now state and explain two principles of justice, and then discuss the appropriateness of these principles for a well-ordered society. They read as follows:

1. Each person has an equal right to the most extensive scheme of equal basic liberties compatible with a similar scheme of liberties for all.
2. Social and economic inequalities are to meet two conditions: they must be (a) to the greatest expected benefit of the least advantaged; and (b) attached to offices and positions open to all under conditions of fair opportunity.

The first of these principles is to take priority over the second; and the measure of benefit to the least advantaged is specified in terms of an index of social primary goods. These goods I define roughly as rights, liberties, and opportunities, income and wealth, and the social bases of self-respect. Individuals are assumed to want these goods whatever else they want, or whatever their final ends. The least advantaged are defined very roughly, as the overlap between those who are least favoured by each of the three main kinds of contingencies. Thus this group includes persons whose family and class origins are more disadvantaged than others, whose natural endowments have permitted them to fare less well, and whose fortune and luck have been relatively less favourable, all within the normal range (as noted below) and with the relevant measures based on social primary goods. Various refinements are no doubt necessary, but this definition of the least advantaged suitably expresses the link with the problem of contingency and should suffice for our purposes here.

I also suppose that everyone has physical needs and psychological capacities within the normal range, so that the problems of special health care and of how to treat the mentally defective do not arise. Besides prematurely introducing difficult questions that may take us beyond the theory of justice, the consideration of these hard cases can distract our moral perception by leading us to think of people distant from us whose fate arouses pity and anxiety. Whereas the first problem of justice concerns the relations among those who in the normal course of things are full and active

participants in society and directly or indirectly associated
together over the whole course of their life.

Now the members of a well-ordered society are free and
equal; so let us first consider the fittingness of the two
principles to their freedom, and then to their equality. These
principles reflect two aspects of their freedom, namely,
liberty and responsibility, which I take up in turn. In regard
to liberty, recall that people in a well-ordered society view
themselves as having fundamental aims and interests which
they must protect, if this is possible. It is partly in the name of
these interests that they have a right to equal consideration
and respect in the design of their society. A familiar historical
example is the religious interest; the interest in the integrity
of the person, freedom from psychological oppression and
from physical assault and dismemberment is another. The
notion of a well-ordered society leaves open what particular
expression these interests take; only their general form is
specified. But individuals do have interests of the requisite
kind and the basic liberties necessary for their protection are
guaranteed by the first principle.

It is essential to observe that these liberties are given by a
list of liberties; important among these are freedom of
thought and liberty of conscience, freedom of the person and
political liberty. These liberties have a central range of
application within which they can be limited and compro-
mised only when they conflict with other basic liberties. Since
they may be limited when they clash with one another, none
of these liberties is absolute; but however they are adjusted to
form one system, this system is to be the same for all. It is
difficult, perhaps impossible, to give a complete definition of
these liberties independently from the particular circumstances, social, economic, and technological, of a given well-
ordered society. Yet the hypothesis is that the general form of
such a list could be devised with sufficient exactness to sustain
this conception of justice. Of course, liberties not on the list,
for example, the right to own certain kinds of property (e.g.,
means of production), and freedom of contract as understood
by the doctrine of laissez-faire, are not basic; and so they are
not protected by the priority of the first principle.[2]

[2] This paragraph confirms H. L. A. Hart's interpretation.
See his discussion of liberty and its priority, *Chicago Law
Review*, April 1973, pp. 536–40.

One reason, then, for holding the two principles suitable for a well-ordered society is that they assure the protection of the fundamental interests that members of such a society are presumed to have. Further reasons for this conclusion can be given by describing in more detail the notion of a free person. Thus we may suppose that such persons regard themselves as having a highest-order interest in how all their other interests, including even their fundamental ones, are shaped and regulated by social institutions. As I noted earlier, they do not think of themselves as unavoidably tied to any particular array of fundamental interests; instead they view themselves as capable of revising and changing these final ends. They wish, therefore, to give priority to their liberty to do this, and so their original allegiance and continued devotion to their ends are to be formed and affirmed under conditions that are free. Or, expressed another way, members of a well-ordered society are viewed as responsible for their fundamental interests and ends. While as members of particular associations some may decide in practice to yield much of this responsibility to others, the basic structure cannot be arranged so as to prevent people from developing their capacity to be responsible, or to obstruct their exercise of it once they attain it. Social arrangements must respect their autonomy and this points to the appropriateness of the two principles.

IV

These last remarks about responsibility may be elaborated further in connection with the role of social primary goods. As already stated, these are things that people in a well-ordered society may be presumed to want, whatever their final ends. And the two principles assess the basic structure in terms of certain of these goods: rights, liberties, and opportunities, income and wealth, and the social bases of self-respect. The latter are features of the basic structure that may reasonably be expected to affect people's self-respect and self-esteem (these are not the same) in important ways.[3] Part

[3] I discuss certain problems in interpreting the account of primary goods in 'Fairness to Goodness,' the *Philosophical Review*, October 1975, pp. 536–554.

(a) of the second principle (the difference principle, or as economists prefer to say, the maximin criterion) uses an index of these goods to determine the least advantaged. Now certainly there are difficulties in working out a satisfactory index, but I shall leave these aside. Two points are particularly relevant here: first, social primary goods are certain objective characteristics of social institutions and of people's situation with respect to them; and second, the same index of these goods is used to compare everyone's social circumstances. It is clear, then, that although the index provides a basis for interpersonal comparisons for the purposes of justice, it is not a measure of individuals' overall satisfaction or dissatisfaction. Of course, the precise weights adopted in such an index cannot be laid down ahead of time, for these should be adjusted, to some degree at least, in view of social conditions. What can be settled initially is certain constraints on these weights, as illustrated by the priority of the first principle.

Now, that the responsibility of free persons is implicit in the use of primary goods can be seen in the following way. We are assuming that people are able to control and to revise their wants and desires in the light of circumstances and that they are to have responsibility for doing so, provided that the principles of justice are fulfilled, as they are in a well-ordered society. Persons do not take their wants and desires as determined by happenings beyond their control. We are not, so to speak, assailed by them, as we are perhaps by disease and illness so that wants and desires fail to support claims to the means of satisfaction in the way that disease and illness support claims to medicine and treatment.

Of course, it is not suggested that people must modify their desires and ends whatever their circumstances. The doctrine of primary goods does not demand the stoic virtues. Society for its part bears the responsibility for upholding the principles of justice and secures for everyone a fair share of primary goods (as determined by the difference principle) within a framework of equal liberty and fair equality of opportunity. It is within the limits of this division of responsibility that individuals and associations are expected to form and moderate their aims and wants. Thus among the members of a well-ordered society there is an understanding that as citizens they will press claims for only certain kinds of things, as allowed for by the principles of justice. Passionate convictions and zealous aspirations do not, as such, give anyone a claim upon social resources or the design of social institutions. For the purposes of justice, the appropriate basis of interpersonal comparisons is the index of primary goods and not strength of feeling or intensity of desire. The theory of primary goods is an extension of the notion of needs, which are distinct from aspirations and desires. One might say, then, that as citizens the members of a well-ordered society collectively take responsibility for dealing justly with one another founded on a public and objective measure of (extended) needs, while as individuals and members of associations they take responsibility for their preferences and devotions.

V

I now take up the appropriateness of the two principles in view of the equality of the members of a well-ordered society. The principles of equal liberty and fair opportunity (part (b) of the second principle) are a natural expression of this equality; and I assume, therefore, that such a society is one in which some form of democracy exists. Thus our question is: by what principle can members of a democratic society permit the tendencies of the basic structure to be deeply affected by social chance, and natural and historical contingencies?

Now since we are regarding citizens as free and equal moral persons (the priority of the first principle of equal liberty gives institutional expression to this), the obvious starting point is to suppose that all other social primary goods, and in particular income and wealth, should be equal: everyone should have an equal share. But society must take organizational requirements and economic efficiency into account. So it is unreasonable to stop at equal division. The basic structure should allow inequalities so long as these improve everyone's situation, including that of the least advantaged, provided these inequalities are consistent with equal liberty and fair opportunity. Because we start from equal shares, those who benefit least have, so to speak, a veto; and thus we arrive at the difference principle. Taking equality as the basis of comparison those who have gained more must do so on terms that are justifiable to those who have gained the least. In explaining this principle, several matters should be kept in mind. First of all, it applies in the first instance to the main public principles and policies that regulate social and economic inequalities. It is used to adjust the system of entitlements and rewards, and the standards and precepts that this system employs. Thus the difference principle holds, for example, for income and property taxation, for fiscal and economic policy; it does not apply to particular transactions or distributions, nor, in general, to small scale and local decisions, but rather to the background against which these take place. No observable pattern is required of actual distributions, nor even any measure of the degree of equality (such as the Gini coefficient) that might be computed from these.[4] What is enjoined is that the inequalities make a functional contribution to those least favoured. Finally, the aim is not to eliminate the various contingencies, for some such contingencies seem inevitable. Thus even if an equal distribution of natural assets seemed more in keeping with the equality of free persons, the question of redistributing these assets (were this conceivable) does not arise, since it is incompatible with the integrity of the person. Nor need we make any specific assumptions about how great these variations are; we only suppose that, as realized in later life, they are influenced by all three kinds of contingencies. The question, then, is by what criterion a democratic society is to organize co-operation and arrange the system of entitlements that encourages and rewards productive efforts? We have a right to our natural abilities and a right to whatever we become entitled to by taking part in a fair social process. The problem is to characterize this process.[5]

At first sight, it may appear that the difference principle is arbitrarily biased towards the least favoured. But suppose, for simplicity, that there are only two groups, one significantly more fortunate than the other. Society could maximize the

[4] For a discussion of such measures, see A. K. Sen, *On Economic Inequality* (Oxford, 1973), chap. 2.
[5] The last part of this paragraph alludes to some objections raised by Robert Nozick in his *Anarchy, State, and Utopia* (New York, 1974), esp. pp. 213–29.

expectations of either group but not both, since we can maximize with respect to only one aim at a time. It seems plain that society should not do the best it can for those initially more advantaged; so if we reject the difference principle, we must prefer maximizing some weighted mean of the two expectations. But how should this weighted mean be specified? Should society proceed as if we had an equal chance of being in either group (in proportion to their size) and determine the mean that maximizes this purely hypothetical expectation? Now it is true that we sometimes agree to draw lots but normally only to things that cannot be appropriately divided or else cannot be enjoyed or suffered in common.[6] And we are willing to use the lottery principle even in matters of lasting importance if there is no other way out. (Consider the example of conscription). But to appeal to it in regulating the basic structure itself would be extraordinary. There is no necessity for society as an enduring system to invoke the lottery principle in this case; nor is there any reason for free and equal persons to allow their relations over the whole course of their life to be significantly affected by contingencies to the greater advantage of those already favoured by these accidents. No one had an antecedent claim to be benefited in this way; and so to maximize a weighted mean is, so to speak, to favour the more fortunate twice over. Society can, however, adopt the difference principle to arrange inequalities so that social and natural contingencies are efficiently used to the benefit of all, taking equal division as a benchmark. So while natural assets cannot be divided evenly, or directly enjoyed or suffered in common, the results of their productive efforts can be allocated in ways consistent with an initial equality. Those favoured by social and natural contingencies regard themselves as already compensated, as it were, by advantages to which no one (including themselves) had a prior claim. Thus they think the difference principle appropriate for regulating the system of entitlements and inequalities.

---

[6] At this point I adapt some remarks of Hobbes. See The *Leviathan*, Chap. 15, under the thirteenth and fourteenth laws of nature.

VI

The conception of equality contained in the principles of justice I have described as Kantian. I shall conclude by mentioning very briefly the reasons for this description. Of course, I do not mean that this conception is literally Kant's conception, but rather that it is one of no doubt several conceptions sufficiently similar to essential parts of his doctrine to make the adjective appropriate. Much depends on what one counts as essential. Kant's view is marked by a number of dualisms, in particular, the dualisms between the necessary and the contingent, form and content, reason and desire, and noumena and phenomena. To abandon these dualisms as he meant them is, for many, to abandon what is distinctive in his theory. I believe otherwise. His moral conception has a characteristic structure that is more clearly discernible when these dualisms are not taken in the sense he gave them but reinterpreted and their moral force reformulated within the scope of an empirical theory. One of the aims of *A Theory of Justice* was to indicate how this might be done.

To suggest the main idea, think of the notion of a well-ordered society as an interpretation of the idea of a kingdom of ends thought of as a human society under circumstances of justice. Now the members of such a society are free and equal and so our problem is to find a rendering of freedom and equality that it is natural to describe as Kantian; and since Kant distinguished between positive and negative freedom, we must make room for this contrast. At this point I resorted to the idea of the original position: I supposed that the conception of justice suitable for a well-ordered society is the one that would be agreed to in a hypothetical situation that is fair between individuals conceived as free and equal moral persons, that is, as members of such a society. Fairness of the circumstances under which agreement is reached transfers to the fairness of the principles agreed to. The original position was designed so that the conception of justice that resulted would be appropriate.

Particularly important among the features of the original position for the interpretation of negative freedom are the limits on information, which I called the veil of ignorance.

Now there is a stronger and a weaker form of these limits. The weaker supposes that we begin with full information, or else that which we possess in everyday life, and then proceed to eliminate only the information that would lead to partiality and bias. The stronger form has a Kantian explanation: we start from no information at all; for by negative freedom Kant means being able to act independently from the determination of alien causes; to act from natural necessity is to subject oneself to the heteronomy of nature. We interpret this as requiring that the conception of justice that regulates the basic structure, with its deep and long-lasting effects on our common life, should not be adopted on grounds that rest on a knowledge of the various contingencies. Thus when this conception is agreed to, knowledge of our social position, our peculiar desires and interests, or of the various outcomes and configurations of natural and historical accident is excluded. One allows only that information required for a rational agreement. This means that, so far as possible, only the general laws of nature are known together with such particular facts as are implied by the circumstances of justice.

Of course, we must endow the parties with some motivation, otherwise no acknowledgement would be forthcoming. Kant's discussion in the *Groundwork* of the second pair of examples indicates, I believe, that in applying the procedure of the categorical imperative he tacitly relied upon some account of primary goods. In any case, if the two principles would be adopted in the original position with its limits on information, the conception of equality they contain would be Kantian in the sense that by acting from this conception the members of a well-ordered society would express their negative freedom. They would have succeeded in regulating the basic structure and its profound consequences on their persons and mutual relationships by principles the grounds for which are suitably independent from chance and contingency.

In order to provide an interpretation of positive freedom, two things are necessary: first, that the parties are conceived as free and equal moral persons must play a decisive part in their adoption of the conception of justice; and second, the principles of this conception must have a content appropriate to express this determining view of persons and must apply to the controlling institutional subject. Now if correct, the argument from the original position seems to meet these conditions. The assumption that the parties are free and equal moral persons does have an essential role in this argument; and as regards content and application, these principles express, on their public face as it were, the conception of the person that is realized in a well-ordered society. They give priority to the basic liberties, regard individuals as free and responsible masters of their aims and desires, and all are to share equally in the means for the attainment of ends unless the situation of everyone can be improved, taking equal division as the starting point. A society that realized these principles would attain positive freedom, for these principles reflect the features of persons that determined their selection and so express a conception they give to themselves.

2 Famine, Affluence and Morality[1]

Peter Singer

As I write this,[2] in November 1971, people are dying in East Bengal from lack of food, shelter, and medical care. The suffering and death that are occurring there now are not inevitable, not unavoidable in any fatalistic sense of the term. Constant poverty, a cyclone, and a civil war have turned at least nine million people into destitute refugees; nevertheless, it is not beyond the capacity of the richer nations to give enough assistance to reduce any further suffering to very small proportions. The decisions and actions of human beings can prevent this kind of suffering. Unfortunately, human beings have not made the necessary decisions. At the individual level, people have, with very few exceptions, not responded to the situation in any significant way. Generally speaking, people have not given large sums to relief funds; they have not written to their parliamentary representatives demanding increased government assistance; they have not demonstrated in the streets, held symbolic fasts, or done anything else directed towards providing the refugees with the means to satisfy their essential needs. At the government level, no government has given the sort of massive aid that would enable the refugees to survive for more than a few days.

[1] Reprinted from *Philosophy and Public Affaires 1*, 3, (spring 1972): 229–43.

[2]. The crisis in Bangladesh that led me to write this article is now of historical interest only, but the world food crisis remains with us. The huge grain reserves that were then held by the United States vanished with a couple of poor harvests. The increased oil prices have increased the cost of fertilizers and fuel in developing countries and have made it difficult for them to produce more food. At the same time their population is continuing to grow. Fortunately, as I write now, there is no major famine anywhere in the world, but poor poeple are still starving in many countries and malnutrition remainds widespread. The need for assistance has therefore hardly diminished and we can be sure that without very substantial assistance from the wealthy nations to the poorer nations there will, again, be major famines. Hence the argument of my article is as relevant today as it was in 1971.

Britain, for instance, has given rather more than most countries. It has, to date, given £14,750,000. For comparative purposes, Britain's share of the nonrecoverable development costs of the Anglo-French Concorde project is already in excess of £275,000,000, and on present estimates will reach £440,000,000. The implication is that the British government values a supersonic transport more than thirty times as highly as it values the lives of the nine million refugees. Australia is another country which, on a per capita basis, is well up in the 'aid to Bengal' table. Australia's aid, however, amounts to less than one-twelfth of the cost of Sydney's new opera house. The total amount given, from all sources, now stands at about £65,000,000. The estimated cost of keeping the refugees alive for one year is £464,000,000. Most of the refugees have now been in camps for more than six months. The World Bank has said that India needs a minimum of £300,000,000 in assistance from other countries before the end of the year. It seems obvious that assistance on this scale will not be forthcoming. India will be forced to choose between letting the refugees starve or diverting funds from her own development programme, which will mean that more of her own people will starve in the future.[3]

These are the essential facts about the present situation in Bengal. So far as it concerns us here, there is nothing unique about this situation except its magnitude. The Bengal emergency is just the latest and most acute of a series of major emergencies in various parts of the world, arising both from natural and from man-made causes. There are also many parts of the world in which people die from malnutrition and lack of food independent of any special emergency. I take Bengal as my example only because it is the present concern, and because the size of the problem has ensured that it has been given adequate publicity. Neither individuals nor governments can claim to be unaware of what is happening there.

What are the moral implications of a situation like this? In

---

[3] There was also a third possibility: that India would go to war to enable the refugees to return to their lands. Since I wrote this paper, India has taken this way out. The situation is no longer that described above, but this does not affect my argument, as the next paragraph indicates.

what follows, I shall argue that the way people in relatively affluent countries react to a situation like that in Bengal cannot be justified; indeed the whole way we look at moral issues—our moral conceptual scheme—needs to be altered, and with it, the way of life that has come to be taken for granted in our society.

In arguing for this conclusion I will not, of course, claim to be morally neutral. I shall, however, try to argue for the moral position that I take, so that anyone who accepts certain assumptions, to be made explicit, will, I hope accept my conclusion.

I begin with the assumption that suffering and death from lack of food, shelter, and medical care are bad. I think most people will agree about this, although one may reach the same view by different routes. I shall not argue for this view. People can hold all sorts of eccentric positions, and perhaps from some of them it would not follow that death by starvation is in itself bad. It is difficult, perhaps impossible, to refute such positions, and so for brevity I will henceforth take this assumption as accepted. Those who disagree need read no further.

My next point is this: if it is in our power to prevent something bad from happening, without thereby sacrificing anything of comparable moral importance, we ought, morally, to do it. By 'without sacrificing anything of comparable moral importance' I mean without causing anything else comparably bad to happen, or doing something that is wrong in itself, or failing to promote some moral good, comparable in significance to the bad thing we can prevent. This principle seems almost as uncontroversial as the last one. It requires us only to prevent what is bad, and not to promote what is good, and it requires this of us only when we can do it without sacrificing anything that is, from the moral point of view, comparably important. I could even, as far as the application of my argument to the Bengal emergency is concerned, qualify the point so as to make it: if it is in our power to prevent something very bad from happening, without thereby sacrificing anything morally significant, we ought, morally, to do it. An application of this principle would be as follows: if I am walking past a shallow pond and see a child drowning in it, I ought to wade in and pull the child out. This will mean getting my clothes muddy, but this is insignificant, while the death of the child would presumably be a very bad thing.

The uncontroversial appearance of the principle just stated is deceptive. If it were acted upon, even in its qualified form, our lives, our society, and our world would be fundamentally changed. For the principle takes, firstly, no account of proximity or distance. It makes no moral difference whether the person I can help is a neighbour's child ten yards from me or a Bengali whose name I shall never know, ten thousand miles away. Secondly, the principle makes no distinction between cases in which I am the only person who could possibly do anything and cases in which I am just one among millions in the same position.

I do not think I need to say much in defence of the refusal to take proximity and distance into account. The fact that a person is physically near to us, so that we have personal contact with him, may make it more likely that we *shall* assist him, but this does not show that we *ought* to help him rather than another who happens to be further away. If we accept any principle of impartiality, universalizability, equality, or whatever, we cannot discriminate against someone merely because he is far away from us (or we are far away from him). Admittedly, it is possible that we are in a better position to judge what needs to be done to help a person near to us than one far away, and perhaps also to provide the assistance we judge to be necessary. If this were the case, it would be a reason for helping those near to us first. This may once have been a justification for being more concerned with the poor in one's own town than with famine victims in India. Unfortunately for those who like to keep their moral responsibilities limited, instant communication and swift transportation have changed the situation. From the moral point of view, the development of the world into a 'global village' has made an important, though still unrecognized, difference to our moral situation. Expert observers and supervisors, sent out by famine relief organizations or permanently stationed in famine-prone areas, can direct our aid to a refugee in Bengal almost as effectively as we could get it to someone in our own block. There would seem, therefore, to be no possible justification for discriminating on geographical grounds.

There may be a greater need to defend the second

implication of my principle—that the fact that there are millions of other people in the same position, in respect to the Bengali refugees, as I am, does not make the situation significantly different from a situation in which I am the only person who can prevent something very bad from occuring. Again, of course, I admit that there is a psychological difference between the cases; one feels less guilty about doing nothing if one can point to others, similarly placed, who have also done nothing. Yet this can make no real difference to our moral obligations.[4] Should I consider that I am less obliged to pull the drowning child out of the pond if on looking around I see other people, no further away than I am, who have also noticed the child but are doing nothing? One has only to ask this question to see the absurdity of the view that numbers lessen obligation. It is a view that is an ideal excuse for inactivity; unfortunately most of the major evils—poverty, overpopulation, pollution—are problems in which everyone is almost equally involved.

The view that numbers do make a difference can be made plausible if stated in this way: if everyone in circumstances like mine gave £5 to the Bengal Relief Fund, there would be enough to provide food, shelter, and medical care for the refugees; there is no reason why I should give more than anyone else in the same circumstances as I am; therefore I have no obligation to give more than £5. Each premise in this argument is true, and the argument looks sound. It may convince us, unless we notice that it is based on a hypothetical premise, although the conclusion is not stated hypothetically. The argument would be sound if the conclusion were: if everyone in my circumstances were to give £5, I would have no obligation to give more than £5. If the conclusion were so

---

[4] In view of the special sense philosophers often give to the term, I should say that I use 'obligation' simply as the abstract noun derived from 'ought', so that 'I have an obligation to' means no more, and no less, than 'I ought to'. This usage is in accordance with the definition of 'ought' given by the *Shorter Oxford English Dictionary*: 'the general verb to express duty or obligation'. I do not think any issue of substance hangs on the way the term is used; sentences in which I use 'obligation' could all be rewritten, although somewhat clumsily, as sentences in which a clause containing 'ought' replaces the term 'obligation'.

stated, however, it would be obvious that the argument has no
bearing on a situation in which it is not the case that everyone
else gives £5. This, of course, is the actual situation. It is more
or less certain that not everyone in circumstances like mine
will give £5. So there will not be enough to provide the
needed food, shelter, and medical care. Therefore by giving
more than £5 I will prevent more suffering than I would
if I gave just £5.

It might be thought that this argument has an absurd
consequence. Since the situation appears to be that very few
people are likely to give substantial amounts, it follows that I
and everyone else in similar circumstances ought to give as
much as possible, that is, at least up to the point at which by
giving more one would begin to cause serious suffering for
oneself and one's dependents—perhaps even beyond this
point to the point of marginal utility, at which by giving more
one would cause oneself and one's dependents as much
suffering as one would prevent in Bengal. If everyone does
this, however, there will be more than can be used for the
benefit of the refugees, and some of the sacrifice will have
been unnecessary. Thus, if everyone does what he ought to
do, the result will not be as good as it would be if everyone did
a little less than he ought to do, or if only some do all they
ought to do.

The paradox here arises only if we assume that the actions
in question—sending money to the relief funds—are
performed more or less simultaneously, and are also
unexpected. For if it is to be expected that everyone is going
to contribute something, then clearly each is not obliged to
give as much as he would have been obliged to had others not
been giving too. And if everyone is not acting more or less
simultaneously, then those giving later will know how much
more is needed, and will have no obligation to give more than
is necessary to reach this amount. To say this is not to deny
the principle that people in the same circumstances have the
same obligations, but to point out that the fact that others
have given, or may be expected to give, is a relevant
circumstance: those giving after it has become known that
many others are giving and those giving before are not in the
same circumstances. So the seemingly absurd consequence of
the principle I have put forward can occur only if people are
in error about the actual circumstances—that is, if they think

they are giving when others are not, but in fact they are giving when others are. The result of everyone doing what he really ought to do cannot be worse than the result of everyone doing less than he ought to do, although the result of everyone doing what he reasonably believes he ought to do could be.

If my argument so far has been sound, neither our distance from a preventable evil nor the number of other people who, in respect to that evil, are in the same situation as we are, lessens our obligation to mitigate or prevent that evil. I shall therefore take as established the principle I asserted earlier. As I have already said, I need to assert it only in its qualified form: if it is in our power to prevent something very bad from happening, without thereby sacrificing anything else morally significant, we ought, morally, to do it.

The outcome of this argument is that our traditional moral categories are upset. The traditional distinction between duty and charity cannot be drawn, or at least, not in the place we normally draw it. Giving money to the Bengal Relief Fund is regarded as an act of charity in our society. The bodies which collect money are known as 'charities'. These organizations see themselves in this way—if you send them a cheque, you will be thanked for your 'generosity'. Because giving money is regarded as an act of charity, it is not thought that there is anything wrong with not giving. The charitable man may be praised, but the man who is not charitable is not condemned. People do not feel in any way ashamed or guilty about spending money on new clothes or a new car instead of giving it to famine relief. (Indeed, the alternative does not occur to them.) This way of looking at the matter cannot be justified. When we buy new clothes not to keep ourselves warm but to look 'well-dressed' we are not providing for any important need. We would not be sacrificing anything significant if we were to continue to wear our old clothes, and give the money to famine relief. By doing so, we would be preventing another person from starving. It follows from what I have said earlier that we ought to give money away, rather than spend it on clothes which we do not need to keep us warm. To do so is not charitable, or generous. Nor is it the kind of act which philosophers and theologians have called 'supererogatory'— an act which it would be good to do, but not wrong not to do. On the contrary, we ought to give the money away, and it is wrong not to do so.

I am not maintaining that there are no acts which are charitable, or that there are no acts which it would be good to do but not wrong not to do. It may be possible to redraw the distinction between duty and charity in some other place. All I am arguing here is that the present way of drawing the distinction, which makes it an act of charity for a man living at the level of affluence which most people in the 'developed nations' enjoy to give money to save someone else from starvation, cannot be supported. It is beyond the scope of my argument to consider whether the distinction should be redrawn or abolished altogether. There would be many other possible ways of drawing the distinction—for instance, one might decide that it is good to make other people as happy as possible, but not wrong not to do so.

Despite the limited nature of the revision in our moral conceptual scheme which I am proposing, the revision would, given the extent of both affluence and famine in the world today, have radical implications. These implications may lead to further objections, distinct from those I have already considered. I shall discuss two of these.

One objection to the position I have taken might be simply that it is too drastic a revision of our moral scheme. People do not ordinarily judge in the way I have suggested they should. Most people reserve their moral condemnation for those who violate some moral norm such as the norm against taking another person's property. They do not condemn those who indulge in luxury instead of giving to famine relief. But given that I did not set out to present a morally neutral description of the way people make moral judgements, the way people do in fact judge has nothing to do with the validity of my conclusion. My conclusion follows from the principle which I advanced earlier and unless that principle is rejected, or the arguments shown to be unsound, I think the conclusion must stand, however strange it appears.

It might, nevertheless, be interesting to consider why our society and most other societies, do judge differently from the way I have suggested they should. In a well-known article, J. O. Urmson suggests that the imperatives of duty, which tell us what we must do, as distinct from what it would be good to do but not wrong not to do, function so as to prohibit behaviour that is intolerable if men are to live together in society.[5] This may explain the origin and continued existence of the present division between acts of duty and acts of charity. Moral attitudes are shaped by the needs of society, and no doubt society needs people who will observe the rules that make social existence tolerable. From the point of view of a particular society, it is essential to prevent violations of norms against killing, stealing, and so on. It is quite inessential, however, to help people outside one's own society.

If this is an explanation of our common distinction between duty and supererogation, however, it is not a justification of it. The moral point of view requires us to look beyond the interests of our own society. Previously, as I have already mentioned, this may hardly have been feasible, but it is quite feasible now. From the moral point of view, the prevention of the starvation of millions of people outside our society must be considered at least as pressing as the upholding of property norms within our society.

It has been argued by some writers, among them Sidgwick and Urmson, that we need to have a basic moral code which is not too far beyond the capacities of the ordinary man, for otherwise there will be a general breakdown of compliance with the moral code. Crudely stated, this argument suggests that if we tell people that they ought to refrain from murder and give everything they do not really need to famine relief, they will do neither, whereas if we tell them that they ought to refrain from murder and that it is good to give to famine relief but not wrong not to do so, they will at least refrain from murder. The issue here is: Where should we draw the line between conduct that is required and conduct that is good although not required, so as to get the best possible result? This would seem to be an empirical question, although a very difficult one. One objection to the Sidgwick-Urmson line of argument is that it takes insufficient account of the effect that moral standards can have on the decisions we make. Given a society in which a wealthy man who gives five percent of his

---

[5] J. O. Urmson, 'Saints and Heroes', in *Essays in Moral Philosophy,* ed. Abraham I. Melden (Seattle and London, 1958), p. 214. For a related but significantly different view see also Henry Sidgwick, *The Methods of Ethics,* 7th edn. (London, 1907), pp. 220–21, 492–3.

income to famine relief is regarded as most generous, it is not surprising that a proposal that we all ought to give away half our incomes will be thought to be absurdly unrealistic. In a society which held that no man should have more than enough while others have less than they need, such a proposal might seem narrow-minded. What it is possible for a man to do and what he is likely to do are both, I think, very greatly influenced by what people around him are doing and expecting him to do. In any case, the possibility that by spreading the idea that we ought to be doing very much more than we are to relieve famine we shall bring about a general breakdown of moral behaviour seems remote. If the stakes are an end to widespread starvation, it is worth the risk. Finally, it should be emphasized that these considerations are relevant only to the issue of what we should require from others, and not to what we ourselves ought to do.

The second objection to my attack on the present distinction between duty and charity is one which has from time to time been made against utilitarianism. It follows from some forms of utilitarian theory that we all ought, morally, to be working full time to increase the balance of happiness over misery. The position I have taken here would not lead to this conclusion in all circumstances, for if there were no bad occurrences that we could prevent without sacrificing something of comparable moral importance, my argument would have no application. Given the present conditions in many parts of the world, however, it does follow from my argument that we ought, morally, to be working full time to relieve great suffering of the sort that occurs as a result of famine or other disasters. Of course, mitigating circumstances can be adduced—for instance, that if we wear ourselves out through overwork, we shall be less effective than we would otherwise have been. Nevertheless, when all considerations of this sort have been taken into account, the conclusion remains: we ought to be preventing as much suffering as we can without sacrificing something else of comparable moral importance. This conclusion is one which we may be reluctant to face. I cannot see, though, why it should be regarded as a criticism of the position for which I have argued, rather than a criticism of our ordinary standards of behaviour. Since most people are self-interested to some degree, very few of us are likely to do everything we ought to do. It would, however, hardly be honest to take this as evidence that it is not the case that we ought to do it.

It may still be thought that my conclusions are so wildly out of line with what everyone else thinks and has always thought that there must be something wrong with the argument somewhere. In order to show my conclusions, while certainly contrary to contemporary Western moral standards, would not have seemed so extraordinary at other times and in other places, I would like to quote a passage from a writer not normally thought of as a way-out radical, Thomas Aquinas.

> Now, according to the natural order instituted by divine providence, material goods are provided for the satisfaction of human needs. Therefore the division and appropriation of property, which proceeds from human law, must not hinder the satisfaction of man's necessity from such goods. Equally, whatever a man has in superabundance is owed, of natural right, to the poor for their sustenance. So Ambrosius says, and it is also to be found in the *Decretum Gratiani*: 'The bread which you withhold belongs to the hungry; the clothing you shut away, to the naked; and the money you bury in the earth is the redemption and freedom of the penniless.'[6]

I now want to consider a number of points, more practical than philosophical, which are relevant to the application of the moral conclusion we have reached. These points challenge not the idea that we ought to be doing all we can to prevent starvation, but the idea that giving away a great deal of money is the best means to this end.

It is sometimes said that overseas aid should be a government responsibility, and that therefore one ought not to give to privately run charities. Giving privately, it is said, allows the government and the noncontributing members of society to escape their responsibilities.

This argument seems to assume that the more people there are who give to privately organized famine relief funds, the less likely it is that the government will take over full responsibility for such aid. This assumption is unsupported, and does not strike me as at all plausible. The opposite view— that if no one gives voluntarily, a government will assume that its citizens are uninterested in famine relief and would not wish to be forced into giving aid—seems more plausible. In

---

[6] *Summa Theologica*, II–II, Question 66, Article 7, in *Aquinas, Selected Political Writings*, ed. A. P. d'Entreves, trans. J. G. Dawson (Oxford, 1948), p. 171.

any case, unless there were a definite probability that by refusing to give one would be helping to bring about massive government assistance, people who do refuse to make voluntary contributions are refusing to prevent a certain amount of suffering without being able to point to any tangible beneficial consequence of their refusal. So the onus of showing how their refusal will bring about government action is on those who refuse to give.

I do not, of course, want to dispute the contention that governments of affluent nations should be giving many times the amount of genuine, no-strings-attached aid that they are giving now. I agree, too, that giving privately is not enough, and that we ought to be campaigning actively for entirely new standards for both public and private contributions to famine relief. Indeed, I would sympathize with someone who thought that campaigning was more important than giving oneself, although I doubt whether preaching what one does not practice would be very effective. Unfortunately, for many people the idea that 'it's the government's responsibility' is a reason for not giving which does not appear to entail any political action either.

Another, more serious reason for not giving to famine relief funds is that until there is effective population control, relieving famine merely postpones starvation. If we save the Bengal refugees now, others, perhaps the children of these refugees, will face starvation in a few years' time. In support of this, one may cite the now well-known facts about the population explosion and the relatively limited scope for expanded production.

This point, like the previous one, is an argument against relieving suffering that is happening now, because of a belief about what might happen in the future; it is unlike the previous point in that very good evidence can be adduced in support of this belief about the future. I will not go into the evidence here. I accept that the earth cannot support indefinitely a population rising at the present rate. This certainly poses a problem for anyone who thinks it important to prevent famine. Again, however, one could accept the argument without drawing the conclusion that it absolves one from any obligation to do anything to prevent famine. The conclusion that should be drawn is that the best means of preventing famine, in the long run, is population control. It would then follow from the position reached earlier that one ought to be doing all one can to promote population control (unless one held that all forms of population control were wrong in themselves, or would have significantly bad consequences). Since there are organizations working specifically for population control, one would then support them rather than more orthodox methods of preventing famine.

A third point raised by the conclusion reached earlier relates to the question of just how much we all ought to be giving away. One possibility, which has already been mentioned, is that we ought to give until we reach the level of marginal utility—that is, the level at which, by giving more, I would cause as much suffering to myself or my dependents as I would relieve by my gift. This would mean, of course, that one would reduce oneself to very near the material circumstances of a Bengali refugee. It will be recalled that earlier I put forward both a strong and a moderate version of the principle of preventing bad occurrences. The strong version, which required us to prevent bad things from happening unless in doing so we would be sacrificing something of comparable moral significance, does seem to require reducing ourselves to the level of marginal utility. I should also say that the strong version seems to me to be the correct one. I proposed the more moderate version—that we should prevent bad occurrences unless, to do so, we had to sacrifice something morally significant—only in order to show that even on this surely undeniable principle a great change in our way of life is required. On the more moderate principle, it may not follow that we ought to reduce ourselves to the level of marginal utility, for one might hold that to reduce oneself and one's family to this level is to cause something significantly bad to happen. Whether this is so I shall not discuss, since, as I have said, I can see no good reason for holding the moderate version of the principle rather than the strong version. Even if we accepted the principle only in its moderate form, however, it should be clear that we would have to give away enough to ensure that the consumer society, dependent as it is on people spending on trivia rather than giving to famine relief, would slow down and perhaps disappear entirely. There are several reasons why this would be desirable in itself. The value and necessity of economic growth are now being questioned not only by conservationists, but by economists as well.[7] There is no doubt, too, that the consumer society has had a distorting effect on the goals and purposes of its members. Yet looking at the matter purely from the point of view of overseas aid, there must be a limit to the extent to which we should deliberately slow down our economy; for it might be the case that if we gave away, say, forty percent of our Gross National Product, we would slow down the economy so much that in absolute terms we would be giving less than if we gave twenty-five per cent of the much larger GNP that we would have if we limited our contribution to this smaller percentage.

I mention this only as an indication of the sort of factor that one would have to take into account in working out an ideal. Since Western societies generally consider one per cent of the GNP an acceptable level for overseas aid, the matter is entirely academic. Nor does it affect the question of how much an individual should give in a society in which very few are giving substantial amounts.

It is sometimes said, though less often now than it used to be, that philosophers have no special role to play in public affairs, since most public issues depend primarily on an assessment of facts. On questions of fact, it is said, philosophers as such have no special expertise, and so it has been possible to engage in philosophy without committing oneself to any position on major public issues. No doubt there are some issues of social policy and foreign policy about which it can truly be said that a really expert assessment of the the facts is required before taking sides or acting, but the issue of famine is surely not one of these. The facts about the existence of suffering are beyond dispute. Nor, I think, is it disputed that we can do something about it, either through orthodox methods of famine relief or through population control or both. This is therefore an issue on which philosophers are competent to take a position. The issue is one which faces everyone who has more money than he needs to support himself and his dependents or who is in a position to take some sort of political action. These categories must include practically every teacher and student of philosophy in

[7] See, for instance, John Kenneth Galbraith, *The New Industrial State* (Boston, 1967); and E. J. Mishan, *The Costs of Economic Growth* (London, 1967).

the universities of the Western world. If philosophy is to deal with matters that are relevant to both teachers and students, this is an issue that philosophers should discuss.

Discussion, though, is not enough. What is the point of relating philosophy to public (and personal) affairs if we do not take our conclusions seriously? In this instance, taking our conclusion seriously means acting upon it. The philosopher will not find it any easier than anyone else to alter his attitudes and way of life to the extent that, if I am right, he is involved in doing everything that we ought to be doing. At the very least, though, one can make a start. The philosopher who does so will have to sacrifice some of the benefits of the consumer society, but he can find compensation in the satisfaction of a way of life in which theory and practice, if not yet in harmony, are at least coming together.

3 The Conversation Between the Generations[1]

Peter Laslett

I choose this somewhat awkward title because it seems to me to be necessary to insist on the uncertainty, the lack of structure, in the connection between the generations. This is due to a large extent of course to the multiple character of the expression 'generation' itself; it is a word with such a tangle of related and overlapping meanings attached to it that it is surprising to find that it goes on being used without qualificatory adjectives. Let us look at a few of the notions which 'generation' covers.

It is both a temporal and a procreative term. In its temporal sense it may mean one or other of the following: all persons between certain ages; all older or all younger than a certain age; all of a particular age. In its procreative sense it may mean all progenitors as contrasted with their own progeny, or in contrast with those who might have been their progeny; it

[1] This essay was originally an address to the Royal Institute of Philosophy in London, published in Vol. 3 of their lectures, edited by Godfrey Vesey in 1970. Since that time the subject has begun to interest political theorists as part of the concern with the trend of world population, along with our effect on the environment and its dangers to the future inhabitants of the world. I have revised the text to some extent with this in mind, but have kept within the limited scope of the original. This was not directed at such cosmic issues as those raised, for example, by the speculations of John Rawls as to what might transpire if all possible present and future humanity could meet behind his veil of ignorance and decide how the business of every 'generation' should be conducted so as to ensure justice as fairness. See the discussions in *A Theory of Justice* (1972) together with applications and criticisms by D. C. Hubin 'Justice and future generations', *Philosophy and Public Affairs,* 1976, and B. Barry, 'Justice between generations', in *Law, Morality and Society*, ed. D. M. J. Hacker and J. Raz, 1977, a very interesting piece. Another treatment of the theme will be found in M. P. Golding, 'Application to future generations', the *Monist,* 1972.

I am grateful to James Fishkin for references and for critical discussion of the issues.

is also the word used when, in these two sub-senses, progeny are meant in contrast to their progenitors. The contrast in question when procreational generations are distinguished need not be between two adjacent generations, for these can consist of great, or great-great-grandfathers and great or great-great-grandchildren. And so on, without limit.

There is a third sense of the word, though this is not quite distinct from the first, the temporal sense. It conveys any collection of people alive at the same time and to whom a particular historical experience is, or was, common, whatever their ages, even if some of them were, or are, parents to others of them. Although these three meanings can be distinguished, and often have to be held distinct if confusion is not to occur, the word 'generation' in ordinary usage often combines two or even all of them. 'His father's generation' will be understood to cover all persons of roughly the same age as the immediate progenitors of the person in question, together with all those sharing the same historical experience as such persons. Alternatively (or even perhaps additionally) all who had children at about the time when his father did could be intended. The interpretation will rely upon the context, though this is seldom specific enough to avoid some degree of ambiguity.

Indeed, in order that the term may enter at all into the generational statements we shall discuss in this essay, the context has to be made to specify the location in place and society of the persons at issue. 'His father's generation' will usually be taken to include Englishmen only, or, if that is previously stated, those of that nationality to which his father belonged. Since the evidence of the context is almost always somewhat vague, it is unlikely to exclude both narrower and wider possibilities. 'His father's generation' might accordingly have to be confined to the indicated members of a certain social class in England, or to a group of such persons in a particular town. Or it might be thought to embrace all relevant Europeans, or an even wider society, such as that conveyed by the (temporal, not procreational) phrase 'the generation of 1914, of the First World War'.

Now these necessary geographical or social-geographical indications tend to be conveyed by suggestion rather than spelt out by the context. It is often impossible to be quite sure who is being taken in and who left out, when any generation is named, temporal or procreative generation that is to say, or, the most usual case, both combined. The one certainty is that the widest possibility of all can scarcely ever be intended, though it decidedly is not logically excluded, that is to say all humanity born in the stated year, or within a particular period, or coeval with someone's parents. For it is obvious that everyone born since 1939, for example even if 'still living' is understood, cannot be a collection of people who could have an attitude towards any other such collection, or share a responsibility for it. Such entities could not enter into an interchange, a conversation between the generations. Yet whenever we talk of posterity, especially posterity in the sense of those who may be affected by the damage we may be doing in our day to the environment which our successors will inherit, we seem to mean generations conceived of in this all-encompassing fashion, in reference to ourselves and with reference to them. How could such global populations of coevals ever have relationships?

A collection comprising 'all living persons who are parents' (or grandparents, or children, or grandchildren)—that is a procreational generation fairly literally defined—is unsatisfactory in a similar way. This in spite of the fact that such persons do share a set of well-defined social roles, and can be assumed to have important common experiences. Only when a temporal and/or procreational set of persons belongs to an established group does it begin to look like a unity capable of an attitude or of a responsibility. Even then, at its most 'structured', so to speak, a generation, say, of Englishmen born between 1919 and 1939 itself falls short of a consensual or action group. This means that a generation can almost never be thought of as a collectivity on its own, and in order to take part in any interchange it is apparently requisite that it be part of a collectivity which exists for other purposes. Unless otherwise indicated this collectivity is usually the whole political society attached to a region—a nationality, that is to say, which includes of course the very old and the very young, whose presence might conflict with what 'generation' intends. The context in which 'generation' appears seems to have to indicate some social grouping which could be called political in order for a usable meaning of the word to appear, even if for the reasons given this social grouping is still not quite what is wanted for the purpose in hand.

There are yet further reasons why 'generation' is difficult to handle. Perhaps the most exasperating habit we have in ordinary conversation is to use the expression in its temporal sense without remembering that each age-set is perpetually changing, being left by the older and joined by the younger. It can have no permanent boundaries, therefore, any more than it can have its own collective life outside the established collectivity of the nation itself, or of parties, societies, clubs, universities, schools. We easily forget, too, that every age-set is itself getting older, and cannot retain its former attitudes unmodified. Even if a certain historical experience moulded its outlook in a particular way when all its members were in their formative years, that outlook itself changes as everyone ages. Since the concept of a generation is elusive as well as confusing, it is difficult to see how one can talk at all convincingly about rights and duties in respect of such an unmanageable entity.

This is, however, what we intend to try to do in the present essay. And the justification must be that palpable consequences for all of us seem to flow from the uses we make of the word 'generation'. These consequences are practical as well as moral. Policies are decided, money is spent, armies are moved, legal judgements are passed and personal sacrifices are made in virtue of the concept of the generation, in addition to the distribution of praise and blame by the narrative historians.

Recognizing as we must that the concept bristles with ambiguities and difficulties of a logical and empirical kind, I am astonished at the ease with which statesmen and administrators, lawyers, philosophers, social scientists and citizens proceed to make judgements, work out policies and take action in respect of the relationship between generations. Let us take up the historian's stance and observe the problems as they are to be seen in past time. It will not be possible to answer many of the questions raised.

Am I obliged by the actions of my predecessors now dead, and if so, what is it that obliges me? A lawyer in response to such a question might well insist that it is the law which requires such compliance. All British citizens are bound by every unrepealed law of their country, no matter how long ago it was enacted. In that way we can be said to be obliged by what our predecessors did.

But this is distinct from being obliged *to* them. The only persons to whom we are obliged are surely those alive along with us now, mutually obliged to keep the law. Since any item in that law is subject to repeal by our generation, even finally one intended by our predecessors as fundamental or constitutional, we are not unconditionally committed to continue to do what was done, and recommended to us as obligatory, by those who came before us in time. It is for our decision, therefore, how far we are required to keep their promises, whether they are to be construed as legal or as semi-legal, as in international treaties. Time present is always sovereign, in respect of what is gone by, and of what is still to come.[2]

Such 'sovereignty' will, of course, have to be exercised with a proper respect for the expectations aroused by past behaviour, as well as by the content of international law, and of the 'natural' justice so beloved of its exponents. At this point questions about past time are seen to involve questions about future time. But I am not aware that the political philosophers have addressed themselves to any searching analysis of these questions, however posed, and the jurists do not seem to have faced the question squarely either.

All that comes to mind is that famous passage in Burke beginning 'Society is indeed a contract'. He goes on to talk about

> a partnership in all science; a partnership in all art; a partnership in every virtue and in all perfection... As the ends of such a partnership cannot be obtained in many generations, it becomes a partnership not only between those who are living, but between those who are dead and those who are to be born.

Burke's easy assumption of ethical continuity between even distant generations may be compared with Richard Hooker's

---

[2] Compare Nozick, *Anarchy, State and Utopia*, 1974, passim and especially p. 153. In spite of the difference in attitude to what he calls 'time-slice principles', we agree that consideration of how in the past an inequitable distribution came into being must be taken into account when deciding on a just distribution now. We disagree in supposing that this should be thought of as *restitution*, and in our appreciation of the ingenious argument in Boris L. Bittker, *The Case for Black Repatriations*, 1973, which I find wholly unconvincing.

statement that 'the act of a public society five hundred years sithence standeth as theirs which are presently of the same society'. Both thinkers betray the unhistorical attitude characteristic of contractarian political thinking, and both are also assuming a metaphysical, revelationary principle of continuity over time no longer at the disposal of late twentieth-century social and political enquiry. We shall return to the significance of this in our final paragraph.

Burke could be said to suggest a reason why I am obliged to earlier generations. We are interconnected, he seems to suppose, through a project which must last for longer than the combined number of years during which we live and which elapse between our lives. But this seems a tenuous link with which to justify rights and duties. It demands that we honour agreements with persons never able to be present so as to tell us what our promise means and how far it extends, quite apart from the crucial issue of whether there could exist an authority which might keep us to our word. We may readily grant that the dead are entitled to respect, even if we find difficulty in defining that respect for political and other purposes. But it is quite another matter to suppose that we are bound to them in a contract-like way, still less that they could be allowed to have made engagements on our behalf. Let it be noted that Burke talks of the ends and advantages of this inter-generational partnership (conceived in a combined temporal and procreational way) but never refers to responsibilities. The transfer of guilt seems not to be in mind. Yet the transfer of guilt between generations is perhaps the commonest form of the conversation we are examining as it goes forward with those in past time, in the historic tense. This can raise disquieting issues, as the following questions may make evident.

Is an American WASP of our day morally responsible for the original enslavement of Blacks, and for the perpetuation, the successive reimposition it might well be called, of white supremacy ever since? Can you be born a white Anglo-Saxon Protestant in that country without incurring this formidable moral liability?

The answer that since a man born into a WASP family is born an American citizen, he is by citizenship legally answerable for this collective guilt, seems to imply the following. First, that the political order of the United States must be possessed of unbroken moral continuity over time: it must be capable of transferring guilt from individual American to individual American, removed from each other by the passage years, and similarly with 'generations' of Americans. Second, that all American citizens, WASPs and otherwise, are involved in the responsibility for the enslavement of black people and their subsequent exploitation. Guilt is not confined to those who are descendants of slave owners, or inheritors of their possessions, nor to those along with that much larger company who themselves now profit from racial subjugation and those with ancestors or relatives in that position. Indeed, unless some juggling with citizenship, its degrees and extent for different classes of person, is undertaken, black American citizens seem themselves to be held guilty of their own moral degradation and that of their forefathers.

Nevertheless foreigners are apparently excluded from the moral interchange which proceeds within the continuing life of every collectivity over time, whatever the descent of those foreigners. It would seem to follow that the many British citizens whose ancestors were slavers have no duties towards American Blacks, while every American is deeply committed to them. This seems to hold notwithstanding most of the ancestry of most Americans of the present day, which was located in countries whose citizens were not involved in the subjugation of Blacks.

The implication here, we may suppose, might be that the enormous moral liability of being a British citizen in some way absolves me from any of the responsibilities incurred by my ancestors in respect of persons who lived within the past of the moral entity we now call America. This is true, apparently, in spite of the fact that I could be living (as the Gladstone family still is?) on the invested proceeds of the great British slave trade to the North American continent.

All this strikes me as highly unpersuasive as well as unrealistic. In implying that to be the subject of legitimate political association a population, like that of America, had and has to have ethical boundaries, it raises all the problems about the arithmetic of the *demos,* as he calls it, which Robert Dahl runs across in his essay in this volume. In assuming an eternal moral person for the State, as Burke seems also to be doing, investing it with moral claims which have no obvious boundaries, I judge it totalitarian in tendency as well, however 'legal' it may be. What is wanted is a relationship between generations which is individual as well as social, and passes through mortal individuals rather than through deathless collectivities.

However, there is a similar unreality, and even more objectionable ethical implications, about making an individual person morally responsible for the acts of his or her procreative predecessors, ancestors that is to say. These are usually impossible to identify beyond a step or two, even in what we call the direct line, and if all lines are taken into account—as they surely have to be if we are to be scrupulous about the transfer of guilt—their numbers are doubled at every step. By the tenth generation backwards, that is at about the time when Englishmen got seriously implicated in slave trading and the imperialist ransacking of the non-European world, the number reaches a thousand. There is no reason why we should stop there, or indeed at any point, and no obvious limit to the extent of the responsibility to be assumed.

Attaching guilt to offspring for the crimes of progenitors, therefore, makes moral bastards of us all. Now to point out the paradoxes and confusions which ensue from supposing that moral responsibility can be transferred like this between temporal generation and temporal generation, or between procreative generation and procreative generation, or between mixtures of both, does not solve any of the difficulties of our topic. But it does draw attention to the enormous extent of the analytic work which has to be done in political philosophy, and the dangers of being preoccupied with a handful of traditional problems. It also underlines the insufficiency of the accepted classics of political theory for this, as for so many of the topics urgently raised by the situation we now find ourselves in. Scripturalism is not enough.

Let us supplement the example of slavery and the American Blacks with another instance of the transfer of moral obliquity from generation to generation, this time where responsibility has been accepted by the later one. In contemporary Germany the present generation of citizens of the Bundesrepublik has been paying good money to Israeli citizens as reparations. The assumption appears to be that this generation acknowledges moral responsibility for the actions of the pre-war generation of Nazi Germans, although Germany was then a different geographical as well as political entity, and not all its citizens were Nazis.

In view of the extraordinary arbitrariness of these circumstances, it seems to me that the actions of the West German taxpayer should not be taken as at all realistic. In so far as he is doing his inter-generational duty in this way, he must be presumed to be choosing to assuage his feelings of guilt about the persecution of the Jews in an almost entirely symbolic fashion.[3] Although this is not the opportunity to analyse the case of the Americans and slavery at the proper length, I suspect that it would turn out that acts of restitution by WASPs to Blacks in the 1970s could only be taken as symbolic as well. To convert the problem into symbolic issues in this way in no way solves it, because we still have to consider how such symbols are nominated, how and why they are effective, the part which propaganda and ideology of all kinds play in the symbol system, and so on. But of one thing we can be certain. Obedience to symbols is scarcely a strict principle of moral entailment.

When generations are involved historically in moral issues, however, there is at least some knowledge both of events and persons. Even this disappears when we turn from the past to the future. If I ask why I should be required to limit my actions and forgo my gratifications now on behalf of those as yet unborn, the answer is subject to all the uncertainties of the historical case with the addition of an irremediable ignorance of who will be benefited. The identity of a thousand of my ancestors could in principle be recovered, but I can know nothing of the tens of thousands of persons who could descend from me within the next few centuries. And we are all equally in the dark about our successors as citizens of Great Britain—or will it be England only? (in my case, perhaps Scotland as well since my wife is Scottish). Or will it be the federation of Europe? Or will nothing corresponding to the country of my citizenship exist at all after a hundred years or so?

Yet no little portion of political life rests on the premise that

[3] For the reparations paid to Jews and to anti-fascists by Germany and Italy since 1945, a topic not adequately treated by scholars, see Bittker, pp. 140–41.

present day political collectivities will persist roughly (how roughly?) as they are into the indefinite future. The speeches of ministers, the propaganda of parties, the actions of planners, the demands of administrators, unhesitatingly assume that men ordinarily recognize the rights of generations of their countrymen yet to come. The additional and significant paradox here is that this assumption is well founded in behaviour. We do in fact respond quite spontaneously to an appeal on behalf of the future. The rulers of 'industrializing' nations, from the Soviets of the 1920s to the struggling peoples of Asia and Africa now, are able to behave with notable ruthlessness towards the men and women of their own day for the sake of their children and grandchildren. These are the very words they use, assimilating the temporal with the procreative meaning of the concept of the generation, though their perorations sometimes continue with the language of the collectivity—big phrases about the Russia, the Ghana, the China, the India of the centuries to come.

Here the indestructible moral entity of the nation state is extending its life forwards in time, with no limit as to period. It is interesting that men should feel reluctant to accept much responsibility for the very distant future, say a century or two ahead, and even more unwilling when it is a question of temporal rather than procreational generations. But there never seems to be any difficulty with a more immediate future. Indeed, keeping promises to do things a month, a year or even a decade ahead is understandably and correctly held to be political commonsense. We are here engaging within our own generation, even with ourselves, and we are prepared to do this backwards as well as forwards, though perhaps to a more limited extent.

But how far forwards, how far back? At this point the time-space occupied by a generation, together with its procreational constitution, become crucial, although, as we have seen, both of these things seem to be irremediably indefinite. Even if we could make up our minds about when one generation ends and another begins, we should still be left with the following problem. Can the moral relationship *between* generations be construed as the same as the moral relationship *within* generations? To solve the problem satisfactorily we should have to be clear whether there is a difference between a responsibility to *all* our predecessors or successors on the one hand and a responsibility to a particular past or future generation on the other, or to a particular set of them. The last two or three back, the next two or three forward, shall we say.

Enough has been said here to show that the solutions to this untidy bundle of thorny problems might involve a great deal of complicated and verbally repetitive discussion, and that it is unrealistic to expect that clear and definite answers could finally be given. This should hardly surprise us, since the problems of political theory and philosophy are always complex and indefinite, especially those to do with obligation. Rather than prolong the analysis of instances and possibilities, I propose to turn to a habit of mind which does exist, so it seems to me, when we think generationally and which does enable us to make both generational entities and the relationship between them rather more concrete things.

It would be going too far to claim that identifying and examining this habit of mind makes it possible to demonstrate propositions about generational relationships in any strict or convincing way. But it can, I believe, be cautiously claimed that reflection of this kind intimates the reasons why, for example, the concept of obligation over any span of more than two procreational generations hardly makes sense. It suggests that moral ties between generations almost inevitably go forward in the time dimension, rarely backwards. It implies that the answer to the question posed in my last paragraph must be a probable negative. We cannot be related with our predecessors and successors in a way which is at all closely analogous to the way in which we are related with our contemporaries, at least outside the generations of our fathers and our children, and this is because it is difficult to see how we can be strictly speaking *obliged* to them at all. Selective sentiment is all that exists to make us feel we have a debt to the early Victorians, shall we say, and the duty which we may feel we owe to the people who will inhabit our country and the rest of the world in the later twenty-first century and after is problematical in character. It has to be construed without benefit of the habit of mind in question.

Perhaps to go so far even in so tentative a way is to promise too much. The manner, I suggest, in which concreteness attaches to generations and the relationships between them is quite straightforward: we extend to whole orders of persons roles performed within the family or, more technically, within what students of historical social structure have come to call the co-resident domestic group. We think we perceive generations in society at large because we tend to see all persons in familial roles; all older men become fathers or father-like, older women mothers and mother-like, coevals are seen as siblings, younger persons and children as offspring; and so on, upwards and downwards.

It is further suggested that this is the context in experience and emotion which prompts us as we construe the meaning of the word 'generation' in the statements discussed in this essay. It makes it easy to proceed, as we find ourselves doing without hesitation or reflection, from the procreational to the temporal sense of the expression. Hence we come to make the quite unjustifiable assumption that there are boundaries to temporal generations, sub-sets of persons in the population at large, as clear-cut as the boundary between parents and children in the family. This is the way, for instance, in which we come to talk of the authority of the older generation, which is parental authority in the household writ large in society. This, I propose, is also why discussions of rights and duties over time tend, as did Edmund Burke, to seize upon just these familial relationships as a way of making some sense of the issues, and why such discussions seem to lose conviction directly the span goes beyond the stretch which includes grandparents and grandchildren.[4]

In spite of the rather imperfect fit between emotional relationships within the family on the one hand and relationships of justice and authority in political society on the other hand, I should like to argue between the two in respect of one particular trait. An individual, it seems to me, believes unquestioningly that he has a right to cherishing, welfare, gratification from his parents entirely gratuitously, without having to do anything for it, without having to pay. This is in fact the outstanding characteristic of the parent–child relationship, for both father and mother lavish gratification on their children without expecting reward. Parents nurture their children as an end in itself, and are

[4] See Rawls, 1972, pp. 128–9, etc.; Golding, 1972, p. 91, etc.; Barry, 1977, p. 299, etc. and (apparently) most of the authors he there cites.

satisfied merely by the act of doing so. There is nothing in the way of exchange in the mutual behaviour of old and young within the family group. It is on this asymmetrical character of these relationships that a tonic stress will be placed here.

Interchange between procreational generations can be translated for the purposes of ethical analysis into the conventional language of reciprocal rights and duties, where a right legitimately claimed is to be met, and cancelled, by a duty correctly performed. The propositions go like this. Parents have duties towards their children, but the fact of procreation gives parents no rights in them. Children have rights in their parents, but no duties towards them, not, that is to say, towards them as their progenitors. The duties in respect of procreation owed by children are paid to their own offspring, that is to say the grandchildren of their parents rather than to their parents themselves. In the ethical exchange between procreational generations, then, duties do meet rights; but not in respect of the same persons.

Hence it is possible to pronounce that duties go forwards in time, but rights go backwards. Duties of parents to children reciprocate rights of parents: rights of children in parents are reciprocated by duties of these children towards their children (i.e. the grandchildren of their own parents). In order for the rights of an individual to be met by duties on the part of another individual, it is necessary to have in view the next generation to that individual, that is the generation of his children, and in order that the duties of those children themselves can be paid to persons having rightful claims it is further necessary for grandchildren to appear. Even when three generations are seen in reciprocal ethical relationship in this way, however, there are still duties which are owing over time, as yet unperformed to the proper persons, and these are the duties of the final, grandchild generation. A crude metaphor would be that of a chain made out of hooks and eyes, where hooks have all to lie one way, and at the point where the chain stops a hook without an eye is always hanging forward.

My proposal is that these principles of ethical reciprocity characteristic of procreational generations, and so of the family group with which we are all familiar, can by inexact analogy be held to apply to temporal generations, that is to generational relationships in society at large, though within one collectivity only. In the same way as children within the family can expect nurture from their parents as a right, conferring no obligation upon them, so can the members of any generation of Englishmen take for granted the material, technical, cultural, social and political benefits which accrue to them from their predecessors. Their 'debt to the past' is to be satisfied by their duties to the future, and 'future' in this last phrase must be construed as 'the foreseeable future' because the distant future is not covered by the analogy. Since, like parents contemplating their own children, the members of a temporal generation spontaneously act as if they had this duty towards their immediate successors, statesmen and others can confidently voice those appeals to posterity which we have cited.

By this analogy there is the same asymmetrical[5] ethical relationship between succeeding temporal generations as there is between succeeding procreational generations, the same hook and eye connection. And in both cases there are discernible limits to the span over which structured generational relationships are effective. These are confined for the most part to the three-generational unit, though it seems permissible to assume that those alive at any one time have a right without obligation to the whole of their inheritance from the past. It is permissible also to look upon these unidirectional, hook-eye linkages extending indefinitely into the future. This is all that is left of Burke's eternal intergenerational 'contract'.

Nevertheless some of the implications of this argument by analogy for the ethical issues between generations which have been discussed so far will be perceived to be quite direct and positive. No living American, or Englishman, no con-

---

[5] This asymmetry, or non-reflexivity, can perhaps be thought of as a complement to that remarked upon in Barry (1977). There he rightly insists that a future 'generation' (never defined or discussed as an entity by him however) has no power over a present one, whilst a present one does have power over a future 'generation'. Barry's problem concerning 'sleepers' (environmental time bombs which do not affect the immediate but drastically affect the remote future) is typical of those which lie outside the scope of the present study. It is in my view of a different logical order and it is important that distinct issues in this difficult discussion should be held distinct.

temporary of ours in the 1970s can be said to have a moral responsibility for the enslavement of the Blacks, nor for any act of discrimination against Blacks which took place before the time of their own 'generation'. No conscientious West German of today is guilty simply because of his citizenship for the persecution of Jews committed by Germans of the 'inter-war generation'. But every American, every German, everyone now alive is strictly obliged to 'the coming generation' for all he now does, and one of the things he must do is to ensure that enslavement, racial discrimination, persecution of the kind which has been analysed, shall never occur, now or within the 'foreseeable future'. This forward obligation may well extend to future generations born later than their own children, but rapidly diminishes as time recedes forwards. It must also be assumed, in accordance with what was laid down at the outset, to be confined to the temporal generations which will succeed in the country of citizenship of the person concerned, but might extend to their succeeding procreative generations, one or two of them, wherever they lived.

Any rights or duties over time other than those referred to in the preceding two paragraphs fall outside the ground covered by the analogy. They must be construed as political rather than as generational. This statement applies to those potential moral responsibilities coming from the past which in course of time have crossed the boundaries of nation states, as for instance those of the descendants of British slave-traders towards the Blacks of the United States in their present situation. I shall have to leave that particular problem at this particular point, together with all others which can be shown to be political in the same way, and turn now to the lack of symmetry which has been claimed to exist in inter-generational rights and duties.

It may be objected against this claim that we all recognize both rights and duties in respect of others, often the same other persons, some of which reciprocate each other, others of which do not, though all are equally valid. The fact, then, that I have to pay to my children the same or similar costs in nurture that my parents paid to me, rather than paying those costs back to the parents themselves, does not of itself imply that I have no duties towards my parents as parents. I may well be bound *both* to bring up my children *and* to support my father and mother after I have acquired the means of doing so—if they are in need. The actual behaviour of particular persons seems to bear this out, especially at the present time. In some societies in India, for example, parents are said to have children in order to ensure support in their later years, support children have a duty to provide. By the analogy we are pursuing what is true of procreational generations within the family group must also be true of temporal generations in a national society at large.

This argument has undoubted force, and if it is pressed might perhaps be thought fatal to this whole attempt to clarify the ethical relationships between generations. There are two sets of considerations which can be put forward, however, in support of the view that the duties of children towards parents, in later life at least, must be looked on as predominantly social or even political in character—as instances in fact of the universal obligation we all have towards contemporaries in need—rather than as generational. The first comes from the nature of affection, familial and otherwise.

Although moralists and lawyers often talk of the duty of loving, even of repaying affection with affection, they carry little conviction with such language. The love which exists in a family group is neither a matter of rights or duties nor of reciprocity, and if it prompts children to support their ageing parents as well as their own dependent offspring, there is little of repayment in it, certainly of settling a procreational debt. To say this, of course, is not to deny that co-operation and interchange go on within the family group: approval and disapproval, reward and punishment, all the practices and expectations which keep associations in being. It is only to insist that dependent children will always receive from their parents immensely more than they give, and that they do not feel required to repay what came to them for love, at any time in their lives.

The second set of considerations bearing upon the duties of children to their parents after they have left the parental home is historical. As a widespread situation this is novel, and characteristic of ourselves in our own time. Though there always have been numbers of such grown and independent offspring with parents alive to whom they could have recognized their obligations, if indeed they felt them, their proportions have grown enormously in very recent years. In earlier times well over half and even approaching two-thirds of all brides and bridegrooms had lost their fathers at the time of marriage. The really crucial situation, in which a person might be called upon to support both ageing dependent parents and expensive offspring, and might have to choose between them, is certainly new in our time. Moreover in the past, at least in English history, there can be no doubt that political pressure had to be brought to bear to require children to support their needy parents, and that many such destitute parents were in fact supported by the State through the Poor Law, even if they had grownup, independent children at the time. Nothing like the same political persuasion had to be used to ensure that parents maintained their offspring.

Recent research has shown that the familistic picture of 'elder generations' being able to count on maintenance by the offspring and kin has been considerably overdrawn.[6] If in our new demographic and familial situation in the late twentieth century in high industrial times we decide that our now surviving parents have a right, an inter-generational right, to repayment for nurture supplied to us when we were children, we are making a deliberate choice. We are electing to regard what was in earlier times ordinarily a right to be claimed from society at large as a right to be claimed from one's own progeny.

On the other hand not everything we know about the attitudes and behaviour of traditional societies supports the general propositions which have been advanced about parents having duties towards their children but no rights in them. Societies still exist in which parents feel themselves at liberty to sell their children, and no more absolute right in a person than this can be imagined. These practices must have been commoner in the past, and children were certainly sold to the highest bidder by proletarian parents in early nineteenth-century London to become chimney boys and the

[6] See Laslett, *Family Life and Illicit Love in Earlier Generations*, 1977, chap. 4. 'The History of ageing and the aged', and its references. Countries and areas of Europe varied in their attitude to the old and in some, especially amongst the Russian peasant serfs for example, grandparents were far commoner in the West and did share households with their offspring.

like. Many of the ancestors of those very same black Americans we have referred to here must have been sold into slavery by their fathers and mothers, who received in return firearms and trinkets from the ruffians who were acting on behalf of the Royal Africa Company of London and other slaving concerns.

These unpleasing facts may serve as a reminder that an argument that proceeds as the present one does from observed behaviour to inferences about what is right is always partial and untidy, quite apart from begging the unsettled and unsettlable question about the relation of what is to what ought to be. In this uneasy situation I can do no more than appeal to what seems to have been the general approved practice, as the old Natural Lawyers used to do. Although men have in the past sold off their progeny, perhaps in some societies on a fairly large scale, and although a few nomadic Africans may still do such things, nearly everyone in the world would now condemn the practice as inhuman and unnatural. Even the much more limited right of a parent to take from his children their early earnings, which may well have been quite common in traditional European society, seems to have had no support in English common law.

It is naturally of considerable interest to our thesis that we are the first 'generation' in which grandparents, parents and grandchildren can expect to be contemporaneous. But this makes very little difference that I can see to their ethical relationships. Grandchildren or great-grandchildren, now appearing in appreciable numbers in our society and assuredly due to become more common, occupy no special ethical status in respect of grandparents or great-grandparents. They owe their biological seniors, as such, no more duties than their parents did, and these duties, I should still insist, derive from their general social obligations. They may suppose that they have legitimate rights of expectation in those more distant biological relatives, but these rights are surely felt to be less secure than those in their parents.

These pro-progenitors and pro-pro-progenitors for their part may feel somewhat reinforced in their sense of duty towards a more distant posterity, but they are also secure in the belief that by and large their inter-generational duty has been done to their own children. It is for these children to take care of those yet to come, and they (the immediate parents) are seen to resent any attempt of their own progenitors to usurp the duties they delight in performing. Even when, for the first time in history, something like a distant posterity comes into existence for old men to do their duty to—real persons at last able to take part in a fairly remote conversation between the generations—there is only a somewhat attenuated sense in which there can be understanding or exchange.

The overriding issue, as we have seen, is whether or not guilt and effective responsibility can be transferred over time, by procreational relationships in the case of individuals, and by analogy with procreational relationships between temporal generations in society at large. The argument has been that guilt cannot be inherited inter-generationally, for who can be made guilty by someone else doing his duty towards him?

As for responsibility, it has been held to be confined for the most part to what has been called the immediate future. If these positions are accepted, then, as has already been stressed, the only remaining basis for such transfers must be political, and it has been stated that the political puzzles presented to the theorist in this way cannot be broached on this occasion. It is worth noting, however, that, since the time of Locke, political theory seems to have held that the principle of continuous responsibility over time is intimately bound up with the inheritance of property.

Most of us may now consider that an argument about social relationships in general which is based on ownership of material things is hardly likely to be reputable. We may wonder for example whether John Rawls was well advised to take the just rate of savings, savings for future generations, as the point of departure for his reflections on inter-generational justice. It seems to me that the one thing any society at any time could be relied upon to do is to save, each individual saving with his own security in mind. This means, death coming as unexpectedly as it does, that they are bound to leave a great deal unspent behind them. Indeed it would be very difficult to find an example from the past where one 'generation' did spend their savings in a way which caused suffering to their successors, even if they may often have produced too many children to live comfortably on available resources. It is much easier to find examples of their consuming or wasting important elements in the environment in the way that the Ancients used up gold, or the Elizabethans the English forests. Robert Nozick of course is far freer with arguments from possessions and property and we cannot entirely escape the issue here.

The right to succeed to property is the most tangible which a child has in his parents, and that right is ordinarily only exercised after the death of the parent, after a procreational generation has completed itself. But what if the property which, in doing his duty to the child, the father bequeathed to him is itself based on injustice? If it consists, to repeat the example, in slaves, or in the money made out of selling and owning slaves?

Nothing which has been advanced here makes it a duty for a man to confer on his children ill-gotten gains; such possessions, by the rules of reciprocity, belong to the persons from whom they were stolen. But if a child should by generational position inherit a disputed possession, the criteria as to whether he should keep that inheritance are scarcely generational.

Such a decision, if the present argument be accepted, should not have been made on the grounds of guilt transferred from a past generation. Who knows how many of his possessions might be forfeit if the exact circumstances of ancestral acquisition were to become known and made into a moral or legal liability to him? It is true that children in such positions sometimes renounce their inheritances because they feel them to be the tainted products of capitalist exploitation or racialist oppression. To act in this way on what I am disposed to call, as with the citizens of Germany and the victimized Jews, a symbolic sense of guilt, is both understandable and praiseworthy. But it does not seem to me that the inheritor of such embarrassing property could be justly condemned for failing to make such renunciation on the grounds that this puts him in the position of his predecessor who did the despoiling. The condemnation would surely be of the politcal and social system which permitted the original injustice, and if the inheritor was held guilty at all, it would be for failing to do his best to alter that system in the present and for the sake of the future. Once more, the duty of the conscientious inheritor goes forwards in time, though the means by which he does his duty are outside the scope of inter-generational relationships. They belong again to politics.

This very tentative discussion leaves us with one final paradox. How can it be, it may be asked, that men act in inter-generational matters without ever apparently questioning them? Why is it that the skein of intricate issues which we have been fingering so gingerly here was never to my knowledge been picked up in the literature of philosophy, ethical or political, before the 1970s? The answer to these questions can be offered with more confidence.

Only yesterday in the political life of man, only fifty or a hundred years ago in the intellectual life of our own society, there was a universally accepted principle of continuity between generations, a revelationary principle. Religious revelation made it possible for time to be held irrelevant and one man in one generation to stand in the place of another man in another generation and if necessary on a special occasion to communicate with him. Political theory and social analysis have scarcely begun to appreciate the void left in their fabric by the entire abandonment of religious belief. The Hegelian metaphysic is no substitute. Existentialists, phenomenologists, logical analysts, veil of ignorance contractarians, are all in a like dilemma when it comes to such a question as the conversation between the generations.

4 Capitalist Man, Socialist Man[1]

Robert E Lane

> What we have here to deal with is a communist society, not as it has *developed* on its own foundation, but, on the contrary, as it *emerges* from capitalist society; which is thus in every respect, economically, morally and intellectually, still stamped with the birthmarks of the old society from whose womb it emerges.—KARL MARX

While a self-destructive economic system might be transformed into an efficient and equitable set of working institutions by a new socialist regime, it is unlikely that a population damaged by its experiences with capitalism (if that were the case) would be prepared for such a transformation. What this implies is that at least two parallel processes are required for change in a socialist direction, economic and psychological. But these may not be in harmony with one another. In the earlier Marxist version the two processes were sequential and harmonious: the economic process leading to breakdown was immanent in the capitalist system and came first; the psychological process leading to the regeneration of man followed upon his release from the repressive, alienating, humanly destructive influences of capitalism. The later incrementalist views of democratic socialism correct the Marxist economics, but retain much of its psychology, indeed, elaborating upon it. But nothing in contemporary psychological research or historical experience reveals a capacity for such rapid human change as these psychologies imply; they represent too plastic a view of human nature. The more nearly correct the analysis of capitalist destruction of human capacities and values, the more certainly wrong the hope of easy and rapid transformation.

We are here concerned with the problem of personality–environment fit, as this may be revealed by the failure of men trained under one system to fit easily into another. The fit depends upon the nature of men's basic needs, their plasticity, and the institutional requirements of each system. Were we to accept the Freudian model of men's

[1] This is a shortened version of 'Waiting for Lefty: The Capitalist Genesis of Socialist Man', *Theory and Society*, 5, 1978.

needs, there would be little hope for improvement under socialism, since these needs are instinctually given and reason has only the most tenuous control over lust and aggression. On the other hand, were we to accept a theory of great plasticity, relying, in some cases, on Darwinian mechanisms of personality selection (autonomous institutional change, selective rewards for adaptation, and selective socialization of the young for the required qualities), the transition might be easy, but the impetus to change would be missing. Capitalist man would already have adapted to his capitalist institutions. A psychological theory of human needs for which socialism would be a more favourable environment than capitalism would, therefore, offer the socialists the greatest grounds for hope. It would promote both change and adaptation.

As contrasted to the plasticity of Platonic or Lockean associationist psychology and to the various instinct theories (sometimes called 'passions') which might be traced from Hobbes through Freud to the sociobiologists, modern experimental psychology seems to offer just such a theoretical underpinning for socialism. These theories, and the research which explores them, are both motivational and cognitive. For example, the theories built around the concepts of 'competence', or 'fate control' suggest that men seek instinctually to control their own environments, just as the socialist seeks to remove from the impersonal market the fates of their members. The theories of 'self-fulfillment', 'ego development', and 'self actualization', also thought to be instinctual, but fragile, are beautifully consonant with Marx's theory of the final stage of communism. Theories of the need for achievement, while not instinctual, indicate that men will often work for intrinsic satisfactions, whether or not they receive monetary rewards—indeed, sometimes extrinsic rewards detract from their efforts and enjoyment. And there is similar hope in cognitive theories. At first maturational, that is, designed to account for the cognitive growth of the individual, these theories and research are now applied to whole populations or societies. They reveal the growth of 'cognitive complexity', or the capacity to entertain multiple concepts and integrate them into new solutions, as men pass from simple to complex societies. The transition from advanced capitalism to socialism would be facilitated by the development of a population whose members were more cognitively complex, for they can entertain ideas contrary to fact; they are not limited by the familiar, the status quo.

But lest one be misled by these research developments providing a psychological underpinning for socialist hopes, one should recall that the record of civilization reveals the long-term persistence of maladaptive solutions to the problem of environment-personality fit. The provision for a benign 'fit' in contemporary capitalism is certainly not clear, a point frequently made by the socialists. But it is even less clear that these motives and skills are enlisted in great social transformations, as three examples will suggest.

Studying displaced Russians after World War II, a Harvard team said:

> Virtually all aspects of the Soviet regime's pattern of operation seem calculated to interfere with the satisfaction of the Russian's need for affiliation. The regime has placed great strain on friendship relations... Many of the primary face-to-face organizations most important to the individual were attacked, or even destroyed by the regime. The break-up of the old village community and its replacement by the more formal, bureaucratic, and impersonal collective farm is perhaps the most outstanding example.

The new regime frustrated the expressiveness, the moral sensibilities, the need for nurturant leadership of its citizens. The transition was, in short, a human disaster.[2]

In the American Southwest the Spanish-Americans have been exposed to the dominant American culture for over a hundred years. Observing their changed value patterns over a fifteen-year period, another Harvard team reported that during that shorter period, 'the acculturation process among these people is progressing at a speed hitherto unknown'. Nevertheless the group has not yet developed the in-dividualistic, mastery over nature and fate, future-oriented, striving orientations which were necessary to accommodate themselves to the dominant culture. On the whole, say these authors, 'the changes to be noted are ... superficial ones made necessary by the demands for adaptation, and they have as yet scarcely touched the deeper convictions of the people'. The prospect is for continued slow acculturation, if the economy makes room for this marginal group, or, 'a fairly thorough-

[2] Alex Inkeles, Eugenia Hanfmann, and Helen Beier, 'Modal Personality and Adjustment to the Soviet Socio-Political System', *Human Relations*, XI (1958), pp. 3–21.

going disorganization both for the group as a whole and for personalities within the group'.[3]

The German workers in the 1930s, says Fromm, were acculturated to an authoritarian society and had developed authoritarian personalities. This meant that they could accept the egalitarian philosophies of the socialist and Communist parties so long as these views were expounded authoritatively by powerful party leaders. Paradoxically, when the egalitarian philosophies were challenged by a stronger authority, they lost their appeal. Humanistic egalitarianism was never resonant with the character structure of the German workers; it was not the content but the apparent strength and power of the source that had appealed to the workers. A stronger and more powerful Nazi party, therefore, easily won their loyalties.[4]

If the Russians, after perhaps 25 years of intensive conditioning, found the morality, the incentive system, the human relations of the Soviet Regime so unpersuasive; if the Spanish Americans after over 100 years of exposure to the American economic culture still found it alien; and if German workers espousing communist or socialist programs were so easily dislodged from their beliefs by an authoritative, voice, how very easy might it be for socialists come to power to assume an idealism, a collectivist orientation, a posture toward authority in the work place that was not there, perhaps reading it off an election record that did not mean that at all? Would a capitalist population, however motivated its members by drives toward self-actualization and competence and however great its cognitive development, be prepared for a new socialist economy?

Capitalist Man, Socialist Man

One way to enter this problem is to compare the idealized versions of man in the two societies, on the grounds that these are but heightened versions of what the systems require or

[3] Florence R. Kluckhohn and Fred L. Strodtbeck, *Variations in Value Orientations* (Evanston, Ill.: Row, Peterson and Co., 1961), pp. 175–257; the quotations are from p. 257.
[4] Erich Fromm, *Escape from Freedom* (New York: Rinehart, 1941), pp. 280–81.

will require. Although Marx himself was partially (but not totally) reticent about the nature of socialist man once the constraints and abuses of the capitalist economy had been removed, there is no dearth of interpreters on this ideal in the current literature. Thus Trotsky, in a lyrical moment, believed that socialist man 'will become immeasurably stronger, wiser, and subtler, his movements more rhythmic, his voice more musical... The average human type will rise to the heights of an Aristotle, a Goethe, a Marx.'[5] Marek Fritzhand, a Polish writer, interprets Marxian socialist man to be one who loves others 'as a natural phenomenon of human life... He feels the welfare of others as his very own'.[6] Bhikhu Parekh, a British interpreter, believes that socialist man will, in accepting the 'human brotherhood', also accept his own powers and talents 'as a social trust' with the implied 'social responsibility for the well-being of [others]', and will work co-operatively, not competitively, for the welfare of all.[7] Erich Fromm, a neo-psychoanalytically oriented writer, develops and endorses Marx's view of man's potentials which would come to flower in a socialist system. Man, in this scheme, is above all self-realizing, in the sense that he has within him creative powers, wide-ranging talents and curiosities, desires and capacities for autonomous self-regulation and self-expression, and naturally seeks mutual and co-operative relations with his fellow men.[8] These and many similar interpretations of man under socialism may lack veridical, even sober, properties, but they all reveal one basic point: man is naturally (in his 'essence', says Marx) a good and wonderful creature, stunted by the institutions of the market. Socialist institutions will set him free.

The same cannot be said of the idealized version, such as it is, of man in capitalist society. Of course, in talking about a future society, the socialist is unrestrained by concrete observations or immediate, practical requirements (and when

---

[5] Quoted in Michael Harrington, *Socialism* (New York: Bantam, 1973), p. 453.
[6] 'Marx's Ideal of Man', in Erich Fromm, ed., *Socialist Humanism* (Garden City, N.Y.: Doubleday/Anchor, 1966), pp. 180–81.
[7] 'Introduction' to his edited volume, *The Concept of Socialism* (New York: Holmes and Meier, 1975), pp. 1–13.
[8] Erich Fromm, 'Marx's Concept of Man', in his edited volume by the same name (New York: Ungar, 1961), p. 1–69.

Marx talks about these, he reverts to an incentive system not
unlike the capitalist one), but even in a like situation, before
the 'triumph' of capitalism, its defenders had more to say
about restraining the passions, channeling self-interest,
balancing anti-social tendencies, than about liberating a
benign essence.[9] Except perhaps, for Montesquieu's favourable opinion of 'the spirit of commerce', and some Scottish
Enlightenment views on promoting the market men's
'personal independence', its apologists viewed the self-
regulating market as a way of harnessing man's selfishness,
rather than as a way of expressing his better qualities. Adam
Smith, for example, had this to say about the 'disadvantages'
of the commercial spirit: 'The minds of men are contracted
and rendered incapable of elevation. Education is despised,
or at least neglected, and the heroic spirit is almost utterly
extinguished.'[10]

It is true that Herbert Spencer and William Graham
Sumner, among others, believed that capitalism nurtured the
virtues of individuation and self-reliance, but the weight is on
the other side. In comparison to 'the democratic character,'
for example, 'the capitalist character' has no moral standing,
and the 'marketing personality' and the 'organization man'
are despised. Capitalist man is a necessity; socialist man is a
fulfillment. Capitalist man grows in spite of the economy that
nurtures him; socialist man grows because of the economic
institutions that foster his growth. And this gives us a clue to
the major problem of the environment-personality fit under
socialism: the socialists require a great deal more of the
human personality than do the capitalists.

But these are figments; they tell us little about real persons
or even about the requirements and possibilities of the two
economic systems.

[9] Albert O. Hirschman, *The Passions and the Interests:
Political Arguments for Capitalism Before Its Triumph*
(Princeton, N.J.: Princeton University Press, 1977).
[10] Adam Smith, *Lectures on Justice, Police, Revenue, and
Arms*, quoted in Hirschman, ibid., pp. 106–7. Compare
Max Weber's mourning over the loss of 'the Faustian
universality of man' under the influence of rising capitalism
in *The Protestant Ethic and the Spirit of Capitalism* (New
York: Charles Scribner's Sons, 1958), p. 180.

The Capitalist Genesis of Socialist Man?

Socialism promises a society where personality development, a sense of community, and egalitarian moral values will flourish. In that sense it is a *high gain* system. But because it demands more of people, and because it breaks down the partial separation of economics and politics characteristic of capitalism, it threatens both inefficiency and the abuse of power. It is also a *high risk* system. These risks include the loss of appropriate work incentives and erosion of innovation, as well as the abuse of power. Let us examine these risks, recognizing that in so doing we slight much of the promise, the high gain, that socialism seems to offer.

Work incentives
The incentive system of a market economy makes no great demands upon men's altruism, orther-regardingness, empathy, or recognition of the brotherhood of man. Rather it employs a durable, reliable, primitive (in the sense of easily taught and easily learned) motivation based on self interest. Although there are doubts about the way the system actually works, it is seen to offer its rewards contingent upon effort, skill, and contribution, in good Skinnerian fashion. This makes reinforcement of the desired acts prompt and automatic, thus inducing the learning that makes the system work.

The incentive system in a socialist economy would rely on similar self interests, too, but there are demands for other motives, and a chorus of voices is raised against selfishness. Furthermore, work would take place under circumstances of security such that it would not be an economic necessity (he who did not work would eat), and it would be positively attractive in itself, offering intrinsic satisfactions, challenges, opportunities to grow, thus enlisting voluntary effort. To a larger extent than under capitalism, individual performance and reward would be separated, partly through rewarding collective or group effort, and partly through de-emphasizing monetary reward itself. Rewards would be more equalitarian because of floors and ceilings on income. The system would seek to elicit co-operative behaviour more than competitive behaviour, but also (and the requirements may be incompatible) each person would have more control over his own work, more autonomy and more responsibility. Workers would participate in more of the decisions affecting their lives and the work place itself would constitute a kind of community. Finally, productivity would have to be high; no (or few) socialist proposals envisage an economically poorer society.

By and large capitalist society has prepared men well for work in the institutions of democratic socialism as described, but there are certain caveats and certain inconsistencies in the socialist demands which signal problems. Assuming that socialist work will thrust responsibility and initiative back down the (inevitable) hierarchy to the individual worker, or to work groups which can only show initiative if the individuals are so disposed, the system requires high levels of individual initiative at the work place. The characterological history of qualities of independence and initiative is interesting. Hunting and fishing societies have the quality more often than do agricultural ones, which tend to be more passive and accepting of routine. Commercial societies, then, had to revive this quality, but early industrialism probably eroded it again among the manual work force. Advanced industrial society revived it again, with its demands for better educated workers to man positions requiring more discretion, and the use of automation to take over many routine jobs.[11] All the relevant measures of 'field independence', 'internal locus of control', and independence from custom and authority reveal advanced technological societies as possessing more of these qualities than the less advanced societies.[12]

[11] See Eva Mueller, *Technological Advance in an Expanding Economy* (Ann Arbor, Mich.: Institute for Social Research, 1969). Robert Blauner proposes a curvilinear theory of work alienation: low in the craft stage, rising through the machine and assembly line stage, declining at the automation stage. See his *Alienation and Freedom* (Chicago: University of Chicago Press, 1964).
[12] For some relevant cross cultural summaries, see Barbara B. Lloyd, *Perception and Cognition: A Cross-Cultural Perspective* (Harmondsworth, England: Penguin, 1972); Jacqueline Goodnow, 'Cultural Variations in Cognitive Skills', in Jerome Hellmuth, ed., *Cognitive Studies*, Volume 1 (New York: Brunner/Mazel, 1970); Stephen Bochner, Richard W. Brislin, and Walter J. Lonner, eds., *Cross-Cultural Perspectives on Learning* (New York:

And so far as we can tell, these tendencies are still accelerating under advanced capitalism, for qualities of initiative seem to be increasingly demanded by management facing conditions of great technological and organizational complexity. If there were any socialist disposition to believe that brotherhood, or collateral authority relationships would improve productivity more than individual initiative, a glance at the Zuni and Navaho economies where collateral relationships prevail, would destroy that disposition; they are well prepared for archaic herding, but not for modern socialism.

Because the socialists propose to establish conditions where men are secure in their jobs, or securely attached to a minimal income whether or not they have jobs, they must rely upon a set of work motives which embrace such concepts as the doing/striving orientation, a work ethic wherein their occupations are viewed as a moral 'calling', competition against an internalized standard of excellence—the need for achievement. Under capitalism these motives have grown and prospered, and in spite of current theories that a hedonistic, advertising-based, erosion of the work ethic has taken place, the secular evidence (attitudes, absenteeism, second jobs, labour force participation, job satisfaction) reveals the work ethic and need achievement to be strong and thriving. In the United States the content of hymns and stories stressed this achievement motive in 1960 to a degree not equalled during the previous hundred years.[13] The work ethic has not been eroded by social security and other welfare state legislation (such as guaranteed annual income); it is a reliable product of capitalism, even welfare state capitalism, available to the socialists when and if they come to power.

The idea of capitalism as fueled by competition in the sense of rivalry between known competitors has been exaggerated; rivalry is not, even theoretically, a part of 'competition' in a perfect market, where no single individual perceives his own acts as affecting that of any particular other. Market economists think of competition as choice: the competition

---

Halsted/John Wiley, 1975), especially (in this volume)
Harry Triandis, 'Cultural Training, Cognitive Complexity and Interpersonal Relations'.
[13] David C. McClelland, *Power, The Inner Experience* (New York: Irvington/John Wiley, 1975), p. 410.

between alternative opportunities. Furthermore, modern
industry requires as much co-operation as competition; it
requires men to work in groups where each depends upon the
action of another. And within a firm, deliberate attempts to
develop co-operative relationships among team workers are
as successful as deliberate efforts to develop a 'spirit of
competition' between rival competitors.[14] Scarcity is more
likely to breed competition than is affluence, at least in
primitive societies, and there is no evidence that individuals
in capitalist societies are more competitive, in the sense of
rivalrous, than others. Moreover, certain kinds of pro-social
(altruistic) behaviour are more common in the capitalist West
than in less developed countries. In spite of the attention
given to it, the competition/co-operation alternative is not a
problem.

But the collectivization of rewards may present
problems—even if 'successful'. It is true that men under
capitalism have developed a clear contingency expectation:
reward will be individual, extrinsic, and dependent upon
effort, contribution, skill; it is the feedback that tells them
their worth. While piece rate systems rarely work, more
carefully devised incentive systems sometimes do and the
entire reward structure is adjusted to these individualized
perceptions and expectations.[15] By separating income from
these contingencies (as above), by emphasizing collective
reward for collective effort, by equalizing rewards within a
narrow range, the socialists propose to alter these expectations. This may be possible, especially if jobs and
organizational climates are adjusted to increase the intrinsic
rewards of work, as Herzberg and the authors of *Work in
America* have proposed and some firms have tried to do, but
there are several caveats.[16] First, all work is both an exchange

[14] Richard M. Steers and Lyman W. Porter, *Motivation
and Work Behavior* (New York: McGraw-Hill, 1975),
Chapters 8–10, 15.
[15] Edward E. Lawler III, *Pay and Organizational
Effectiveness: A Psychological View* (New York: McGraw-
Hill, 1971).
[16] Frederick Herzberg, *Work and the Nature of Man*
(New York: Mentor/New American Library, 1973); *Work
in America*, Report of a Special Task Force to the
Secretary of Health, Education, and Welfare (Cambridge,
Mass.: MIT Press, n.d.).

of effort for satisfaction and, except in ascriptive systems, a means of establishing one's worth in one's own eyes. But it appears that praise from a supervisor, honour among co-workers, community esteem and media recognition will serve as well. To make these other rewards serve the function of pay incentives, however, offers few advantages, and the special disadvantage that they are more loosely tied to performance, the contingency link is more easily broken and, therefore, they may lose their power to motivate and may increase the sense of inequity: my benefit/effort ratio is smaller than someone else's.

Secondly, the collective rewards are certainly motivating, especially under the circumstances the socialists propose: participation in decisions, contribution to outcomes, sharing in the benefits. But these apply to face-to-face groups, not larger collectivities. Now it is the case that building these strong face-to-face cellular units in an enterprise can increase total productivity, but it is also the case that they can reduce productivity: the stronger the cell the greater the deviance from the norm. It is by no means certain, therefore, that creating small collectively rewarded units in an enterprise will serve the cause of the larger socialist undertaking. And it is certainly true that attempting to rely upon appeals to the public interest or general societal goals, except under external threat, are ineffective. A sympathetic observer of the Cuban effort to enlist volunteer unpaid teams of agricultural workers noted that the effort ended in a military type dragooning of reluctant participants.[17] In sum, the capitalist *Gesellschaft* has not destroyed the possibility of small scale *Gemeinschaft*, but neither capitalism nor any other system can prepare the socialists to convert an entire society into a working *community*.

As for the de-emphasis on money, a theme in all socialist writing since Marx, one could argue that the process is already taking place. This inference follows from studies showing the rise of post-materialist values in economically developing Western societies[18]; from studies of contributions

[17] René Dumont, cited in Michael Harrington, *Socialism*, p. 291.
[18] Ronald Inglehart, 'The Silent revolution in Europe: Intergenerational Changes in Post-Industrial Societies', *American Political Science Review*, LXV (1971), pp. 991–1017.

to an overall sense of well-being by various life 'domains' showing that family, friends, and non-working activities contribute more to happiness than does income, and, incidentally, revealing the very loose relationship between actual pay and satisfaction with pay[19]; from the rising cohorts of better educated workers seeking challenge and developmental opportunities more than pay and security in their occupational life and related studies showing that 'interesting work' contributes more to job satisfaction than does pay. Beyond a certain level, both within nations and between nations, pay is only an indicator of achievement; it is not sought by achievers for what it will buy but rather for what it tells them about themselves. Other indicators may (or may not) serve as well. The success motive, that is, is malleable and the socialists might simply harness it for other purposes. In conformity with economic laws, capitalism, by making real money, purchasing power, more plentiful decreases its value relative to other sources of satisfaction.

Innovation

The market creates incentives for invention, and, more important perhaps, for implementing invention and discovery; it provides capital for innovators, and multiple decision centers for experimentation, with varied risk preferences thus distributed throughout the economy. It creates penalties for failure to innovate. It further encourages innovation by exempting the innovating firms from the social costs of human obsolescence or redundancy, cultural disamenities, community dislocation, and the destruction of valued traditions, thrusting these costs onto individuals and governments. Thus it institutionalizes protections against human tendencies to prefer the familiar, to protect the established status hierarchies and interpersonal relations; it forces men to review and revise their routines. By rewarding innovators it creates them. But this institutionalization of innovation might be threatened by shifting power from units which themselves profit from innovation to units of government where the profit accrues to others, unless the

[19] Angus Campbell, Philip E. Converse, and Willard L. Rodgers, *The Quality of American Life* (New York: Russell Sage, 1976), pp. 76, 304, 374.

men who run the system have internalized the qualities which make them receptive to change.

These qualities would include:

> (1) the *capacity* for innovative thinking, implying cognitive complexity and the ability to imagine conditions contrary to fact;
>
> (2) an *evaluative* support of novelty and change implied, for example, in disagreement with the standard personality measurement question, 'If you try to change things very much, you will usually make them worse;'
>
> (3) characterological *autonomy* such that one is not at the mercy of either conventional authority or public opinion, that is, lack of conformism or an obedience orientation;
>
> (4) *tolerance of ambiguity*, of heterodoxy, and a willingness to entertain and 'play along with' a discrepant idea, and
>
> (5) to make these capacities and attitudes and values effective, a belief in the *effectiveness of one's own actions*, the absence of powerlessness/helplessness syndrome.

Wherever they have been measured, these traits are stronger in modern Western societies than in traditional societies, and as mentioned, they seem to be the product of a Western-type education. Within developing societies they are associated with exposure to modern industrial and commercial institutions[20]; within Western societies they tend to increase with education and, to some extent, with income. There is very little and conflicting evidence, however, that they are associated with any particular occupations, commercial or otherwise, except that they tend to increase with level of management in managerial hierarchies.

The trend data, to the extent that we have them, similarly represent a progressive improvement within the (American) capitalist system in generating a receptivity to change. Thus, there is direct evidence of the decline in authoritarianism, with its conventionalism and intolerance of ambiguity, evidence of a decline in parental support for conformism and other-directedness, a measured increase in tolerance for heterodoxy, and scattered indications of relaxed parental and peer group control over opinions, a process of sociological release or individuation.[21] The close relationship between

---

[20] Alex Inkeles and David H. Smith, *Becoming Modern* (Cambridge, Mass.: Harvard University Press, 1974).
[21] Nevitt Sanford, 'Authoritarian Personality in Contemporary Perspective', in Jeanne N. Knutson, ed.,

education (especially college education) and cognitive complexity, internal locus of control, and preferred range of novelty suggests, with some reservations, that these have also increased. These qualities have thrived under capitalism, but there is nothing which links them to capitalist institutions *per se*. There is, therefore, no reason to believe that they would wither under socialism.

Further, they are generally associated with two circumstances that the socialists might even enhance: a nurturant (but also 'critical') family socialization, and a degree of security and perceived lack of threat (the very opposite of some hard-line views of the uses of insecurity). The American capitalist variant is witnessing a disintegration of child care which can only be repaired by intelligent governmental policy. And, for all its affluence, capitalism promotes a sense of insecurity and, as many commentators have noted, a sense of scarcity. In both respects there are reasons to believe the socialists would do better.

On the other hand, qualities of innovativeness are concentrated in the better educated, the better off, the higher management.[22] To the extent that the socialists lodge investment or other strategic decisions in workers' councils they may create a conservative, change-resistant feature in their decision processes.

Finally, since socialism is sometimes associated (mistakenly, I think) with bureaucracy, it is useful to note first that in studies of welfare policies it is the bureaucrats, not the unions or the politicians, that have taken the lead in innovation,[23] and second, that studies of policy flexibility find

Handbook of Political Psychology (San Francisco: Jossey-Bass, 1973), p. 165; Otis Dudley Duncan, Howard Schuman, and Beverly Duncan, *Social Change in a Metropolitan Community* (New York: Russell Sage, 1973), p. 39; James A. Davis, 'Communism, Conformity, Cohorts, and Categories: American Tolerance in 1954 and 1972–73', *American Journal of Sociology*, 81 (1975), pp. 491–513; Vern L. Bengsten, 'Generation and Family Effects in Value Socialization', *American Sociological Review*, 40 (June 1975), pp. 358–71.

[22] Herbert M. Lefcourt, *Locus of Control* (New York: Erlbaum/Wiley, 1976), p. 114.

[23] Hugh Heclo, *Modern Social Politics in Britain and Sweden* (New Haven: Yale University Press, 1974).

that in some important respects bureaucrats are more flexible than those in other settings.[24]

The problem of innovativeness under socialism does not disappear in the light of these findings; but they do suggest that the characerological base for innovation under socialism has been created by innovative capitalism.

Authority

To some extent the market economy separates governmental and economic power, at least it does so more than socialist or partially socialized economies do. Further, within the private sector, power is decentralized, either by competition or by countervailing power. Authority over what shall be produced is vested in some uncertain balance between producers (producer sovereignty) and consumers (consumer sovereignty). Authority over whom to employ and what wages to offer is divided among employers, constrained by efficiency (non-particularistic) considerations, government regulations, and union power. Thus to some degree, at least, power is dispersed, constraints are institutionalized. And to that extent the constraint on power does not depend upon the conscience, the values of the powerful. Nor does it depend upon the volunteered, socially motivated attendance or vigilance or participation of the subjects of industrial power: if workers have little voice, they have the option of 'exit'— they can find another employer. Thus control of power in a capitalist economy, however adequate or inadequate, makes fewer demands on the personal qualities of either the powerful or the less powerful; it is institutionalized.

A socialist system, even if it decentralizes, even if it creates participant citizen and worker institutions, must, in order to implement its policies of planning and intelligent social guidance, have more power at the centre. The exception to this concentration of power lies in worker self-management within firms, but this requires volunteered vigilance, willingness to confront authority, balanced judgement at or near the bottom of the status hierarchy. In both cases, then, in the case of the institutionally less constrained central officials who must have internalized controls and interpret 'the public

[24] Melvin L. Kohn, 'Bureaucratic Man: A Portrait and an Interpretation', *American Sociological Review*, 36 (1971), pp. 461–74.

interest', and in the case of the worker self-managers who must have strengths of character to deal with authority without tension, the demands upon the individual personality are substantial.

The personal qualities that form internal restraints against the abuse of power share much in common with the ones that facilitate innovation, but they go beyond them. (1) The cognitively simple tend to be rule-bound and authoritarian. While often just as 'intelligent' as the cognitively complex, they tend to see only one solution to a problem, usually the conventional or 'authoritative' one. Groups made up of the cognitively simple tend to be less democratic than groups of the complex; a group cannot rise above the level of its members.[25] Thus *cognitive complexity* is a protection against authoritarianism and the abuse of power. And the findings and inferences leading us to conclude above that under modern capitalism cognitive complexity has increased offers the first hint of the capitalist genesis of this socialist (and democratic) requirement.

(2) The control of power implies the capacity to stand outside the conventional morality and the 'law and order' mentalities which the powerful employ to justify their rule, and standing outside, to generate and employ an independent morality. This capacity is embraced in the concept of post-conventional *moral reasoning* which has recently been measured and tested under a variety of circumstances. Generally, post-conventional moral reasoning is more common in advanced capitalist countries than in less developed countries; the levels increase with amount of formal education, with college education a condition of the higher levels. While there is no indication of historical increases in post-conventional moral reasoning among the working class, there is indication that middle-class levels may have increased in the past generation—at least in one American sample the middle-class sons of middle-class fathers achieved a higher level of moral reasoning than their fathers.[26]

[25] Harold M. Schroder, M. J. Driver, and S. Streufert, *Human Information Processing* (New York: Holt, Rinehart & Winston, 1967), pp. 3–41.
[26] Lawrence Kohlberg and R. Kramer, 'Continuities and Discontinuities in Childhood and Adult Moral Development', *Human Development*, 12 (1969), pp. 103–5.

(3) Because *authoritarianism* implies the preference of hierarchical situations where human relations are characterized by dominance and submission, because it defines the world as composed of glorified in-groups and denigrated out-groups, and because it rejects 'tenderness' in favour of toughness and aggression, and is uncomfortable with democratic leadership, the measured decline in authoritarianism represents a contribution to the world the socialists hope to create.

(4) The 'good Germans' who went along with Hitler were thought to be uniquely *obedient to authority* until Stanley Milgram showed that most normal, decent Americans would obediently give potentially lethal shocks to relatively unknown others when told to do so, not because of aggressiveness, but because they abdicated responsibility for their own acts.[27] Moreover survey evidence revealed that when Lieutenant Calley shot old men, women and children in a Viet Nam village under the impression that these were his orders, most Americans believed he was justified in the shooting and that they would have done the same thing.[28] The evidence is frightening and seems to call for further institutionalized checks against abuse of authority, not the internalized constraints the socialist scheme requires. But consider two modifying circumstances. First, the two personality qualities that restrained Milgram's subjects from 'malignant obedience' were high levels of moral reasoning and low authoritarianism, dealt with above. Second, Milgram closes his book with this quotation from Laski: '... the condition of freedom in any state is always a widespread and consistent skepticism of the canons upon which power insists.' For a decade the unthinking acceptance of American institutions, including capitalist ones, has been declining[29];

[27] Stanley Milgram, *Obedience to Authority* (New York: Harper and Row, 1974).
[28] Herbert C. Kelman and Lee Hamilton Lawrence, 'Assignment of Responsibility in the Case of Lt. Calley: Preliminary Report of a National Survey', *Journal of Social Issues*, 28 (1972), pp. 177–212.
[29] Louis Harris for the U.S. Senate Subcommittee on Intergovernmental Relations, *Confidence and Concern: Citizens View American Government* (Cleveland: Regal Books/King's Court Communications, 1974), p. 7.

the beginning of 'a widespread and consistent skepticism' may, if nurtured, temper malignant obedience.

(5) Since democratic control of institutions begins with *democratic interpersonal relations,* Tocqueville's belief that, for the Americans, 'Democracy has gradually penetrated into their customs, their opinions, and their forms of social intercourse; it is to be found in the details of their daily life as well as in the laws', offers the socialists modest hope for the one country of which they may despair. Whether or not this democratic social intercourse has persisted is hard to say; on the one hand there are documented reports of increased amoral manipulative interpersonal relations;[30] on the other hand the measures of interpersonal trust have remained constant for twenty years and, something Tocqueville would not have anticipated, there have been increases in friendships between blacks and whites, as well as other evidence of increased tolerance.[31]

(6) In the discussion of innovation, we discussed the sense that a person is the author of his own acts, a causal agent, the controller of his own fate. We also discussed the problem of conformity. The rise of 'internality' and the decline of conformity will serve the control of power as it serves to implement change. Perhaps of all the features discussed here, this one is the most important.

(7) Finally, the control of power requires active participation in power-controlling agencies: workers' councils, campaign committees, voluntary organizations of all kinds. Advanced capitalism as reflected in the record of the United States shows a mixed performance: a decline in proportion of the work force in unions combined with an increase, especially by the poor and disadvantaged, in voluntary organizations of all (other) kinds; a decline in voter turnout combined with an increase in other forms of electoral participation; a decline, too, in sense of political efficacy combined with an increase in political competence, as

[30] Richard Christie and Florence Geis, *Studies in Machiavellianism* (New York: Academic Press, 1970), pp. 315–21.
[31] *Political Indicator Time Series,* 1952–1970 (Ann Arbor, Mich.: Center for Political Studies of the University of Michigan, 1972).

reflected in better knowledge of the relationship between issues and parties, and between ideologies and issues.[32]

But on the specific question of participation in voluntary organizations designed to modify management control of the factory, a study by John Witte of an experiment in limited worker self-management in an American plant is revealing. Compared to the members of Yugoslav workers' councils, the Americans initiated more actions, spoke up more, challenged management more often, exercised, within the modest domain alloted to them, more influence. One important reason is that in the American case there was a difference of only two years of formal education between the worker council members and management members while in the Yugoslav plants there was a difference of eight years. Another important finding was that in the American plant it was the ambitious workers who did not believe that they could realistically expect a promotion who took the lead in the council initiatives.[33] A third important difference, reminiscent of Tocqueville's observation, was the historical culture of hierarchy and rank which the Yugoslavs inherited and had to transform, but which was absent in the American case. Quite independent of the influence of market institutions on personality, this suggests that a high level of worker education, a democratic culture, *and* the availability of personal ambition for voluntaristic worker control of management activities combine to offer the socialists promise for a participative system controlling the abuse of power.

[32] Herbert Hyman and Charles F. Wright, 'Trends in Voluntary Association Memberships of American Adults', *American Sociological Review*, 36 (1971), pp. 191–206; Sidney Verba and Norman H. Nie, *Participation in America: Political Democracy and Social Equality* (New York: Harper & Row, 1972), pp. 250–52; Philip E. Converse, 'Public Opinion and Voting Behavior', in Fred I. Greenstein and Nelson W. Polsbey, eds., *Handbook of Political Science* (Reading, Mass.: Addison-Wesley, 1975), Vol. 4, pp. 98–111.
[33] John Witte, *Democracy, Authority, and Alienation in Work: Worker's Participation in an American Corporation*, Dissertation, Yale University Library, 1978.

Conclusions

Marx was quite right: it is a mistake to press socialist institutions upon a society that is not ready for them, but the 'readiness' consists of the psychological qualities required to work a democratic socialist system and to protect it from degeneration into poverty, stasis, or the abuse of power.[34] Further, Marx may have been right about the immanent qualities of self-destruction in capitalism, but these are not economic; rather they deal with the tendencies of advanced capitalism to create values, especially among certain portions of the professional middle class, which the system itself cannot fulfill. And, as others have argued, under these circumstances it will be the universities and not the factories that generate discontent, for, true to their mission, they rehearse for their members alternative value schemes.

There are some ironies here. Of all the qualities which seemed most central to the prosperity of the socialist cause, something close to individualism is the most important: the individual's belief that outcomes are contingent upon his acts, his autonomy from collective pressure and authoritative command, his capacity for independent moral reasoning, his belief in himself and his own powers. Only such 'individualized individuals', generated by complex and nurturant institutions, can work a collectivist system. Further, it is affluence and security, not scarcity and threat, which create the possibility of generating such qualities. There may be other roads to socialism, such as the Tanzanians, the Chinese, the Cubans are embarked upon; but they will not be democratic socialisms unless these societies first create the conditions of autonomy, and then the autonomous persons themselves. Western affluence may not be necessary, but

[34] There is an ironic historical reversal in this 'correction' of Marx; according to Robert Tucker, the post 1845 Marx represented a direct translation into social terms of the concepts of self-alienation elaborated in the 1844 Paris manuscripts. Instead of the divided self we have the divided society, sociologizing of Marx's earlier psychology. What is suggested here is a return trip. See Tucker's *Philosophy and Myth in Karl Marx* (Cambridge: Cambridge University Press, 1961).

something like Western individualism (in the sense described) will be. For innovation and for the control of power the individual must have 'a place to stand' outside of the collectivity.

And so to return to the original concept of the fit between institutions and personality, there is hope, but not certainty, that advanced capitalist society has shaped a personality that would fit, with transitional strain, the proposed socialist institutions.

5 Paternalism[1]

Gerald Dworkin

I take as my starting point the 'one very simple principle' proclaimed by Mill in *On Liberty* ...

> That principle is, that the sole end for which mankind are warranted, individually or collectively, in interfering with the liberty of action of any of their number, is self-protection. That the only purpose for which power can be rightfully exercised over any member of a civilized community, against his will, is to prevent harm to others. He cannot rightfully be compelled to do or forbear because it will be better for him to do so, because it will make him happier, because, in the opinion of others, to do so would be wise, or even right.[2]

This principle is neither 'one' nor 'very simple.' It is at least two principles: one asserting that self-protection or the prevention of harm to others is sometimes a sufficient warrant and the other claiming that the individual's own good is *never* a sufficient warrant for the exercise of compulsion either by the society as a whole or by its individual members. I assume that no one, with the possible exception of extreme pacifists or anarchists, questions the correctness of the first half of the principle. This essay is an examination of the negative claim embodied in Mill's principle—the objection to paternalistic interferences with a man's liberty.

I

By paternalism I shall understand roughly the interference with a person's liberty of action justified by reasons referring exclusively to the welfare, good, happiness, needs, interests or values of the person being coerced. One is always well advised to illustrate one's definitions by examples, but it is

[1] Reprinted from *The Monist* 56, 1 (January 1972): pp. 64–84. The article has been shortened and there are some minor amendments.
[2] J. S. Mill, *Utilitarianism* and *On Liberty*, ed. by Mary Warnock (London: Fontana Library Edition, 1962), p. 135. All further quotes from Mill are from this edition unless otherwise noted.

not easy to find 'pure' examples of paternalistic interferences. For almost any piece of legislation is justified by several different kinds of reasons, and even if historically a piece of legislation can be shown to have been introduced for purely paternalistic motives, it may be that advocates of the legislation with an anti-paternalistic outlook can find sufficient reasons justifying the legislation without appealing to the reasons which were originally adduced to support it. Thus, for example, it may be that the original legislation requiring motorcyclists to wear safety helmets was introduced for purely paternalistic reasons. But the Rhode Island Supreme Court recently upheld such legislation on the grounds that it was 'not persuaded that the legislature is powerless to prohibit individuals from pursuing a course of conduct which could conceivably result in their becoming public charges', thus clearly introducing reasons of a quite different kind. Now I regard this decision as being based on reasoning of a very dubious nature, but it illustrates the kind of problem one has in finding examples. The following is a list of the kinds of interferences I have in mind as being paternalistic.

II

(1) Laws requiring motorcyclists to wear safety helmets when operating their machines.

(2) Laws forbidding persons from swimming at a public beach when lifeguards are not on duty.

(3) Laws making suicide a criminal offence.

(4) Laws making it illegal for women and children to work at certain types of jobs.

(5) Laws regulating certain kinds of sexual conduct, e.g., homosexuality between consenting adults in private.

(6) Laws regulating the use of certain drugs which may have harmful consequences to the user but do not lead to anti-social conduct.

(7) Laws requiring a license to engage in certain professions, with those not receiving a license subject to fine or jail sentence if they do engage in the practice.

(8) Laws compelling people to spend a specified fraction of their income on the purchase of retirement annuities (Social Security).

(9) Laws forbidding various forms of gambling (often justified on the grounds that the poor are more likely to throw away their money on such activities than the rich who can afford to).

(10) Laws regulating the maximum rates of interest for loans.
(11) Laws against duelling.

In addition to laws which attach criminal or civil penalties to certain kinds of action there are laws, rules, regulations, and decrees which make it either difficult or impossible for people to carry out their plans and which are also justified on paternalistic grounds. Examples of this are:

(1) Laws regulating the types of contracts which will be upheld as valid by the courts, e.g., (an example of Mill's to which I shall return) no man may make a valid contract for perpetual involuntary servitude.

(2) Not allowing as a defense to a charge of murder or assault the consent of the victim.

(3) Requiring members of certain religious sects to have compulsory blood transfusions. This is made possible by not allowing the patient to have recourse to civil suits for assault and battery and by means of injunctions.

(4) Civil commitment procedures when these are specifically justified on the basis of preventing the person being committed from harming himself. (The District of Columbia Hospitalization of the Mentally Ill Act provides for involuntary hospitalization of a person who 'is mentally ill, and because of that illness, is likely to injure *himself* or others if allowed to remain at liberty.' The term injure in this context applies to unintentional as well as intentional injuries.)

(5) Putting fluorides in the community water supply.

All of my examples are of existing restrictions on the liberty of individuals. Obviously one can think of interferences which have not yet been imposed. Thus one might ban the sale of cigarettes, or require that people wear safety belts in automobiles (as opposed to merely having them installed), enforcing this by not allowing motorists to sue for injuries even when caused by other drivers if the motorist was not wearing a seat belt at the time of the accident.

I shall not be concerned with activities which, though defended on paternalistic grounds, are not interferences with the liberty of persons, e.g., the giving of subsidies in kind rather than in cash on the grounds that the recipients would not spend the money on the goods which they really need, or not including a $1,000 deductible provision in a basic protection automobile insurance plan on the ground that the people who would elect it could least afford it. Nor shall I be concerned with measures such as 'truth-in-advertising' acts and the Pure Food and Drug legislation, which are often attacked as paternalistic but should not be considered so. In these cases all that is provided is information which it is presumed that rational persons are interested in having in order to make wise decisions. There is no interference with the liberty of the consumer unless one wants to stretch a point beyond good sense and say that his liberty to apply for a loan without knowing the true rate of interest is diminished. It is true that sometimes there is sentiment for going further than providing information—for example, when laws against usurious interest are passed preventing those who might wish to contract loans at high rates of interest from doing so, and these measures may correctly be considered paternalistic.

III

Bearing these examples in mind, let me return to a characterization of paternalism. I said earlier that I meant by the term, roughly, interference with a person's liberty for his own good. But as some of the examples show, the class of persons whose good is involved is not always identical with the class of persons whose freedom is restricted. Thus, in the case of professional licensing it is the practitioner who is directly interfered with and it is the would-be patient whose interests are presumably being served. Not allowing the consent of the victim to be a defense to certain types of crime primarily affects the would-be aggressor, but it is the interests of the willing victim that we are trying to protect. Sometimes a person may fall into both classes, as would be the case if we banned the manufacture and sale of cigarettes and a given manufacturer happened to be a smoker as well.

Thus we may first divide paternalistic interferences into 'pure' and 'impure' cases. In 'pure' paternalism the class of persons whose freedom is restricted is identical with the class of persons whose benefit is intended to be promoted by such restrictions. Examples: making suicide a crime, requiring passengers in automobiles to wear seat belts, requiring a Jehovah's Witness to receive a blood transfusion. In the case of 'impure' paternalism in trying to protect the welfare of a class of persons we find that the only way to do so will involve restricting the freedom of other persons besides those who are benefitted. Now it might be thought that there are no cases of 'impure' paternalism since any such case could always be justified on non-paternalistic grounds, i.e., in terms of preventing harms to others. Thus we might ban cigarette manufacturers from continuing to manufacture their product on the grounds that we are preventing them from causing illness to others in the same way that we prevent other manufacturers from releasing pollutants into the atmosphere, thereby causing danger to the members of the community. The difference is, however, that in the former but not in the latter case the harm is of such a nature that it could be avoided by those individuals affected if they so chose. The incurring of the harm requires, so to speak, the active co-operation of the victim. It would be mistaken theoretically and hypocritical in practice to assert that our interference in such cases is just like our interference in standard cases of protecting others from harm. At the very least someone interefered with in this way can reply that no one is complaining about his activities. It may be that impure paternalism requires arguments or reasons of a stronger kind in order to be justified, since there are persons who are losing a portion of their liberty and they do not even have the solace of having it be done 'in their own interest.' Of course in some sense, if paternalistic justifications are ever correct, then we are protecting others, we are preventing some from injuring others, but it is important to see the differences between this and the standard case.

Paternalism then will always involve limitations on the liberty of some individuals in their own interest, but it may also extend to interferences with the liberty of parties whose interests are not in question.

IV

I shall begin for dialectical purposes by discussing Mill's objections to paternalism and then go on to discuss more positive proposals.

An initial feature that strikes one is the absolute nature of Mill's prohibitions against paternalism. It is so unlike the carefully qualified admonitions of Mill and his fellow Utilitarians on other moral issues. He speaks of self-protection as the *sole* end warranting coercion, of the individual's own goals as *never* being a sufficient warrant. Contrast this with his discussion of the prohibition against lying in *Utilitarianism*:

> Yet that even this rule, sacred as it is, admits of possible exception, is acknowledged by all moralists, the chief of which is where the withholding of some fact . . . would save an individual . . . from great and unmerited evil.[3]

The same tentativeness is present when he deals with justice.

> It is confessedly unjust to break faith with any one: to violate an engagement, either express or implied, or disappoint expectations raised by our own conduct, at least if we have raised these expectations knowingly and voluntarily. Like all the other obligations of justice already spoken of, this one is not regarded as absolute, but as capable of being overruled by a stronger obligation of justice on the other side.[4]

This anomaly calls for some explanation. The structure of Mill's argument is as follows:

(1) Since restraint is an evil, the burden of proof is on those who propose such restraint.

(2) Since the conduct which is being considered is purely self-regarding, the normal appeal to the protection of the interests of others is not available.

(3) Therefore, we have to consider whether reasons involving reference to the individual's own good, happiness, welfare, or interests are sufficient to over-come the burden of justification.

(4) We either cannot advance the interests of the individual by compulsion, or the attempt to do so involves evil which outweighs the good done.

(5) Hence, the promotion of the individual's own interests does not provide a sufficient warrant for the use of compulsion.

Clearly the operative premise here is (4) and it is bolstered by claims about the status of the individual as judge and appraiser of his welfare, interests, needs, etc.

> With respect to his own feelings and circumstances, the most ordinary man or woman has means of knowledge im-measurably surpassing those that can be possessed by any one else.[5]

[3] Mill, *Utilitarianism* and *On Liberty*, p. 174.
[4] Ibid., p. 299.
[5] Ibid., p. 207.

> He is the man most interested in his own well-being: the interest which any other person, except in cases of strong personal attachment, can have in it, is trifling, compared to that which he himself has.[6]

These claims are used to support the following generalizations concerning the utility of compulsion for paternalistic purposes.

> The interferences of society to overrule his judgement and purposes in what only regards himself must be grounded on general presumptions; which may be altogether wrong, and even if right, are as likely as not to be misapplied to individual cases.[7]

> But the strongest of all the arguments against the interference of the public with purely personal conduct is that when it does interefere, the odds are that it interferes wrongly and in the wrong place.[8]

> All efforts which the individual is likely to commit against advice and warning are far outweighed by the evil of allowing others to constrain him to what they deem is good.[9]

Performing the utilitarian calculation by balancing the advantages and disadvantages, we find that:

> Mankind are greatest gainers by suffering each other to live as seems good to themselves, than by compelling each other to live as seems good to the rest.[10]

From which follows the operative premise (4).

This classical case of a utilitarian argument with all the premises spelled out is not the only line of reasoning present in Mill's discussion. There are asides, and more than asides, which look quite different, and I shall deal with them later. But this is clearly the main channel of Mill's thought and it is one which has been subjected to vigorous attack from the moment it appeared—most often by fellow Utilitarians. The link that they have usually seized on is, as Fitzjames Stephen put it, the absence of proof that the

> mass of adults are so well acquainted with their own interests and so much disposed to pursue them that no compulsion or

---

[6] Ibid., p. 206.
[7] |Ibid., p. 207.
[8] Ibid., p. 214.
[9] Ibid., p. 207.
[10] Ibid., p. 138.

restraint put upon them by any others for the purpose of promoting their interest can really promote them.[11]

Even so sympathetic a critic as Hart is forced to the conclusion that:

> In Chapter 5 of his essay Mill carried his protests against paternalism to lengths that may now appear to us as fantastic ... No doubt if we no longer sympathize with this criticism this is due, in part, to a general decline in the belief that individuals know their own interest best.[12]

Mill endows the average individual with

> too much of the psychology of a middle-aged man whose desires are relatively fixed, not liable to be artificially stimulated by external influences; who knows what he wants and what gives him satisfaction or happiness; and who pursues these things when he can.[13]

Now it is interesting to note that Mill himself was aware of some of the limitations on the doctrine that the individual is the best judge of his own interests. In his discussion of government intervention in general (even where the intervention does not interfere with liberty but provides alternative institutions to those of the market), after making claims which are parallel to those just discussed, e.g.,

> People understand their own business and their own interests better, and care for them more, than the government does, or can be expected to do,[14]

he goes on to an intelligent discussion of the 'very large and conspicuous exceptions' to the maxim that:

> Most persons take a juster and more intelligent view of their own interest, and of the means of promoting it than can either be prescribed to them by a general enactment of the legislature, or pointed out in the particular case by a public functionary.[15]

[11] J. F. Stephen, *Liberty, Equality, Fraternity* (New York: Henry Holt & Co. [1873]), p. 24.
[12] H. L. A. Hart, *Law, Liberty and Morality* (Stanford, Cal.: Stanford University Press, 1963), p. 32.
[13] Ibid., p. 33.
[14] J. S. Mill, *Principles of Political Economy*, vol. 2 (New York: P. F. Collier and Sons, 1900), p. 448.
[15] Ibid., p. 458.

Thus there are things

> of which the utility does not consist in ministering to inclination, nor in serving the daily uses of life, and the want of which is least felt where the need is greatest. This is peculiarly true of those things which are chiefly useful as tending to raise the character of human beings. The uncultivated cannot be competent judges of cultivation. Those who most need to be made wiser and better, usually desire it least, and, if they desired it, would be incapable of finding the way to it by their own lights.
>
> ... A second exception to the doctrine that individuals are the best judges of their own interest, is when an individual attempts to decide irrevocably now what will be best for his interest at some future and distant time. The presumption in favour of individual judgement is only legitimate, where the judgement is grounded on actual, and especially on present, personal experience; not where it is formed antecedently to experience, and not suffered to be reversed even after experience has condemned it.[16]

The upshot of these exceptions is that Mill does not declare that there should never be government interference with the economy, but rather that

> ... in every instance, the burden of making out a strong case should be thrown not on those who resist but on those who recommend government interference. Letting alone, in short, should be the general practice: every departure from it, unless required by some great good, is a certain evil.[17]

In short, we get a presumption, not an absolute prohibition. The question is: Why doesn't the argument against paternalism go the same way?

I suggest that the answer lies in seeing that in addition to a purely utilitarian argument Mill uses another one as well. As a Utilitarian Mill has to show, in Fitzjames Stephen's words, that:

> Self-protection apart, no good object can be attained by any compulsion which is not in itself a greater evil than the absence of the object which the compulsion obtains.[18]

To show this is impossible—one reason being that it isn't true. Preventing a man from selling himself into slavery (a paternalistic measure which Mill himself accepts as legitimate), or from taking heroin, or from driving a car without

[16] Mill, *Principles*, 2:459.   [17] Ibid., 451.
[18] Stephen, *Liberty*, p. 49.

wearing seat belts, may constitute a lesser evil than allowing him to do any of these things. A consistent Utilitarian can only argue against paternalism on the grounds that it (as a matter of fact) does not maximize the good. It is always a contingent question that may be refuted by the evidence. But there is also a non-contingent argument which runs through *On Liberty*. When Mill states that

> there is a part of the life of every person who has come to years of discretion, within which the individuality of that person ought to reign uncontrolled either by any other person or by the public collectively,

he is saying something about what it means to be a person, an autonomous agent. It is because coercing a person for his own good denies this status as an independent entity that Mill objects to it so strongly and in such absolute terms. To be able to choose is a good that is independent of the wisdom of what is chosen. A man's 'mode of laying out his existence is the best, not because it is the best in itself, but because it is his own mode.'[19]

> It is the privilege and proper condition of a human being, arrived at the maturity of his faculties, to use and interpret experience in his own way.[20]

As further evidence of this line of reasoning in Mill, consider the one exception to his prohibition against paternalism.

> In this and most civilized countries, for example, an engagement by which a person should sell himself, or allow himself to be sold, as a slave, would be null and void; neither enforced by law nor by opinion. The ground for thus limiting his power of voluntarily disposing of his own lot in life, is apparent, and is very clearly seen in this extreme case. The reason for not interfering, unless for the sake of others, with a person's voluntary acts, is consideration for his liberty. His voluntary choice is evidence that what he so chooses is desirable, or at least endurable, to him, and his good is on the whole best provided for by allowing him to take his own means of pursuing it. But by selling himself for a slave, he abdicates his liberty; he forgoes any future use of it beyond that single act.
>
> He therefore defeats, in his own case, the very purpose which is the justification of allowing him to dispose of himself. He is no longer free; but is thenceforth in a position which has no longer the presumption in its favour, that

[19] Mill, *Utilitarianism* and *On Liberty*, p. 197.
[20] Ibid., p. 186.

would be afforded by his voluntarily remaining in it. The principle of freedom cannot require that he should be free not to be free. It is not freedom to be allowed to alienate his freedom.[21]

Now leaving aside the fudging on the meaning of freedom in the last line, it is clear that part of this argument is incorrect. While it is true that *future* choices of the slave are not reasons for thinking that what he chooses then is desirable for him, what is at issue is limiting his immediate choice; and since this choice is made freely, the individual may be correct in thinking that his interests are best provided for by entering such a contract. But the main consideration for not allowing such a contract is the need to preserve the liberty of the person to make future choices. This gives us a principle—a very narrow one—by which to justify some paternalistic interferences. Paternalism is justified only to preserve a wider range of freedom for the individual in question. How far this principle could be extended, whether it can justify all the cases in which we are inclined upon reflection to think paternalistic measures justified, remains to be discussed. What I have tried to show so far is that there are two strains of argument in Mill—one a straightforward Utilitarian mode of reasoning, and one which relies not on the goods which free choice leads to but on the absolute value of the choice itself. The first cannot establish any absolute prohibition but at most a presumption (and indeed a fairly weak one) given some fairly plausible assumptions about human psychology; the second, while a stronger line of argument, seems to me to allow on its own grounds a wider range of paternalism than might be suspected. I turn now to a consideration of these matters.

V

We might begin looking for principles governing the acceptable use of paternalistic power in cases where it is generally agreed that it is legitimate. Even Mill intends his principles to be applicable only to mature individuals, not those in what he calls 'non-age.' What is it that justifies us in interfering with children? The fact that they lack some of the emotional and cognitive capacities required in order to make

[21] Ibid., pp. 235–236.

fully rational decisions. It is an empirical question to just what extent children have an adequate conception of their own present and future interests, but there is not much doubt that there are many deficiencies. For example, it is very difficult for a child to defer gratification for any considerable period of time. Given these deficiencies and given the very real and permanent dangers that may befall the child, it becomes not only permissible but even a duty of the parent to restrict the child's freedom in various ways. There is, however, an important moral limitation on the exercise of such parental power which is provided by the notion of the child eventually coming to see the correctness of his parent's interventions. Parental paternalism may be thought of as a wager by the parent on the child's subsequent recognition of the wisdom of the restrictions. There is an emphasis on what could be called future-oriented consent—on what the child will come to welcome, rather than on what he does welcome.

The essence of this idea has been incorporated by idealist philosophers into various types of 'real-will' theory as applied to fully adult persons. Extensions of paternalism are argued for by claiming that in various respects, chronologically mature individuals share the same deficiencies in knowledge, capacity to think rationally, and the ability to carry out decisions that children possess. Hence in interfering with such people we are in effect doing what they would do if they were fully rational. Hence we are not really opposing their will, hence we are not really interfering with their freedom. The dangers of this move have been sufficiently exposed by Berlin in his *Two Concepts of Liberty*. I see no gain in theoretical clarity nor in practical advantage in trying to pass over the real nature of the interferences with liberty that we impose on others. Still, the basic notion of consent is important and seems to me the only acceptable way of trying to delimit an area of justified paternalism.

Let me start by considering a case where the consent is not hypothetical in nature. Under certain conditions it is rational for an individual to agree that others should force him to act in ways which, at the time of action, the individual may not see as desirable. If, for example, a man knows that he is subject to breaking his resolves when temptation is present, he may ask a friend to refuse to entertain his requests at some later stage.

A classical example is given in the Odyssey when Odysseus

commands his men to tie him to the mast and refuse all future orders to be set free, because he knows the power of the Sirens to enchant men with their songs. Here we are on relatively sound ground in later refusing Odysseus's request to be set free. He may even claim to have changed his mind, but since it is just such changes that he wished to guard against we are entitled to ignore them.

A process analogous to this may take place on a social rather than individual basis. An electorate may mandate its representatives to pass legislation which, when it comes time to 'pay the price', may be unpalatable. I may believe that a tax increase is necessary to halt inflation though I may resent the lower pay cheque each month. However, in both this case and that of Odysseus the measure to be enforced is specifically requested by the party involved and at some point in time there is genuine consent and agreement on the part of those persons whose liberty is infringed. Such is not the case for the paternalistic measures we have been speaking about. What must be involved here is not consent to specific measures, but rather consent to a system of government, run by elected representatives, with an understanding that they may act to safeguard our interests in certain limited ways.

I suggest that since we are all aware of our irrational propensities, deficiencies in cognitive and emotional capacities and avoidable and unavoidable ignorance, it is rational and prudent for us to in effect take out 'social insurance policies.' We may argue for and against proposed paternalistic measures in terms of what fully rational individuals would accept as forms of protection. Now, clearly since the initial agreement is not about specific measures, we are dealing with a more-or-less blank cheque and therefore there have to be carefully defined limits. What I am looking for are certain kinds of conditions which make it plausible to suppose that rational men could reach agreement to limit their liberty even when other men's interests are not affected.

Of course, as in any kind of agreement schema, there are great difficulties in deciding what rational individuals would or would not accept. Particularly in sensitive areas of personal liberty, there is always a danger of the dispute over agreement and rationality being a disguised version of evaluative and normative disagreement.

Let me suggest types of situations in which it seems

plausible to suppose that fully rational individuals would agree to having paternalistic restrictions imposed upon them. It is reasonable to suppose that there are 'goods' such as health which any person would want to have in order to pursue his own good—no matter how that good is conceived. This is an argument that is used in connection with compulsory education for children, but it seems to me that it can be extended to other goods which have this character. Then one could agree that the attainment of such goods should be promoted even when not recognized to be such, at the moment, by the individuals concerned.

An immediate difficulty that arises stems from the fact that men are always faced with competing goods and that there may be reasons why even a value such as health—or indeed life—may be overriden by competing values. Thus the problem with the Jehovah's Witness and blood transfusions. It may be more important for him to reject 'impure substances' than to go on living. The difficult problem that must be faced is whether one can give sense to the notion of a person irrationally attaching weights to competing values.

Consider a person who knows the statistical data on the probability of being injured when not wearing seat belts in an automobile and knows the types and gravity of the various injuries. He also insists that the inconvenience attached to fastening the belt every time he gets in and out of the car outweighs for him the possible risks to himself. I am inclined in this case to think that such a weighing is irrational. Given his life-plans which we are assuming are those of the average person, his interests and commitments already undertaken, I think it is safe to predict that we can find inconsistencies in his calculations at some point. I am assuming that this is not a man who for some conscious or unconscious reasons is trying to injure himself, nor is he a man who just likes to 'live dangerously'. I am assuming that he is like us in all the relevant respects but just puts an enormously high negative value on inconvenience—one which does not seem compre-hensible or reasonable.

It is always possible, of course, to assimilate this person to creatures like myself. I also neglect to fasten my seat belt and I concede such behaviour is not rational, but not because I weigh the inconvenience differently from those who fasten the belts. It is just that having made (roughly) the same calculation as everybody else, I ignore it in my actions. [Note: a much better case of weakness of the will than those usually given in ethics texts.] A plausible explanation for this deplorable habit is that although I know in some intellectual sense what the probabilities and risks are, I do not fully appreciate them in an emotionally genuine manner.

We have two distinct types of situation in which a man acts in a non-rational fashion. In one case he attaches incorrect weights to some of his values; in the other he neglects to act in accordance with his actual preferences and desires. Clearly there is a stronger and more persuasive argument for paternalism in the latter situation. Here we are really not—by assumption—imposing a good on another person. But why may we not extend our interference to what we might call evaluative delusions? After all, in the case of cognitive delusions we are prepared, often, to act against the expressed will of the person involved. If a man believes that when he jumps out the window he will float upwards—Robert Nozick's example—would we not detain him, forcibly if necessary? The reply will be that this man doesn't wish to be injured, and if we could convince him that he is mistaken as to the consequences of his action he would not wish to perform the action. But part of what is involved in claiming that a man who doesn't fasten his seatbelts is attaching an irrational weight to the inconvenience of fastening them is that if he were to be involved in an accident and severely injured, he would look back and admit that the inconvenience wasn't as bad as all that. So there is a sense in which if I could convince him of the consequences of his action he also would not wish to continue his present course of action. Now the notion of consequences being used here is covering a lot of ground. In one case it's being used to indicate what will or can happen as a result of a course of action, and in the other it's making a prediction about the future evaluation of the consequences— in the first sense—of a course of action. And whatever the difference between facts and values—whether it be hard and fast or soft and slow—we are genuinely more reluctant to consent to interferences where evaluative differences are the issue. Let me now consider another factor which comes into play in some of these situations which may make an important difference in our willingness to consent to paternalistic restrictions.

Some of the decisions we make are of such a character that they produce changes which are in one or another way irreversible. Situations are created in which it is difficult or impossible to return to anything like the initial state at which the decision was made. In particular, some of these changes will make it impossible to continue to make reasoned choices in the future. I am thinking specifically of decisions which involve taking drugs that are physically or psychologically addictive and those which are destructuve of one's mental and physical capacities.

I suggest we think of the imposition of paternalistic interferences in situations of this kind as being a kind of insurance policy which we take out against making decisions which are far reaching, potentially dangerous and irreversible. Each of these factors is important. Clearly there are many decisions we make that are relatively irreversible. In deciding to learn to play chess I could predict, in view of my general interest in games, that some portion of my free time was going to be pre-empted and that it would not be easy to give up the game once I acquired a certain competence. But my whole life style was not going to be jeopardized in an extreme manner. Further, it might be argued that even with addictive drugs such as heroin one's normal life-plans would not be seriously interfered with if an inexpensive and adequate supply were readily available. So this type of argument might have a narrower scope than appears to be the case at first.

A second class of cases concerns decisions which are made under extreme psychological and sociological pressures. I am not thinking here of the making of the decision as being something one is pressured into—e.g., a good reason for making duelling illegal is that unless this is done many people might have to manifest their courage and integrity in ways in which they would rather not do so—but rather of decisions such as that to commit suicide which are usually made at a point where the individual is not thinking clearly and calmly about the nature of his decision. In addition, of course, this comes under the previous heading of all-too-irrevocable decisions. Now there are practical steps which a society could take if it wanted to decrease the possibility of suicide—for example, not paying social security benefits to the survivors or, as religious institutions do, not allowing such persons to be buried with the same status as natural deaths. I think we may count these as interferences with the liberty of persons to attempt suicide, and the question is whether they are justifiable.

Using my argument schema the question is whether rational individuals would consent to such limitations. I see no reason for them to consent to an absolute prohibition, but I do think it is reasonable for them to agree to some kind of enforced waiting period. Since we are all aware of the possibility of temporary states, such as great fear or depression, that are inimical to the making of well-informed and rational decisions, it would be prudent for all of us if there were some kind of institutional arrangement whereby we were restrained from making a decision which is (all too) irreversible. What this would be like in practice is difficult to envisage, and it may be that if no practical arrangements were feasible then we would have to conclude that there should be no restriction at all on this kind of action. But we might have a 'cooling off' period, in much the same way that we now require couples who file for divorce to go through a waiting period. Or, more farfetched, we might imagine a Suicide Board composed of a psychologist and another member picked by the applicant. The Board would be required to meet and talk with the person proposing to take his life, though its approval would not be required.

A third class of decisions—these classes are not supposed to be disjoint—involves dangers which are not either sufficiently understood or appreciated correctly by the persons involved. Let me illustrate, using the example of cigarette smoking, a number of possible cases.

(1) A man may not know the facts—e.g., smoking between 1 and 2 packs a day shortens life expectancy 6.2 years, the costs and pain of the illness caused by smoking, etc.
(2) A man may know the facts, wish to stop smoking, but not have the requisite will power.
(3) A man may know the facts but not have them play the correct role in his calculation because, say, he discounts the danger psychologically because it is remote in time and/or inflates the attractiveness of other consequences of his decision which he regards as beneficial.

In case 1 what is called for is education, the posting of warnings, etc. In case 2 there is no theoretical problem. We are not imposing a good on someone who rejects it. We are simply using coercion to enable people to carry out their own goals. (Note: There obviously is a difficulty in that only a subclass of individuals affected wish to be prevented from doing what they are doing.) In case 3 there is a sense in which we are imposing a good on someone since, given his current appraisal of the facts, he doesn't wish to be restricted. But in another sense we are not imposing a good since what is being claimed—and what must be shown or at least argued for—is that an accurate accounting on his part would lead him to reject his current course of action. Now we all know that such cases exist, that we are prone to disregard dangers that are only possibilities, that immediate pleasures are often magnified and distorted.

If in addition the dangers are severe and far-reaching, we could agree to allow the state a certain degree of power to intervene in such situations. The difficulty is in specifying in advance, even vaguely, the class of cases in which intervention will be legitimate.

A related difficulty is that of drawing a line so that it is not the case that all ultra-hazardous activities are ruled out, e.g., mountain climbing, bull fighting, sports car racing, etc. There are some risks—even very great ones—which a person is entitled to take with his life.

A good deal depends on the nature of the deprivation—e.g., does it prevent the person from engaging in the activity completely or merely limit his participation?—and how important to the nature of the activity is the absence of restriction when this is weighed against the role that the activity plays in the life of the person. In the case of automobile seat belts, for example, the restriction is trivial in nature, interferes not at all with the use or enjoyment of the activity, and does, I am assuming, considerably reduce a high risk of serious injury. Whereas, for example, making mountain climbing illegal completely prevents a person from engaging in an activity which may play an important role in both his life and his conception of the person he is.

In general the easiest cases to handle are those which can be argued about in the terms which Mill thought to be so important—a concern not just for the happiness or welfare, in some broad sense, of the individual, but rather a concern for the autonomy and freedom of the person. I suggest that we would be most likely to consent to paternalism in those instances in which it preserves and enhances for the individual his ability to rationally consider and carry out his own decisions.

I have suggested in this essay a number of types of situations in which it seems plausible that rational men would agree to granting the legislative powers of a society the right to impose restrictions on what Mill calls 'self-regarding' conduct. However, rational men knowing something about the resources of ignorance, ill will and stupidity available to the lawmakers of a society—a good case in point is the history of drug legislation in the United States—will be concerned to limit such intervention to a minimum. I suggest in closing two principles designed to achieve this end.

In all cases of paternalistic legislation there must be a heavy and clear burden of proof placed on the authorities to demonstrate the exact nature of the harmful effects (or beneficial consequences) to be avoided (or achieved) and the probability of their occurrence. The burden of proof here is twofold—what lawyers distinguish as the burden of going forward and the burden of persuasion. That the authorities have the burden of going forward means that it is up to them to raise the question and bring forward evidence of the evils to be avoided. Unlike the case of new drugs where the manufacturer must produce some evidence that the drug has been tested and found not harmful, no citizen has to show with respect to self-regarding conduct that it is not harmful or promotes his best interests. In addition, the nature and cogency of the evidence for the harmfulness of the course of action must be set at a high level. To paraphrase a formulation of the burden of proof for criminal proceedings—better ten men ruin themselves than one man be unjustly deprived of liberty.

Finally, I suggest a principle of the least restrictive alternative. If there is an alternative way of accomplishing the desired end without restricting liberty, then although it may involve great expense, inconvenience, etc., the society must adopt it.

6 Procedural Democracy

Robert A Dahl

If one makes certain minimal assumptions about a human association, I shall argue here, then one must also accept the reasonableness of certain criteria for evaluating how that association governs itself. These criteria specify democratic procedures, and an association that satisfied all of the criteria would be fully democratic in its procedures.

However, since their origins in classical Greece, democratic ideas have been plagued by the problem of inclusion: what persons have a rightful claim to be included as citizens with full and equal rights to participate in governing the association? My strategy will be to leave this problem initially unsolved in order to set out the assumptions and the criteria of procedural democracy. I shall then examine several well known solutions to the problem—those advanced by Schumpeter, Locke, Rousseau and Mill—and show that they are defective. I shall conclude by offering what seems to me a more satisfactory solution to the problem of inclusion.

I Assumptions

Let me start by assuming that each of a number of persons has in mind the idea of forming an association for certain purposes, or changing an already existing association in order to adapt to conditions as they now understand them. Among other things, the association will have rules, or will make decisions about rules, that are to be binding on the members. Anyone to whom the rules apply is defined as a member. Thus being subject to the rules and decisions of the association is an essential characteristic of membership; it is sufficient to distinguish members from non-members.

Suppose one believes that the following assumptions are valid:

> (A1) There is a need among the members or putative members[1] for *binding decisions* on at least some matters, and

---

[1] Hereafter, in the case of an association not yet formed, member means putative member.

so for a process that will eventuate in binding decisions on these matters.

This condition has two aspects. First, at least some of the purposes the members have in mind can be satisfactorily attained if and only if at least some members are influenced to act, or not to act, in certain ways.[2] Second, the actions necessary to these purposes can be brought about if, and only if, there exists a procedure by means of which the members, or some of them, can decide on a rule, policy, purpose, principle, act, or pattern of conduct with which members will be obliged to act consistently. The obligation to act consistently with the rule is imposed on *all* members in the sense that even when acts by particular members or offices are specified, all members are required not to act in such a way as to impede or prevent that particular act.

In order to bring about the acts they seek, rule makers might create an expectation that violators of the rule will be punished by officials. Conceivably, however, decisions might be binding without punishments by officials or other members. It might be enough to evoke an expectation of divine or magical sanctions. Or the mere process of enacting and announcing a rule might cause enough members to adopt it as a principle of conduct so as to produce a quite satisfactory level of compliance. In short, the need for binding decisions, and for procedures to bring them about, does not imply that the association is necessarily coercive, employs the threat of violent sanctions to bring about compliance, or possesses other characteristics that are often used to distinguish a state from other sorts of associations.

(A2) A process for making binding decisions ought to include at least two stages: setting the agenda and deciding the outcome.

Setting the agenda is the part of the process during which the matters are selected on which decisions are to be made (including a decision not to decide the matter). Deciding the outcome, or the *decisive stage,* is the time during which the process culminates in an outcome, signifying that a rule has definitely been adopted or rejected. If setting the agenda is, so to speak, the first say, the decisive stage is the last say, the final word, the controlling decision, the moment of sovereignty

[2] Hereafter expressions like 'acting' are meant to include not acting in certain ways.

with respect to the matter at hand. Until the decisive stage is completed, the process of decision-making is tentative; it may lead to discussion, agreements, even outcomes of votes; but these are all preliminary, may be over-ruled at the decisive stage, and are not binding on the members. Decisions are binding only at the conclusion of the decisive stage.

(A3) Binding decisions should be made only by members.

That is, no person who is not a member is properly qualified, in the broadest sense, to make, or participate in making, decisions that will be binding on members. I say nothing about the possible grounds for such a belief, which are many. It may be, for example, that the founders of the association have managed to include among the members everyone who is considered to be fully qualified, or everyone who must be included if the rule is to be useful, or everyone whose interests are affected. But other reasons would also suffice.

(A4) Equally valid claims justify equal shares.

That is, if the claims made on behalf of A,B,C ... to an object of value, X, are judged to be equally valid, then any procedure for allocating X to A,B,C ... must give equal regard to the claims of each.

Because this principle seems to have well-nigh universal acceptability, one might suspect that it is tautological. I think it falls just short of a tautology, but it is close enough to being so as to make its contradiction seem quite fundamentally arbitrary. Thus suppose that Christopher, Ann, and Jane each claims the last piece of pie; they agree (or I hold) that their claims are equally valid; that is, there are no grounds for asserting that, say, Christopher's claims are superior to Ann's or Jane's; or that either Ann's or Jane's are better. Then they must also agree (or I must insist) that any procedure for allocating the piece of pie must give equal regard to the claims of each. The principle does not specify a particular procedure. Several procedures might therefore be thought to satisfy the principle equally well: The piece of pie might be divided equally among them, or awarded according to a random process, etc.

Even with the addition of this elementary principle of fairness, the conditions set out so far do not constitute grounds for asserting that an association ought to be governed by democratic procedures. If a single member were judged by all the others to be definitely more qualified than they to make decisions on all the matters which the association is to deal with, or if there were a graded hierarchy of competencies, then to say that the association ought to be governed by the one person, or by a graded hierarchy, would not be inconsistent with the judgment that all the preceding conditions also hold.

In order for democratic procedures to be required, it is sufficient to add one additional and highly crucial assumption:

> (A5) The claims of a significant number of members as to the rules, policies, etc., to be adopted by binding decisions are valid and equally valid, taken all around, and no member's claims are, taken all around, superior or overriding in relation to the claims of this set of members.

This set of members I am going to call the demos. Members of the demos are citizens, though this usage is not meant to imply that they are necessarily citizens of a state.

A 'significant number' must, of course, be more than one member; otherwise democratic procedures would not be required nor could the procedures be democratic. What constitutes a sufficiently large number or proportion, however, has been an issue of great theoretical and practical importance. It is directly bound up with the question of whose claims are valid and equally valid. These issues are central to the problem of inclusion: what persons have a rightful claim to be included in the demos? Since this question is too important to be closed off merely by stipulation, I want to defer it for the time being. Meanwhile, the grounds that would properly justify having one's claims accepted as equally valid are not at issue here. I shall simply assume that one arrives at such a judgement somehow; whether the grounds are reasonable or unreasonable is not at this point a matter of concern. In this way a controversial issue in the history of democratic ideas and practises can be set aside for consideration later on.

I I   Criteria

Suppose, then, some collection of persons wish to form an association, and one believes that the five assumptions described above are valid with respect to this group. Then it is reasonable to hold that the procedures by which the demos is to arrive at its decisions ought to meet certain criteria, which I am going to call the criteria of procedural democracy.

When I say that the procedures ought to meet certain criteria, I mean that if one believes in the assumptions, then one must reasonably affirm the desirability of the criteria; conversely, to reject the criteria is in effect to deny that the assumptions apply.

One additional point. The criteria do not specify any *particular* procedure, such as majority rule. Specific procedures cannot be extracted from the criteria. The criteria are standards against which proposed procedures are to be evaluated. They do not eliminate all elements of judgment in evaluation. I think it should not be surprising that democratic theory, like most other normative theories, cannot furnish completely unambiguous answers in all concrete situations in which a choice has to be made between alternative proposals.

Political Equality
First, all proposed procedures for making binding decisions must be evaluated according to *the criterion of political equality*. That is, the decision rule for determining outcomes at the decisive stage must take into account, and take equally into account, the expressed preferences of each member of the demos as to the outcome. The expression of preferences as to the outcome at the decisive stage is, of course, what we usually mean by 'voting' and 'a vote'; thus the criterion of political equality specifies that at the decisive stage each citizen has an equal vote.

To reject this criterion would be to deny at least one of two premises discussed earlier. Either equally valid claims do not justify equal shares, or it is not true that the claims of a significant number of members are valid and equally valid.

However, the criterion does not explicitly embody a particular method of voting or elections. It is not reducible solely to the principle of one man one vote, or to the principle that each citizen should have an equal vote in districts of equal numbers of voters, potential voters, or residents, or to a system of proportional representation based on equal votes. To adopt the criterion implies that specific procedures like these ought to be evaluated according to the extent to which they satisfy the conclusions. How preferences may best be expressed and what the specific rules should be for taking preferences into account, and equally into account, are questions requiring additional judgments; but procedures judged to meet the criterion better ought to be preferred over those that meet it worse. Obviously the requirement that the better be preferred to the worse holds even if all the procedures proposed are in some respects defective.

Nor does the criterion explicitly specify the majority principle. It requires only that the majority principle and alternatives to it be evaluated according to the criterion, and the solution that best meets the criterion of political equality be adopted. Whether majority voting is the best, or always the best, is thus left open.

Effective Participation

The second criterion according to which all proposed procedures must be evaluated is the criterion of *effective participation*. According to this criterion, throughout the process of making binding decisions, one must have an adequate opportunity, and an equal opportunity, for expressing his or her preferences as to the final outcome. Thus citizens must have adequate and equal opportunities for placing questions on the agenda, and for expressing reasons for endorsing one outcome rather than another. For to deny any citizen adequate opportunities for effective participation means that their preferences cannot be known, or cannot be correctly known, and hence cannot be taken into account. And if some citizens have less opportunity than others, then their preferences as to the final outcome are less likely to be taken equally into account. But not to take their preferences as to the final outcome equally into account is to reject the criterion of political equality, and thus to deny the condition of roughly equal qualification, taken all around.

Any specific procedures, then, must be evaluated according to the adequacy of the opportunities they provide for, and the relative costs they impose on, expression and participation by the demos in making binding decisions. Other things being equal, procedures that meet the criteria better are to be preferred over those that meet it less well. Once again, the requirement that the better be chosen over the worse clearly applies even if all the options are thought to be imperfect in some respect. Thus having the agenda for the assembly determined by a council of 500, chosen by lot, as in classical Athens, would meet the criterion better than having the agenda set single handedly by Pericles or Creon, even if the system of selection by lot involved some minor departures from a strictly random selection in which every citizen had an exactly equal chance of being selected.

I think it is consistent with historic usage to say that any association satisfying these two criteria is, at least to that extent, *procedurally democratic*. To put it somewhat formally, in order to leave room for some important distinctions to come, I want to call such an association *procedurally democratic* (or a *procedural democracy*) in a *narrow sense*. The criteria enable one to evaluate a large number of possible procedures. They are not decisive in cases where a procedure is better according to one criterion and worse by the other. Moreover, any evaluation would ordinarily require additional judgements about the facts of the particular situation, or about general tendencies and regularities of human behaviour and action. Nonetheless, the criteria are far from vacuous. Although I will not introduce a rigourous argument here, it would be hard to deny that procedures providing for decisions by a randomly selected sample of citizens would satisfy the criteria better than a procedure by which one citizen makes binding decisions for all the rest, or that a voting scheme allocating one vote to each citizen would be better than a scheme in which some citizens had ten votes and others none. I do not mean to imply that judgements about alternatives like these could invariably result from a perfectly rigourous argument ending in a completely unassailable conclusion.

Enlightened Understanding

As I have already suggested, judgements about the existence, composition, and boundaries of a demos are highly contestable. Thus one might simply challenge such judgements outright by asserting that some citizens are more qualified than the rest to make the decisions required. This objection of course raises a fundamental challenge to procedural democracy and is generally a premise in a counter-argument for aristocracy, meritocracy, or rule by a qualified elite. It is not this fundamental objection that I wish to consider at the moment, but rather a second kind of objection which might run rather like this:

> I agree—the objector might say—that the citizens are equally well qualified, taken all around. I agree also that none among them, or among the other members, or among non-members are so definitely better qualified as to warrant their making the decisions instead of the demos. Yet for all that, I think the citizens are not as well qualified as they might be. They make mistakes about the means to the ends they want; they also choose ends they would reject if they were more enlightened. I agree then that they ought to govern themselves by procedures that are satisfactory according to the criteria of procedural democracy, narrowly defined. Yet a number of different procedures will satisfy the criteria about equally well; among these, however, some are more likely to lead to a more enlightened demos—and thus to better decisions— than others. Surely these are better procedures, and ought to be chosen over the others.

One might object, I suppose, that enlightenment has nothing to do with democracy. But I think this would be a foolish and historically false assertion. It is foolish because democracy has usually been conceived as a system in which 'rule by the people' makes it more likely that 'the people' will get what it wants, or what it believes is best, than alternative systems, like aristocracy, in which an elite determines what is best. But to know what it wants, or what is best, the people must be enlightened, at least to some degree. And because advocates of democracy have invariably recognized this, and placed great stress on the means to an informed and enlightened demos, such as education and public discussion, the objection is also historically false.

I propose therefore to amplify the doctrine of procedural democracy by adding a third criterion. Unfortunately, I do not know how to formulate the criterion except in words that are rich in meaning and correspondingly ambiguous. Let me, however, offer this formulation for *the criterion of enlightened understanding*:

> In order to express his or her preferences accurately, each citizen ought to have adequate and equal opportunities for

> discovering and validating, in the time permitted by the need
> for a decision, what his or her preferences are on the matter to
> be decided.

This criterion implies, then, that alternative procedures for making decisions ought to be evaluated according to the opportunities they furnish citizens for acquiring an understanding of means and ends, and of oneself and other relevant selves. Yet if the criterion is accepted, ambiguous as it may be, I think it would be hard to justify procedures that cut off or suppressed information which, were it available, might well cause citizens to arrive at a different decision; or gave some citizens much easier access than others to information of crucial importance; or presented citizens with an agenda of decisions that had to be decided without discussion, though time was available; and so on. To be sure, these may look like easy cases; but a great many political systems—perhaps most—operate according to the worse not the better procedures.

Control of the Agenda

If an association were to satisfy all three criteria, it could properly be regarded as a *full procedural democracy with respect to its agenda* and *in relation to its demos.* the criteria are to be understood as aspects of the best possible political system, from a democratic point of view; while no actual system could be expected to satisfy the criteria perfectly, systems could be judged more democratic or less, and to that extent better or worse, according to how nearly they meet the criteria.

Yet to say that a system is governed by fully democratic procedures 'with respect to an agenda' and 'in relation to a demos' suggests the possibility that the three criteria are incomplete. The two qualifying clauses imply the possibility of restrictions—of democratic decision-making processes limited to a narrow agenda, or responsive to a highly exclusive demos, or both. To judge whether a demos is appropriately inclusive and exercises control over an appropriate agenda evidently requires additional standards. The catch is that the condition of equal qualification is of indefinite range: it need apply only to certain matters or to some members of an association. Obviously, to say that some persons are sufficiently well qualified to govern themselves on some matters is not to say that all persons are sufficiently competent to govern themselves on all matters.

Thus the conditions set out earlier are no longer sufficient for generating the additional criteria we need. To remedy this defect in the conditions, I now propose a change of strategy. I shall propose a fourth criterion, and show what sort of judgement as to equality would impose this criterion.

In order to see more clearly why a fourth criterion is needed, let us suppose that Philip of Macedon, having defeated the Athenians at Chaeronea, deprives the Athenian assembly of the authority to make any decisions on matters of foreign and military policy. The citizens continue to assemble some forty times a year and decide on many matters; but on some of the most important questions they must remain silent. With respect to 'local' matters, the Athenian polis is no less democratic than before; but with respect to foreign and military affairs, the Athenians are now governed hierarchically by Philip or his minions.

Again: let us imagine that during the Nazi occupation of Norway, Hitler had allowed the Norwegians to use their democratic political institutions for one or two matters— driving speeds for civilian traffic, let us say—but nothing else. If the Norwegians had gone along with this arrangement, we might conclude that while they had retained some nominal degree of 'democracy', in a broad sense they had lost it. Save for one subject of minor importance, Norwegians would be denied the opportunity to make binding decisions on the matters they felt important and fully qualified to decide for themselves. If we were to take as valid their own judgement as to their competence, then we must also hold that the criteria of procedural democracy ought to apply to all the questions they feel are important and not merely to trivial matters. For to say that some persons outside the demos should be able to prevent the demos from deciding for itself which questions it wishes to put on the agenda of things to be decided according to the criteria of procedural democracy is to deny at least one of the original premises: binding decisions ought to be made only by members, equally valid claims justify equal shares, and no member's claims are, taken all around, superior or overriding in relation to the claims of the demos.

These considerations suggest an additional criterion, *final control of the agenda by the demos:*

> The demos must have the exclusive opportunity to make decisions that determine what matters are and are not to be decided by means of procedural democracy.

The criterion of final control is perhaps what is also meant when we say that in a democracy the people must have the final say, or must be sovereign. A system that satisfies this criterion as well as the other three could be regarded as *a full procedural democracy in relation to its demos.*

According to this criterion, a political system would be procedurally democratic even if the demos decided that it would not make every decision on every matter, but instead chose to have some decisions on some matters made, say, in a hierarchical fashion by judges or administrators. As long as the demos could effectively retrieve any matter for decision by itself, the criterion would be met. In this respect, then, the doctrine of procedural democracy allows more latitude for delegation of decision-making than would be permissible by Rousseau's eccentric definition of democracy in the *Social Contract.* By defining democracy so as to make delegation impermissible, Rousseau could hardly avoid concluding, as he did, that democracy (in his sense) would be impossible among human beings, though perhaps satisfactory for gods.

Thus the criterion of final control does not presuppose a judgement that the demos is qualified to decide *every* question requiring a binding decision. It does presuppose a judgement that the demos is qualified to decide (1) which matters do or do not require binding decisions, (2) of those that do, which matters the demos is qualified to decide for itself, and (3) the terms on which the demos delegates authority. To accept the criterion as appropriate is therefore to imply that the demos is the best judge of its own competence and limits. Consequently, to say that certain matters ought to be placed beyond the final reach of the demos—in the sense that the demos ought to be prohibited from dealing with them at all—is to say that on these matters the demos is not qualified to judge its own competence and limits.

Let me now phrase our revised assumption as follows:

> (A5.1) *The Full Condition of Equal Qualification.* With respect to all matters, citizens are qualified, and equally well qualified, taken all around, to decide which matters do or do not require binding decisions; of those that do, which matters

108   *Robert A Dahl*

the demos is qualified to decide for itself; and the terms on which the demos delegates authority.

By *delegation* I mean a revocable grant of authority, subject to recovery by the demos. Empirically, of course, the boundaries between delegation and alienation are not always sharp, and what begins as delegation might end as alienation. But the theoretical distinction is nonetheless crucial.

In a system of full procedural democracy decisions about delegation would be made according to democratic procedures. But alienation would clearly violate the criterion of final control, and would be inconsistent with the judgement that the full condition of equal qualification existed among a demos.[3]

The criterion of final control completes the requirements for full procedural democracy in relation to a demos. If all the members of some set of persons are judged equally qualified, in the full sense, and if the other conditions set out earlier are held to exist among them, then the procedures according to which these persons, the demos, make binding decisions ought to be evaluated according to the four criteria. If citizens were reasonable, they would select the procedures that best meet the criteria.

III   The Problem of Inclusion

The criteria of procedural democracy assume the existence of a demos of qualified citizens. However, neither the existence of a demos nor the scope of its competence can be settled satisfactorily merely by assumption. Any specific claim of either kind would surely be highly contestable. Thus the assumptions have allowed me to by-pass two inter-related problems:

[3] In this respect the criterion comes closer to meeting Rousseau's restrictions in the *Social Contract* than might first appear. Rousseau would allow a sovereign people to grant executive power to (1) itself or a majority ('democracy'), (2) a minority ('aristocracy'), or (3) a single person ('monarchy'). What the people may not do is alienate its sovereignty, the power to make laws. Although 'democracy' in sense (1) is impractical, all three forms of delegating executive power are equally legitimate because, and as long as, the people does not alienate any of its sovereignty. Cf. particularly Book 2, Chapters 1 and 6, and Book 3, Chapter 6.

(1) The problem of inclusion: What persons have a rightful claim to be included in the demos?
(2) The scope of its authority. What rightful limits are there on the control of a demos? Is alienation ever permissible?

Finding solutions is particularly difficult for two reasons. First, not only is it hard to find much direct confrontation with these problems by democratic theorists, but political and moral theory is typically expressed in universalistic terms—'all men', 'all persons'—that belie the need for boundaries even as the theory prescribes limits on conduct. Second, the two problems are interdependent; a solution to one seems to depend on a solution to the other.

Thus the extent to which a particular demos ought to have final control over the agenda evidently depends on a prior judgement as to the scope of matters which the demos is qualified to decide. In this sense, judgements as to the scope of the agenda and the composition of the demos are interdependent. A judgement as to the competence of the demos bears on the scope of its agenda; and the nature of an agenda bears on a judgement as to the composition of the demos. The demos being given, the scope of its agenda can be determined. The scope of an agenda being given, the composition of an appropriate demos to make decisions on those matters can be determined. But in principle the one cannot be determined independently of the other.

In this essay, however, I intend to explore only the first problem. I shall argue that we cannot successfully deal with it without directly meeting the question of competence and openly confronting the view that a meritorious elite of exceptional knowledge and virtue ought to govern. This rival idea, which the Greeks called aristocracy and I shall call meritocracy, seems to me to constitute the greatest challenge to democracy, both historically and in the present world. I shall show that insofar as democratic theorists like Locke and Rousseau evaded taking direct and explicit issue with the challenge of meritocracy, they allowed a lethal defect to remain in the foundations of democratic ideas.

What properly constitutes a demos? Who must be included in a properly constituted demos, and who may or must be excluded from it?

The question of inclusion in (or exclusion from) the demos would scarcely present a serious challenge if a demos could enact rules that were binding only on itself. In that case, an outsider might still argue that a demos was acting unwisely or unjustly toward itself; but this would hardly give the outsider a justifiable claim to be included. Some associations do escape the problem in this way. The rules of an association might be binding only on its demos, either because all members of the association are also citizens, in which case the association is fully inclusive, or because every member is free to leave the association at any time with no great difficulty, in which case a member who objects to a rule can simply escape the application of the rule by withdrawing from the association.

It is by no means true of every association, however, that its demos can enact rules that are binding only on itself. A trade union might enforce a rule preventing non-members from working at a particular trade or workplace. An even more obvious and certainly more important exception is of course the state. Even if a state met all four of the criteria for procedural democracy and thus were a full procedural democracy in relation to its citizens, it could enact laws that were enforceable against persons who were not citizens, did not have the right to participate in making the laws, and had not given their consent either explicitly or implicitly to the laws they were forced to obey. Indeed every state has done so in the past, and there are grounds for thinking that all states will continue to do so in the future.

If some persons are excluded from the demos of a state, and yet are compelled to obey its laws, do they have a justifiable claim to be included in the demos or else to be excluded from the domain of enforcement? How inclusive should the demos be? Are there criteria for judging when, if ever, exclusion is rightful or inclusion is obligatory?

Citizenship as Wholly Contingent

One response is that the grounds for deciding who ought to be included in a demos are inherently particularistic and historical, often indeed primordial, and cannot be set forth as general principles. Thus citizenship is wholly contingent on circumstances that cannot be specified in advance. This is Schumpeter's solution.

Although democratic ideas often yield rather ambiguous answers to the question of inclusion, Schumpeter was an exception. It is an 'inescapable conclusion', he asserted, that we must 'leave it to every populus to define himself' [sic]. He rested his argument on an incontestable historical fact: what had been thought and legally held to constitute a 'people' has varied enormously, even among 'democratic' countries. What is more, there are no grounds for rejecting any exclusion whatsoever as improper: 'it is not relevant whether we, the observers, admit the validity of those reasons or of the practical rules by which they are made to exclude portions of the population; all that matters is that the society in question admits it.' He pressed his argument relentlessly. The exclusion of Blacks in the American South does not allow us to say that the South was undemocratic. The rule of the 'Bolshevik party' in the Soviet Union 'would not *per se* entitle us to call the Soviet Republic undemocratic. We are entitled to call it so only if the Bolshevik party itself is managed in an undemocratic manner—as obviously it is.'[4]

The last two examples beautifully illustrate the absurdities to which we may be led by the absence of any criterion for defining the *demos*. It is undeniable that in the United States, southern Blacks were excluded from the *demos*. But surely *to that extent* the South was undemocratic: *undemocratic in relation to its Black population*. Suppose that in the South, as in Rhodesia or South Africa, Blacks had been a preponderant majority of the population. Would Schumpeter still have said that the Southern states were 'democratic'? Is there not some number or proportion of a population below which a 'people' is not a demos but rather an aristocracy, oligarchy, or despotism? If the rulers numbered 100 in a population of 100 million, would we call the rulers a demos and the system a democracy? On Schumpeter's argument, Britain was already a 'democracy' by the end of the eighteenth century—even though only one adult in twenty could vote.

Consider the monumental implications of the second example, in which Schumpeter asserts that 'the Soviet Republic' would be a democracy if only the ruling party itself were internally democratic. Schumpeter imposes no minimum limits on the relative size of the party. Suppose it were one per cent of the population? Or suppose that the Politburo were internally democratic, and ruled the party,

[4] The whole discussion occurs in less than three pages (243–5) in Joseph A. Schumpeter, *Capitalism, Socialism, and Democracy* (New York: Harper and Bros., 1942, 1947).

which ruled over the State, which ruled over the people. Then the members of the Politburo would constitute the Soviet *populus,* and the Soviet State would be, on Schumpeter's interpretation, a democracy.

His definition thus leaves us with no particular reason for wanting to know whether a system is 'democratic' or not. Indeed, if a demos can be a tiny group that exercises a brutal despotism over a vast subject population, then 'democracy' is conceptually, morally, and empirically indistinguishable from autocracy. Thus Schumpeter's solution is truly no solution at all, for its upshot is that there are simply no principles for judging whether anyone is unjustly excluded from citizenship. But the argument leads, as we have seen, to absurdities.

These consequences follow because Schumpeter failed to distinguish, indeed insisted on conflating, two different kinds of propositions:

System X is democratic in relation to its own demos.

System Y is democratic in relation to everyone subject to its rules.

Perhaps because he was convinced by historical experience that no state like Y had ever existed or was likely to, he felt that any 'realistic' theory of democracy, such as he proposed, could scarcely require that a 'democracy' be a system like Y. For if this requirement were imposed, then no democratic state would, or probably ever could, exist. But by carrying historicism and moral relativism to their limits, he obliterated the possibility of any useful distinction between democracy, aristocracy, oligarchy, and one-party dictatorship.

Citizenship as a categorical right

Schumpeter's solution, or rather non-solution, was to allow a demos to draw any line it chooses between itself and other members. Suppose instead that one were to insist that no one subject to the rules of the demos should be excluded from the demos. Then the demos and the members (in the language used here) would be identical.

It is possible to interpret Locke, Rousseau, and a long succession of writers they influenced as advancing a solution along these lines.[5] The argument is grounded on the moral

[5] I do not mean to suggest that Locke and Rousseau (or later writers) presented similar views on democracy, for

axiom that no person ought to be governed without his consent, or, with Rousseau, required to obey laws that are not of his own making in some genuine sense. In developing the argument writers have found it useful to distinguish between the initial act of forming the polity, (society, association, community, city, or state) and the subsequent process of making and enforcing the rules of the polity. Thus both Locke and Rousseau held that the initial formation required the agreement of everyone who has to be subject to it; thereafter, however, laws could be enacted and enforced if they were endorsed by a majority. Both sought to explain why, even though unanimity is required in the first instance, thereafter a majority is sufficient. I wish to ignore this question, for my concern here is a different one: in speaking of agreement by 'all' or a 'majority', what is the collection of persons to which they refer? Does 'the consent of every individual' and 'the determination of the *majority*' of such individuals[6] literally refer to *every* member, in the sense that a majority must be *a majority of every person subject to the laws?*

Clearly, neither Locke nor Rousseau meant to imply this conclusion. To begin with, children are of course to be excluded from the demos. The exclusion of children from the demos is so often taken as unproblematical that one hardly notices how much the claim to citizenship based on categorical right is embarrassed by this simple exclusion: for it is made on the grounds that children are not competent to govern themselves or the community. Yet if we permit the exclusion of children from the demos (and who seriously does not?) then we allow a contingent element, based on

---

they were of course very different. Thus Locke permitted the delegation and even the indefinite alienation by the demos of the power to make laws. (*Second Treatise,* Ch. X and Ch. XIX, par. 243.) Rousseau, as we saw above, did not. However, because their differences are not directly relevant to the argument of this section, I ignore them here.

[6] The phrases are from Locke's *Second Treatise of Government,* Chapter VIII, 'Of the Beginning of Political Societies', par. 95–7, and *passim,* in John Locke, *Two Treatises of Government,* ed. by Peter Laslett, 2nd ed., (Cambridge: Cambridge University Press, 1967).

qualifications for governing, to limit the universality of the claim based on categorical right. Never mind; let us momentarily ignore this embarrassment, though I intend to return to it.

Suppose, then, that the claim based on a categorical right is revised to read: all *adults* subject to the laws of a state should be members of the demos of that state. Citizenship is no longer fully coextensive with membership; but all adult members are citizens by categorical right. Did Rousseau and Locke mean to justify such a claim?

Certainly Rousseau did not, though it is easy to see why the *Social Contract* is sometimes understood as saying so. There Rousseau occasionally appears to be asserting an unqualified right to membership in the demos.[7] But Rousseau makes it clear that he means no such thing. Thus he lauds Geneva, even though its demos consisted of only a small minority of the population. Children were, of course, excluded. But so too were women. What is more, a majority of adult males were also excluded from the Genevan demos. Rousseau was well aware of these exclusions. Yet he neither condemned them as inconsistent with his principles, nor provided grounds on which they might be justified. Rather, he seems simply to have taken them for granted.

Rousseau may, in fact, have anticipated Schumpeter's solution. In arguing that it is wrong to take the government of Venice as an instance of true aristocracy, he remarks that although the ordinary people in Venice have no part in the government, there the nobility takes the place of the people. This is Schumpeter's populus defining itself. Rousseau then goes on to show that Venice and Geneva are truly alike. Thus the government of Venice is actually no more aristocratic than that of Geneva! (Book IV, Chapter 3).

What Rousseau does not feel it important to say is that in both cities the great bulk of the people subject to the laws were not only excluded from the execution and administration of the laws (the *government,* in Rousseau's terminology) but also from any participation in *making* the laws. In neither republic were the people—that is, most people— entitled to assemble in order to vote on the laws, or even to vote for representatives who would make the laws. In both cities, most people were thus subject to laws which they had

[7] For example, in Book I, Chapters 4 and 6.

no part in making.[8] One might conclude that neither republic could be legitimate in Rousseau's eyes. But this was not his conclusion, nor did he even hint at such an inference.

What Rousseau seems to have assumed, as other advocates of democracy had done since the Greek city states of antiquity, is that a large number of persons in any republic— children, women, foreigners, and many male adult residents—will be subjects but are not qualified to be citizens. In this way, Rousseau himself undermined the categorical principle of inclusion that he appeared to set forth in the *Social Contract.*

Locke's language in *The Second Treatise* is as categorical and universalistic as Rousseau's, if not more so.[9] Yet his apparent assertion of an unqualifed and categorical claim was limited both explicitly and implicitly by a requirement as to competence. Naturally, children were excluded; I shall return later to Locke's argument on 'paternal power.' It is highly doubtful that he meant women to be included as a

---

[8] In Venice, the number of noblemen, who alone had rights to participate in the government, were from one to two per cent of the population of the city, and, if the mainland population is included, around one-tenth of one per cent. In 1797, there were 1090 noblemen, 137,000 residents of the city, and 2.2 million people on the mainland. The number of noblemen was never larger than about 2000. James C. Davis, *The Decline of the Venetian Nobility as a Ruling Class* (Baltimore: The Johns Hopkins Press, 1962), Table 1, p. 58.

In Geneva the percentage, though not as tiny, was small. Of the five orders subject to the laws, only males in the top two orders participated in making laws: 'at the top, the "citizens", who had the legal right to hold office, and of whom Rousseau was one; next, the "burghers", who had the right to vote but not to hold office.' Together, the citizens and burghers were 'some 1,500 in number' in a population of 25,000. Moreover, the top offices were monopolized by a few families. R. R. Palmer, *The Age of the Democratic Revolution, A Political History of Europe and America,* 1760–1800 (Princeton: Princeton University Press, 1959), p. 36. Palmer remarks that 'Rousseau himself, in all the study he made of Geneva politics at Neuchatel, showed no interest in the Natives. The Natives, however, (were) three-quarters of the population who were not Burghers.' (p. 137)
[9] For example, *Second Treatise,* Ch. VIII, §93.

matter of right.[10] As to adult males, he explicitly excluded 'lunatics and idiots [who] are never set free from the government of their parents.'[11] In addition, 'slaves, ... being captives taken in a just war, are by the right of nature subjected to the absolute dominion and arbitrary power of their masters.' He probably intended to exclude servants as well.[12] Thus a claim to citizenship was not categorical but, as it turns out, contingent on a judgement as to the relative qualifications of a person for participating in the government of the commonwealth. Like Rousseau, Locke torpedoed his own view (if indeed it was his view) that every person subject to the laws made by the demos possesses a categorical and unqualified right to membership in the demos.

Citizenship as contingent on competence

Locke and Rousseau appear to have advanced two different principles on which a claim to citizenship might be grounded. One is explicit, categorical, and universal; the other is implicit, contingent, and limiting:

> *Categorical Principle:* Every person subject to a government and its laws has an unqualified right to be a member of the demos (i.e., a citizen).
>
> *Contingent Principle:* Only persons who are qualified to govern, but all such persons, should be members of the demos (i.e., citizens).

If some persons subject to the laws are not qualified to govern, then obviously the two principles lead to contradictory conclusions. Which principle should take precedence? As we have seen, Locke and Rousseau held, at least implicitly, that the second principle takes precedence over the first.

What was only or mainly implicit in the arguments of Locke and Rousseau was made explicit by John Stuart Mill. Mill openly confronted the conflict he believed to exist between the two principles. Like his predecessors he also insisted that in case of conflict the first must give way to the second.

[10] See his discussion on the status of women in 'conjugal society', Ch. VIII, §§78–84. '... it seems highly improbable that Locke was thinking in terms of extending those rights to women.' Willmoore Kendall, *John Locke and the Doctrine of Majority Rule* (Urbana: Univ. of Illinois Press, 1941, p. 121, fn. vi.).

[11] Ch. VI, §60.

[12] Ch. VII, §85.

To be sure, on a careless reading Mill could be interpreted as favouring the categorical principle.[13] Yet although on casual inspection his language has a universalistic tone, in fact Mill does not endorse a categorical principle of general inclusion. It is hardly surprising that he argues, not from principles of right, but rather from considerations of social utility. His judgements are meant to reflect a balancing of social utilities and disutilities. And while his argument is powerful, it does not lead him to a categorical principle but to a contingent and contestable judgement about social utility. If the question is one of social utility, however, then relative competence is also a factor to be weighed.

As every reader of *Representative Government* soon discovers, it was Mill himself who undermined his own argument for universal inclusion by posing a counter-argument based on considerations of competence. In the course of his discussion, he gave explicit and careful recognition that the criterion of competence must take priority over any principle, whether categorical or utilitarian, that makes inclusion in the demos a matter of general right among all adults subject to the laws. At a minimum, he argued, to demonstrate that persons are qualified to engage in governing requires a showing that they have 'acquired the commonest and most essential requisites for taking care of themselves, for pursuing intelligently their own interests and those of the persons most nearly allied to them.' It was Mill's judgement that in the England of his day, many categories of adults could not meet this standard and ought therefore to be denied the suffrage until they acquired the competence they at that time lacked.[14]

By giving priority to the criterion of competence, recognizing the contingent and socially specific nature of judgements about competence, and accepting a restricted

[13] For example, *Considerations on Representative Government* Third Edition (1865), ed. by Currin V. Shields (New York: The Liberal Arts Press, 1958), pp. 42, 55, 131. A much fuller exposition of Mill's ideas about the conflict between 'the principle of participation' and 'the principle of competence', which draws on a wide variety of Mill's work, is Dennis F. Thompson, *John Stuart Mill and Representative Government* (Princeton: Princeton University Press, 1976).
[14] Ibid., pp. 131–8.

118   *Robert A Dahl*

demos as the consequence of his own judgement as to the
qualifications of fellow Englishmen, Mill brought into the
open a problem that has been glossed over by some of his
most illustrious predecessors. Yet in justifying an exclusionary demos Mill did no more than to make implicit what
had generally been implicit in all previous democratic theory
and practice.

The formal opportunities for participation available to
citizens in the democratic city-states of Greece, the
universalistic language in which democratic beliefs are often
presented, and the emphasis on participation by Rousseau
and Mill have induced some writers to interpret 'classical'
democratic ideas as much less 'elitist' than they actually
were.[15]

In classical Athens itself, the demos could hardly have
consisted of more than a third of the free adults, a sixth of all
free persons, and a seventh—or less—of the total population.
In relation to its own demos, the Athenians may have come
about as close as any people to procedural democracy, and
possibly a good deal closer than any modern state. But the fact
is that the Athenian demos, as a modern admirer rather
nonchalantly admits, was 'a minority elite.'[16]

[15] For examples, see Peter Bachrach's comments on
'classical democratic theory' and its contrasts with 'elitist
theory' in *The Theory of Democratic Elitism* (Boston:
Little, Brown, 1967), pp. 2–9. And Carole Pateman,
Participation and Democratic Theory (Cambridge:
Cambridge University Press, 1970), who presents
Rousseau and John Stuart Mill as 'two examples of
"classical" democratic theorists, whose theories provide
us with the basic postulates of a theory of participatory
democracy'. (p. 21.)
[16] M. I. Finley, *Democracy, Ancient and Modern* (New
Brunswick: Rutgers University Press, 1973). The remark
is made in the context of slavery; he does not mention
that the exclusion of women and resident foreigners made
the demos an even more restrictive 'minority elite'. All
the conjectures about the relative size of the citizen body
and the level of their participation in public affairs look
very fragile to me. I have taken the estimates above from
A. H. M. Jones, *Athenian Democracy* (Oxford: Basil
Blackwell, 1969), pp. 78–9. As to actual participation,
scholarly guess work looks even shakier. Though
sympathetic to the Athenian democracy, Jones concludes
that 'contrary to general belief, the average assembly was
attended mainly by the relatively well-to-do citizens ...'

One might choose to dismiss these limits as transitory deficiencies in a revolutionary new political idea which transcended the historical limits of actual practice. But as we have seen, Locke and Rousseau accepted, and Mill defended, the principle that a demos might properly exclude large numbers of adults who are subject to laws made by the demos. Thus the attempt to ground 'participatory democracy' on Mill and his predecessors is fatally flawed. Participation indeed. But only for the qualified! And in principle the qualified might be a tiny minority. Thus it is not only Schumpeter's solution that would permit the demos to shrink into a ruling elite. Rousseau himself, as we saw, regarded Geneva and Venice both as true republics, governed 'by the people', even though in both cities the demos constituted a minority of the adults: in Venice about one-tenth of one per cent of the population!

Modern admirers of 'classical' democratic ideas seem to have reversed the relation between citizenship and competence as it was generally understood from the Greeks to Mill. In the 'classical' perspective not every adult, much less every person, was necessarily qualified to govern and thus to enter into the demos. Rather, the demos consisted of all those who *were* qualified to govern. It was precisely because citizens were a qualified minority of the whole people that they were entitled to govern and could on the whole be counted on to govern well.

As a consequence, 'classical' ideas leave the intellectual defence of procedural democracy lethally vulnerable. Consider the standing of the case for procedural democracy if the criterion of competence is given priority over a categorical and universal principle of right.

If everyone subject to law has a categorical right to participate in the process of making laws, if the requirement of consent is universal and uncontestable, then the case for democracy is very powerful and the case against exclusionary

---

(Ibid. p. 36. See also pp. 50, 55, and the discussion 104–7). However, unlike the Assembly and the Council, the magistracies chosen by lot 'were filled by quite humble citizens'. (p. 104.) I cannot help suspecting that an Athenian Survey Research Centre would have turned up a good deal of evidence of citizen apathy and non-participation.

alternatives—aristocracy, meritocracy, rule by a qualified elite, monarchy, dictatorship, and so on—is correspondingly weakened. If the claim to citizenship is a categorical and universal right of all human beings, then among any human group a demos always exists and that demos must always be inclusive. To put it in another way, among any body of persons who wish to establish or maintain an association having a government capable of making binding decisions, the condition of equal qualification, the most crucial of the conditions for procedural democracy set forth earlier, must necessarily exist.

But if the criterion of competence overrides a claim based on rights, then the argument for democracy rests on mushy grounds. Citizenship depends on contingent judgements, not categorical rights. And the contingent judgements need not lead to universal inclusion. Indeed, as we have seen, the boundaries between democracy on the one side and meritocracy on the other become fuzzy and indeterminate. The arguments for the one or the other become indistinguishable except for a crucial judgement as to the relative magnitude of the competent members, the citizenry or ruling group.

I V   Towards A Criterion of Inclusiveness

Three questions arise: First, is it possible to get around the principle of competence in deciding on the inclusiveness of the demos? Second, if not, is it possible to avoid the contingent and contestable nature of a judgement as to competence? Third, if again not, can we develop strong criteria that such a judgement ought to satisfy?

That we cannot get round the principle of competence in deciding on the inclusiveness of the demos is decisively demonstrated by the exclusion of children. It is virtually never argued, no doubt because it would be so obviously untenable to do so, that children either must be members of the state's demos, or else ought not to be subject to laws made by the demos. So far as I am aware, no one seriously contends that children should be full members of the state's demos. An eight-year-old child can hardly be enlightened enough to participate equally with adults in deciding on laws to be enforced by the government of the state. Yet these laws are enforced on children—without their explicit or implied consent. It is often held—and legal systems tend to reflect the force of the argument—that because of their limited competence children should not be subject to exactly the same laws as adults; they cannot, for example, enter into legally enforceable contracts. Yet they are not wholly exempt from the enforcement of all laws.

Children therefore furnish us with a clear instance of violation of the principle that a government must rest on the consent of the governed, or that no one should be subject to a law not of one's own choosing, or subject to a law made by an association not of one's own choosing. Yet this violation is nearly always taken for granted; or else it is interpreted as not actually a violation. One way of interpreting it is to say that the principle of consent applies only to adults. But this is to admit that some persons who are subject to the rules of a state can nevertheless be properly excluded from the demos of the state.

On what grounds? The only defensible ground on which to exclude children from the demos is that they are not yet fully capable of the 'exercise of reason', to use the common phrase. The need to exclude children on this ground was of course perfectly obvious to early democratic theorists. Locke devotes a whole chapter to Paternal Power. After reminding us of 'that equal right that every man hath to his natural freedom, without being subject to the will or authority of any other man', he immediately turns to the exceptions, of which children are the most numerous, obvious, and important.[17]

The example of children is sufficient to show that the criterion of competence cannot reasonably be evaded, that any reasonable bounding of a demos must, by excluding children, necessarily exclude a large body of persons subject to the laws, and that any assertion of a universal right of *all* persons to membership in a demos cannot be sustained. It might be argued, however, that children constitute a comparatively well-defined and unique exception.[18] Thus

[17] *The Second Treatise, op. cit.*, par. 55 and 63 (pp. 28, 31). In the *Social Contract*, Rousseau also recognizes, though merely in passing, the authority of the father over children 'before they reach the age of reason'. *op. cit.*, p. 239.
[18] Douglas Rae has commented that children may be thought of as having a life-time bundle of rights, some of

once a distinction is allowed between children and adults, all *adults* subject to the laws must be included. The categorical principle might then be re-stated as follows:

> *Modified Categorical Principle:* Every adult subject to a government and its laws must be presumed to be qualified as, and has an unqualified right to be, a member of the demos.

There are, however, at least two sources of difficulty with the modified categorical principle. First, the boundary between childhood and adulthood is itself something of a difficulty. There is the well known arbitrariness of imposing a dichotomy—child/adult—on what is clearly a continuous process of development; we may reasonably disagree about whether one becomes qualified at 21, or 18, or whatever. There are also the troublesome cases for which experience, even when joined with compassion, points to no clear solution. As Locke put it:

> ... if, through defects that may happen out of ordinary course of nature, any one comes not to such a degree of Reason wherein he might be supposed capable of knowing the Law, and so living within the rules of it, he is never capable of being a Free Man, ... but is continued under the Tuition and Government of others all the time his own understanding is incapable of that charge. And so Lunatics and Idiots are never set free from the government of their Parents ...[19]

Thus the modified categorical principle runs the risk of circularity by defining 'adult' as persons who are presumed to be qualified to govern.

A second source of difficulty with the modified principle is caused by the presence in a country of foreigners who might be adult by any reasonable standards, who are subject to the laws of the country in which they temporarily reside, but who are not thereby qualified to participate in governing.

Suppose that France is holding an election on Sunday and I, an American, arrive in Paris on Saturday as a tourist. Would anyone argue that I should be entitled to participate in the election—much less acquire all the other political rights of

---

which they become eligible for as they mature. Locke seems to make a similar point in the paragraphs cited above. By contrast, for excluded adults 'the bonds of ... subjection' never 'quite drop off, and leave a man at his own free disposal'.

[19] *Second Treatise*, par. 60, *op. cit.,* p. 30.

French citizenship? I think not. On what grounds could I properly be excluded? On the ground that I am unqualified.[20]

To sum up:

(1) Schumpeter's solution to the problem of the composition of the demos is unacceptable because it effectively erases the distinction between democracy and a non-democratic order dominated by a collegial elite.

(2) A categorical principle of inclusion that overrides the need for a judgement as to competence is also unacceptable, for it is rendered untenable by such cases as children, feeble-minded persons, and foreigners of temporary residence. In so far as Locke and Rousseau advanced a categorical principle, their defense of it is unconvincing. However, evidence suggests that they recognized these objections and never intended their argument to be taken as a rejection of the priority of a criterion of competence.

(3) Because a judgement as to competence is contingent on weighing evidence and making inferences as to the intellectual and moral qualifications of specific categories of persons, a decision based on competence is inherently open to question. To be sure, a reasonable argument may be presented in behalf of a particular judgement as to the proper boundaries of inclusion and exclusion. But the exact location of any boundary is necessarily a highly debatable judgement. Thus Mill presented persuasive reasons to justify the particular exclusions he advocated; yet probably few

[20] Suppose I were able to demonstrate that I had carefully studied the issues, parties, candidates, and the like. My exclusion would seem rather less justified. Still, a French citizen might say, 'you will hardly be in France long enough to justify your inclusion. Your coming here is voluntary; you acknowledge by coming your willingness to obey our laws; you will have left the country before the election will effect any changes in existing laws; consequently you will not bear any responsibility for your choices. Therefore you are, in that respect, *morally* unqualified to participate in this election.' This seems to me a powerful rebuttal to my claim. However, the force of the objection derives mainly from the fact that I may not be subject to the laws my participation might have helped to bring about. To this extent, I am not a member in the sense defined earlier, and consequently I *ought* to be excluded under the assumption (No. 3) that binding decisions should be made only by members.

contemporary democrats would accept his exclusions as reasonable.

In short, if Schumpeter's solution leads to absurdities, those found in earlier democratic ideas, whether in classical antiquity or in the works of early modern theorists like Locke, Rousseau, and Mill, provide all too fragile a foundation for the doctrine of procedural democracy. Even though we must accept the need for, and the contingent and contestable nature of a judgement as to competence, we are in need of further criteria that will help to reduce the arbitrariness of such a judgement.

Further Requirements

I now want to argue that a reasonable criterion of inclusion in a system of procedural democracy in relation to its demos must pass three tests. At the outset, a criterion of inclusion must satisfy the general principle of fairness that constitutes one of the conditions of procedural democracy: equally valid claims justify equal shares. Consequently if C_a is a citizen, and if another member, M, is about as well qualified as C_a, then either M must be included in the demos or C_a must be excluded from it. If C_a is excluded, then the same test must be applied in comparing the claims of C_a with any other citizen, C_i. And so on, until a fair boundary can be staked out.

Assuming that a boundary of inclusion and exclusion meets the general principle of fairness, several additional tests may reasonably be required. The reasonableness of these tests rests, however, on two additional principles, which I shall refer to as *equal consideration* and *burden of proof*. I do not propose to consider whether or how these principles might be derived from antecedent considerations. Although the burden of proof principle reflects a judgement as to human experience, I doubt whether it is wholly verifiable, at least as a practical matter. And the principle of equal consideration is a moral orientation so fundamental that it is hard to see how one might go about the task of demonstrating its validity to an adversary. Fortunately, the principle itself is widely accepted. I want to introduce it initially as a principle of universal application and then narrow it to include only the members of the association.

> *Equal consideration (universal inclusion).* No distribution of
> socially allocated entities, whether actions, forebearances, or

objects, is acceptable if it violates the principle that the good or interest of each human being is entitled to equal consideration.[21]

The principle does not depend on an assumption as to whether one's good is distinguished from one's interests, or whether 'good' or 'interest' refer to want-regarding or ideal-regarding principles.[22] It simply asserts that the good or interest of each person, whatever they may be, ought to be given equal consideration in social allocations. If A and B are human beings, if some entity X is socially allocated, if X is equally beneficial to A and to B, and if no benefits to others need to be taken into account, then the principle holds that there are no grounds for upholding a claim that X ought to go to A rather than B, or B rather than A. Whatever principle of distribution is adopted, it must not incorporate a bias toward either A or B. Thus if X is indivisible, the most appropriate solution might be to toss a coin. But to claim that because A is stronger than B or A has discovered X first, then A ought to have X, would not be acceptable.

To universalize the principle of equal consideration, however, poses a host of theoretical and practical problems that I do not wish to deal with here. Moreover, universality is not necessary in order to arrive at a reasonable solution to the problem of the composition of the demos. A much less inclusive version applying only to the *members* will prove satisfactory.

> *Equal Consideration for all members:* No distribution of socially allocated entities, whether actions, forbearances, or objects, is acceptable if it violates the principle that the good or interest of each member is entitled to equal consideration.

[21] This assumption is, I think, roughly equivalent to, though not necessarily identical with, a widespread if contestable judgement that forms a fundamental ground for a good deal of moral theory. For instance, Hugo Adam Bedau specifies a not dissimilar notion that he calls 'the doctrine of metaphysical egalitarianism' in J. Roland Pennock and John W. Chapman, *Equality* (New York: Atherton Press, 1976), p. 17. Stanley I. Benn asserts the 'principle of equal consideration of interests', ibid., p. 67. It is probably at least a second cousin to Rawls's assumption of human equality based on the capacity for moral personality. *op. cit.*, p. 506.

[22] Brian Barry, *Political Argument* (London: Routledge and Kegan Paul, 1965), pp. 38–9 and 173ff.

If one accepts the principle of equal consideration of all members, then of course one must also hold that a criterion of inclusion is unacceptable if it violates this principle. However, the import of the principle is further amplified by an additional assumption that also reflects a widely held though not strictly universal judgement:

> *Burden of Proof:* In the absence of a compelling showing to the contrary everyone is assumed to be the best judge of his or her own good or interests. Thus if A holds that her good consists of X, not Y, and B insists that A's good consists of Y, not X, then A's judgement is to be accepted unless the validity of B's judgement can be satisfactorily demonstrated.[23]

For any given member, M, an association that meets the criteria of procedural democracy in relation to its demos can satisfy the principle of equal consideration in one of two ways. M may be a citizen; that is, M is already included in the demos, in which case equal consideration is insured by procedural democracy. Alternatively, if M is excluded from the demos the principle of equal consideration can be satisfied if, but only if, the citizens give as much consideration to M's good or interest as to their own. However, the demos cannot reasonably be expected to give equal consideration to M unless (1) it *knows* at least as much about M's good as about its own, and (2) it will in fact *act* on this knowledge in such a way as to give equal consideration to M's good or interests. But the burden of proof principle requires a compelling showing that the demos definitely is a better judge than M as to M's own interests. The second test that M's exclusion must meet is precisely such a showing.

If the second test is met satisfactorily, M's exclusion will

---

[23] The principle is analogous to, though not identical with, the first of the two principles that according to Mill are,

> 'of as universal truth and applicability as any general propositions which can be laid down respecting human affairs. The first is that the rights and interests of every and any person are only secure from being disregarded when the person interested is himself able, and habitually disposed, to stand up for them ... Human beings are only secure from evil at the hands of others in proportion as they have the power of being, and are, *self-protecting* ...' *op. cit.*, p. 43.

still violate the principle of equal consideration if the demos cannot reasonably be expected to *act* so as to give equal consideration to M. Thus, given the burden of proof, a positive showing is necessary that the demos has in fact given equal consideration to M's interests in the past and will continue to do so in the future; or, though it has neglected M's good in the past, there are nevertheless compelling reasons for believing that the demos has recently changed in this respect, or is about to change and will care equally for M's good in the future.

The arguments used in the past to justify the exclusions from full citizenship in the state of various categories of adults—the unpropertied, women, racial minorities, for example—would, I think, fail to meet these three tests. Experience has shown that any group of adults excluded from the demos will be lethally weakened in its own defence; and an exclusive demos will fail to protect the interests of those who are excluded.

> We need not suppose that when power resides in an exclusive class, that class will knowingly and deliberately sacrifice the other classes to themselves; it suffices that, in the absence of its natural defenders, the interest of the excluded is always in danger of being overlooked, and, when looked at, is seen with very different eyes from those of the persons whom it directly concerns.[24]

Mill was surely right. In rejecting the conclusion his own premises pointed to—the enfranchisement of the working classes—Mill's justification failed all three tests. 'Universal teaching must precede universal enfranchisement', he wrote. But it was not until *after* the extension of the suffrage in 1868 that Parliament passed the first act establishing public elementary schools. The historical record since then demonstrates even more fully that when a large class of adults is excluded from citizenship their interests will almost certainly not be given equal consideration. Perhaps the most convincing evidence is provided by the exclusion of Southern Blacks from political life in the United States until the late 1960s.

Though one might argue from numerous cases of child neglect that all too many children fall under III.2, there are reasonable grounds for holding that in general the exclusion

[24] Mill, *op. cit.*, pp. 44–45.

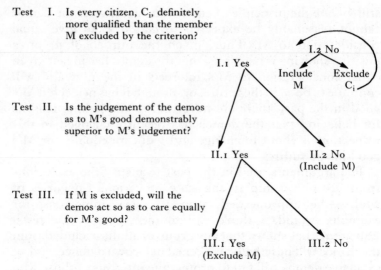

Test I. Is every citizen, C_i, definitely more qualified than the member M excluded by the criterion?

I.1 Yes

I.2 No

Include   Exclude
M C_i

Test II. Is the judgement of the demos as to M's good demonstrably superior to M's judgement?

II.1 Yes   II.2 No
                  (Include M)

Test III. If M is excluded, will the demos act so as to care equally for M's good?

III.1 Yes   III.2 No
(Exclude M)

Figure 6.1 Three Tests for a Criterion of Inclusion

of children meets the tests. The bonds between children and adults are unique in the human species. For one thing, while most citizens may not understand from their own direct experiences what it is like to be a member of an excluded class, race, or sex, every adult has once been a child. Moreover, many adults are closely tied to children by bonds of love, nurturance, pity, joy, compassion, and hope. Among adults these bonds are far too weak to ensure enough mutuality of interests and understanding to ensure that members of a demos will protect the interests of other adults who are excluded. Consequently, as children approach 'the age of reason' the justification for their guardianship by parents, community, and state weakens and finally fails to meet the two tests.

What then of III.2? For example, what of the child in a community of uncaring adults? In this case, it is not possible for a procedural democracy to arrive at a satisfactory solution. Yet since the existing state of affairs violates the principle of equal consideration, an obligation arises for all who accept that principle to search for and bring about changes that will remedy the situation. There is an obligation to raise the level of M's competence or the enlightenment and compassion of the demos or both. Meanwhile III.2 ought to be viewed as a morally intolerable state of affairs.

A Criterion of Inclusion

These considerations provide reasonable grounds for adopting a criterion that approaches universality among adults. It is not only very much less arbitrary than Schumpeter's solution but far more inclusive than the restricted demos that was accepted, implicitly or explicitly, by Mill, Rousseau, Locke, and the Greek *polis*.

> (C.5) *Inclusiveness:* The demos must include all adult members of the association except transients.

Admittedly the definition of adults and transients is a potential source of ambiguity. Probably no definition of the term adult can be completely watertight. In general, however, every member ought to be considered an adult who does not suffer from a severe mental disability or whose punishment for disobeying the rules is not reduced because he or she is younger than a given age. The meaning of the criterion seems to me to be clear enough: A demos that permitted the concept of adulthood to be manipulated in order to deprive certain persons of their rights—dissenters, for example—to that degree would simply fail to meet the criterion of inclusiveness. Obviously this criterion, like others, can never be self-enforcing.

Taken with the other four criteria, inclusiveness completes the requirements for procedural democracy. To the extent that a system approaches all five criteria, it is fully democratic in a procedural sense. The argument is summarized in Table 6.1.

V   Comments

The argument for procedural democracy holds that if one believes in the half dozen assumptions in Table 6.1, then reason requires one to hold that an association should adopt procedures for making binding decisions that will satisfy the five criteria of procedural democracy.

I take it for granted that in the real world no system will fully meet these criteria. At best any actual polity is likely to be something of an approximation to procedural democracy. My guess is that any approximation will invariably fall pretty far short of meeting the criteria. However, I have not tried to specify thresholds of attainment above which a system may

Table 6.1.   The Argument for Procedural Democracy in Schematic Outline

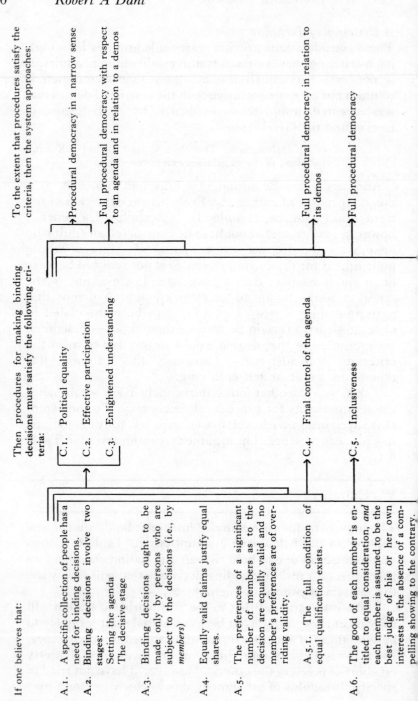

If one believes that:

A.1. A specific collection of people has a need for binding decisions.

A.2. Binding decisions involve two stages:
Setting the agenda
The decisive stage

A.3. Binding decisions ought to be made only by persons who are subject to the decisions (i.e., by *members*)

A.4. Equally valid claims justify equal shares.

A.5. The preferences of a significant number of members as to the decision are equally valid and no member's preferences are of over-riding validity.

A.5.1. The full condition of equal qualification exists.

A.6. The good of each member is entitled to equal consideration, *and* each member is assumed to be the best judge of his or her own interests in the absence of a compelling showing to the contrary.

Then procedures for making binding decisions must satisfy the following criteria:

C.1.   Political equality
C.2.   Effective participation
C.3.   Enlightened understanding

C.4.   Final control of the agenda

C.5.   Inclusiveness

To the extent that procedures satisfy the criteria, then the system approaches:

Procedural democracy in a narrow sense

Full procedural democracy with respect to an agenda and in relation to a demos

Full procedural democracy in relation to its demos

Full procedural democracy

properly be called a procedural democracy, for that exercise promises to be rather sterile. Instead, the criteria serve as standards against which one may compare alternative procedures in order to judge their relative merits according to the criteria of procedural democracy: to compare different systems in order to judge their relative approximations to procedural democracy; and to compare a given system over time in order to judge whether its trend, if any, is toward or away from procedural democracy. I do not hold that the criteria of procedural democracy fully define the notion of a good polity or good society. But to the extent that procedural democracy is worthwhile, then judgements of the sort I just mentioned bear directly on the relative worth or goodness of political arrangements.

The doctrine thus serves the task of clarification and prescription, of appraising and choosing among alternatives. For an example, suppose that I am a member of an association, and I believe that the conditions of procedural democracy exist among us but that my fellow members have not understood why the criteria of procedural democracy ought to apply to our processes of decision-making. My task is clarification: if we believe these things to be true, I would say to them, then we must reasonably adopt the criteria of procedural democracy. Or clarification might go in the other direction. Since you deny the validity of the criteria, I would say, then it must be that you reject one or more of these assumptions as valid among us. Which of the assumptions do you reject, and on what grounds?

Nor need I be a member of an association in order to arrive at judgements and recommendations as to the procedures the association ought to employ. If I judge that the conditions exist, then I must also conclude that the association should be procedurally democratic, whether or not I am a member.

As I have already said, I think that objections to procedural democracy will most often come to rest on a denial of the condition of equal qualification. This is why I have dealt at such length with that assumption. Sooner or later, to advocate procedural democracy requires a direct confrontation with its main alternative, which historically, today, and doubtless far into the future, is the doctrine of meritocracy. This enduring rival to democratic ideas is the view that adults in general are not qualified to govern, that the task of governing ought properly to be lodged with a meritorious minority, an elite possessing superior knowledge and virtue.

Many defenses of democracy imply that democracy is always better than meritocracy. Yet even the most committed adherents of democracy have usually shrunk from insisting that every kind of human association must always follow democratic procedures.

In setting out the doctrine of procedural democracy I have not assumed that the condition of equal qualification always holds. Yet I would have to believe the doctrine irrelevant if I did not believe that the condition exists in at least some important associations.

Whether or not the state is the most important of all human associations, it is surely highly crucial. It is crucial because of its extraordinary influence, power, and authority, and thus the capacity of those who govern the state to control the resources, structures, agendas, and decisions of all other associations within the boundaries of the state. A people that alienates its final control over the agenda and decisions of the government of the state runs a very high risk of alienating its final control over other important associations as well.

I have not tried to show here what kinds of institutional arrangements procedural democracy would require for governing the state. Partly, though not wholly, in response to democratic ideas, a set of institutions for the government of the state has evolved during the last two centuries. The common features of these institutions have been called polyarchy. The institutions of polyarchy provide a much better approximation to procedural democracy among a numerous people, I believe, than the more exclusionary and authoritarian systems they replaced or serve as existing alternatives to polyarchy in the present world. Yet it seems clear to me that the institutions of polyarchy are not sufficient for a close approximation to procedural democracy.

However, I refrain here from arguing whether they are necessary, or how polyarchies might be further democratized, or whether radically different kinds of political institutions could provide a closer fit to procedural democracy.

A people that adhered to the doctrine of procedural democracy in the government of the state would also want to employ that doctrine in determining how other associations ought to be governed. For reasons I have already indicated, the doctrine bars a universalistic and *a priori* judgement that procedural democracy is best for all associations. But every system for governing any association ought to be tested against the doctrine, to determine whether the conditions are present; and, if they are, the relative merits of existing and alternative arrangements for satisfying the criteria.

As with the state, the question of what government is best for other associations will turn most frequently on a contestable and contingent judgement as to the relative competence of the members to govern. If, as I believe, a wise and humane people that sought to govern the state according to the criteria of procedural democracy would also employ the principles of equal consideration and burden of proof in making judgements about the relative qualifications of members to govern other associations, then it appears to me that many hierarchic or meritocratic arrangements would have to give way to procedural democracy.

7 A Principle of Simple Justice

Douglas W Rae

In this essay, I wish to justify and vindicate a principle of simple justice. I will justify this principle by showing why it represents the general interests of all who must accept its implications, given an initial presumption of equality in their claims upon social resources. This justification is cast in the form of a social contract—a meeting among the hypothetical classes of society—in which the agents reject all other principles including utilitarian maximization, pure egalitarianism, and John Rawls's conception of 'maximin justice'. Only my proposal is consistent with the shared interests of all agents, hence can be said to express the general interest of the community they represent. This justification is meant to establish that the proposed rule of simple justice is a uniquely best solution to the problem of simple justice. The essay's second task is to vindicate the principle by showing its implications, as measured by a logically independent and intuitively appealing 'minimal test', to be acceptable. This minimal test is very simple: No principle should ever ask us to divide less less equally when we could instead divide more more equally. Put another way, no principle should ever violate equality and (utilitarian) maximization *at once*. I will show that my rule avoids this obvious defect.

It will also be seen that the proposed principle is a second cousin to Rawls's idea of maximin justice, and that my argument supports Rawls's argument in its general spirit. I will nevertheless venture to criticize Rawls's doctrine by showing one of its main defects: maximin justice fails the minimal test I propose. Whoever adopts maximim justice must commit himself to the possibility that both equality and the maximisation of totals should be violated at a single stroke. First, I shall pause to say what I mean by the problem of *simple* justice.

I The Problem of Simple Justice

A principle of simple justice says very little. It provides neither a general blueprint of right, nor even a complete specification of justice for any one historical society. The question of simple justice can, as a first approximation, be put as follows: How should allocation be carried out in a community of equals? By a 'community of equals,' I do not mean a community whose members must always receive equal shares of a given value, but merely a community whose members all enjoy *prima facie* equal claims to that value. It may turn out that some receive more than others, but their initial claims are all on par. Indeed, a second formulation of our question is this: When, if ever is inequality permissible in a community of *(prima facie)* equals? As I will argue later, the only ground for treating moral equals unequally is that their universally shared interests are promoted by such inequalities.

A principle of simple justice presupposes that two fundamental questions have been resolved, and have been resolved in particular ways. First, a *community of justice* must be understood before one sets out to apply any account of simple justice. It must be understood that such a community has well-defined boundaries. The community of man, or even of all sentient creatures, may be the proper referent of simple justice. Perhaps instead only particular national communities, or even mere families, are in some instances subjects of simple justice. The principle I wish to propose, like all of its alternatives, must presume that such a community has been chosen. And this presumption is obviously important, for justice inside each of two or more small communities does not at all imply justice within the larger population which includes them. Justice for each of two races or classes considered separately assures no justice for the larger societies which they jointly populate. One can make a house beautiful by decorating its rooms one at a time; one cannot, however, make a society just by applying justice to its castes and classes one at a time. If they have no other value, societies such as South Africa serve to illustrate this simple point. I will, for this reason, be thinking about communities of justice corresponding at least to full national societies. The community of justice must also be so conceived as to contain *prima facie* moral equals. Each person must at birth have an equal *prima facie* claim to the use of society's accumulated capital, shared knowledge, consumer product. If one does not admit this much, then he is not interested in *simple* justice, and is perhaps not interested in justice at all.

But *what* is to be justly allocated? Are we thinking about utility in Bentham's sense, about its marginal cousin in neoclassical economics, about labour value in classical and Marxian economics, about Rawlsian 'primary goods,' about money, seats in a lifeboat, drams of rum, . . . whatever? This is obviously a fundamental decision, for one can accept *any* principle of simple justice and still freely determine practical exactions by altering the *numèraire* of justice—i.e., *what* it is whose distribution is being enumerated. By way of familiar example, a 'just' allocation of 'money per unit of production' under a piece-work system would mean one thing, while a just allotment of 'money per hour' of labour under a wage system would mean something else, even if the principle pointed up by the word 'just' remained unaltered. Another import of the *numèraire* is trivialization. If one applies justice to dividing the social storehouse of peanuts, and not to land or capital, he is talking justice in only a trivial way. One may, moreover, believe that different values are subject to different principles of allocation, and that some are not proper objects of simple justice. Consider 'romantic love,' 'praise,' and 'honour.' If things of this general sort are allocated by simple justice, they may *perish for that reason.* This is because such things as praise require a violation of the egalitarian premise with which simple justice begins. It is not the task of simple justice to define and delineate the *numèraire* of justice, and one may suppose that the *numèraire* is sensitive to historical and cultural vagaries not contemplated by the idea of simple justice. But not just *any* answer will do and a principle of simple justice requires some *numèraire* meeting four general specifications:

(1) *Nontriviality:* Given the historical, cultural, and material structure of a community, the *numèraire* of justice must importantly correspond to the wants or interests (or both) of most members.

(2) *Divisibility:* Simple justice is concerned with social sharing, and can be applied only to some *numèraire*

which is capable of division into shares. The *numèraire* must not, for example, be an indivisible prize.

(3) *Comparability:* It must be possible to compare the shares given to particular agents, and these comparisons must be precise enough that we can perform two elementary operations: (i) decide whether a given individual share has been increased, diminished, or left alone, and (ii) decide which of two possible allocations is more nearly equal in its overall treatment of individuals.

(4) *Singularity:* The task of simple justice is not to evaluate 'trade-offs' between two or more values, but to evaluate the allocation of single values. The *numèraire* may be complex in that the comparison of shares takes simultaneous account of two or more simpler values, but must itself be singular.

In the analysis given below, I will assume a simple cardinal scale with interpersonal comparisons. In giving examples, I will let '100 units' for Smith mean that he has a quite generous entitlement, and let '1 unit for Jones' suggest that he receives next to nothing. These numbers should be taken merely as illustrations. As the attentive reader will guess, I intend not to review such dismal quarrels as occur in welfare economics over just such comparisons as these.

So far, then, I have marked off two forms of simplicity in principles of the sort I propose to discuss. They are simple with respect both to subject and object, community and *numèraire*. Justice for whom, in sharing what? Both questions must be answered separately and in the right ways before a principle of simple justice begins its work. Simple principles are also inattentive to many further questions, three of which require brief mention. First, a simple principle does not tell us anything about the problem of transition from a basically unjust society to a basically just one. It gives no account of political tactics, and omits to tell us what price must be paid (in bloodshed, say) for the initial establishment of justice. Second, like Rawl's principles (and unlike Nozick's), simple principles attend to end-states which should be aimed at, not at historical chains of movement. These dynamical considerations would need to be treated as further specifications of right, and might sometimes limit the legitimate means by which simple justice could be brought about. In leaving out such possible constraints, a simple principle of justice does not warrant the conclusion that just *any* scheme of movement is legitimate provided it ends in

justice. A simple principle is merely agnostic in this way.
Finally, a simple principle fails to specify the historically
definite institutions under which justice ought be adminis-
tered. Two societies, both just in their allocation of a given
numèraire, might administer this question in very different
ways, and these differences are of no direct interest in the
formulation of a simple principle.

It follows from what I have said here that simple principles
are only part of what one would need in a general and
historically focused account of justice. They are, nevertheless, essential parts. One could answer all the *other* questions
discussed here in the finest detail without having really begun
to address the central problem of social justice. For this, he
would also require a principle of simple justice.

II Justification for a Principle

I now wish to justify a simple principle by showing that it
alone specifies the conditions for just inequality among *prima
facie* equals in such a way as to fully take account of their
shared interests. For this purpose let me set out a sort of social
contract—I'll call it a 'court of allocation'—in which
delegates for the hypothetical classes or strata in a society are
asked to choose between possible allocations. Where the
delegates for all these classes or strata agree without dissent
that one allocation X is better than another allocation Y, I will
infer that this choice reflects the universal interest of all these
classes or strata. Where no such unanimity is forthcoming, I
will infer that such a decision does not reflect the universal
interest of all. In order to account for the *prima facie* equality
of all, I will organize the court of allocation so that
disagreements are always settled in favour of the more equal
allocation. Thus, only those diminutions of equality which
are consistent with the general interest of all classes will be
agreed. We will then 'observe' a series of particular decisions
in this court of allocation and ask what general principle
prescribes *all* the decisions made. I will show that one
principle does so while all others fail, and claim that this
establishes that principle as the uniquely best principle of
simple justice.

II.I   *The court of allocation*
Imagine a group of agents, each representing a hypothetical
social stratum. These strata form a weak hierarchy of relative
advantage in the form,

$$a \geqslant b \geqslant c, \ldots, \geqslant m$$

Thus, agent *a* knows that his 'constituency' will be at least as
well off as all others, and perhaps better off. Agent *m* knows
that his constituency will never be better off than anyone
else's constituency, no matter what he does to promote its
interests. These agents represent the top and bottom strata
while others represent middling strata. Since all strata are
represented, all interests can have a voice in all decisions
taken. But these strata have a merely hypothetical standing in
two ways. First, they may be only potentially rather than
actually stratified. A weak hierarchy admits of the case in
which *a* is not better treated than *m*, so that all stand in perfect
equality. In this case, the strata serve only to indicate a
ranking as it *would* look if inequalities were introduced.
Second, these strata bear a merely hypothetical relationship
to particular positions or groupings in society. In a society of
rich bankers and poor shoemakers, *a* would indicate the
former and *m* would denote the latter; in a society of rich
shoemakers and poor bankers, the order would be reversed.
So the agents represent particular interests in a only a very
thin sense. The agents for the *i*th stratum represent those
positions in society which, in a particular allocation, rank *i*th.
And, if a particular allocative choice happened to reverse
orderings, the same agent, representing the same stratum,
might be required to promote the interests of two or more
distinct groupings—for example, the bankers who happen to
rank *i*th in one allocation and the prostitutes who rank *i*th in
another. The agents must concern themselves with a formal
stratum no matter what concrete social content it takes on at a
given moment. This reflects my view that simple justice
never depends on differences of the sort which distinguish
bankers, shoemakers, and prostitutes, but depends instead on
the *relative generosity* with which mere *persons* are treated.
   Like Rawlsian parties to the social contract, these agents do
not, therefore, have knowably concrete interests. But they do
have distinguishable interests and in this way differ from
their counterparts in Rawls's argument. If Rawls tries to use

uncertainty to make each party an agent for us all, this argument uses limited knowledge—agents know *which* strata they are to represent—as a way to represent us all piecemeal. Our conflicts of interest are thus represented by the conflicts which arise among the interests promoted by these agents.

Each agent is concerned always to promote the interests of the stratum he represents, and no agent has any other concern. In judging any particular allocative choice, each agent must prepare himself to face a hypothetical interrogation by the particular persons who turn out to occupy the positions whose interests fall under his domain in any given decision. He must always be prepared to show truthfully that he has agreed only to those decisions which would best serve the interests of these persons. And the agents are to assume that these persons derive no benefit from the losses of others through either envy or smugness. This rules out two main strategies of agency, for it will not do, as preparation for interrogation, that I should either: (1) act on a principle of malice or compassion for other strata and their agents, or (2) engage in 'log-rolling' whereby the interests of my stratum in one case are sacrificed to those of my stratum in another. In each case, I may find myself unable to explain my performance to those whose interests I have surrendered.

The agents just introduced have motives for their decisions, but no particular decisions to make. Notice, first of all, that justice is not concerned merely with particular allocations but with *choices* among them. If there were only a single feasible outcome for any given society, then allocation would hardly present a point of contention and the problem of simple justice would vanish. What must be justified, then, is always a claim that one outcome should be imposed *instead* of another. Our agents, therefore, are not to be asked questions in the form, 'Is allocation X correct?' They are instead asked to answer questions in the form, 'Given a choice between allocations X and Y, which is better?' We will imagine the agents as forming a court of allocations in which each 'case' is a choice among alternative allocations.

The agents are not asked to say which of the two is more *just*, but which choice they feel impelled to advocate given the interests of the stratum they happen to represent. Suppose, for instance, that the judge for class C is asked to rule on the following case:

Share for Stratum	Allocation X	Allocation Y
A	—	—
B	—	—
C	5 units	6 units
D. . .	—	—
M	—	—

Our agent will find this very incomplete table entirely adequate, for it permits him to answer the question *on behalf of his stratum* without regard to any other stratum. He is no advocate of justice, but of a particular stratum's interests. What we learn about justice will come not directly from the pronouncements of single agents, but from the *pattern* of judgements reached by such agents under a suitably designed system for aggregating these particular judgements into fair collective judgements by the court as a whole.

Recall that simple justice applies to *prima facie* equals, and information about *equality* will be wholly ignored by the agents. Attention to this feature of the problem must therefore be lodged in the decision-making procedure of the court itself. By way of preliminary explication, imagine two contrasting ideal types. First, consider a society in which men and women enjoy only those benefits of social collaboration which may be shared in perfect equality. To each position is given the same claim on society's product. Second, think of a society in which the incumbent of a single position—Rex, if you like—holds a monopoly claim on the full social product. The incumbent need share a portion only in order to keep alive his contemporaries with a view to further profit. Between these two cases lies a continuum of inequality, and we may think of allocations as points arrayed along this span. Similarly, allocative choices may be understood in one essential aspect as movements along this continuum, bringing society closer to one or the other of these polar cases.

The individual agents have no responsibility for positioning the allocations along this continuum, but the court's decision-making procedure is deliberately biased in the following way. Suppose that one allocation is more equal than the other in a given choice. Then,

       (1) *Any agent is entitled unilaterally to impose the more equal alternative as the decision of the court,*

and   (2) *The less equal allocation may be imposed as the decision of the court only if some agents judge it better and none judge it worse than the more egalitarian alternative.*

This amounts, in effect, to requiring unanimous consent in any choice which diminishes equality. The purpose in this structural feature should also be apparent. Only those furtherances of inequality which express the general interest of all can possibly become decisions of the court. All other such approvals of inequality must be vetoed by one or more agent, and cannot possibly become decisions of the court. The process of decision-making serves thus as a 'filter' for precisely those furtherances of inequality which can be justified in accordance with the general interests of a community, rather than the merely particular interests of given strata within it. No stratum will be able to insist on promoting its more than equal claims at the expense of others. This decision-making scheme is the means by which the particularistic views of agents for particular strata are folded together in forming a just *pattern* of decisions corresponding to simple justice.

II.II   *The court's decisions*
The method of analysis is simple. We consider possible principles of simple justice, and test their implications against the 'case law' of this court. Nearly any principle will agree with the court's view some of the time, but that isn't enough. An acceptable principle of simple justice must *always* agree with the decisions of the court. The court and its constituent agents do not *think* about justice, for that is our job in the section which follows. Notice, before we begin, that I claim a single principle to be *uniquely acceptable*. It is nice to reject particular principles, and we will begin in this way, but eventually we must try to dispatch all but *one*. Begin with an obviously weak proposal:

> *Proposal 1: Particularism: Maximize the reward given some particular group in society.*

This would mean doing our best by a particular race or caste, or functional grouping, or class defined through ownership and labour. It should be obvious that at least one agent to the allocations court must favour all proposals of this kind, no matter which group is to benefit. The agent for society's first stratum will find pleasure in this suggestion, for the privileged group must become society's highest stratum, and his task of agency must be dispatched splendidly by whatever judgements are reached under this maxim. Thus, he would be pleased by outcome Y in this choice:

Positions	Allocations	
	X	Y
Bankers	50	100
A	50	10
B	50	10

But it is impossible to imagine that agents for lower strata will permit this, and indeed they will not. For it would be an unpardonable breach of agency to permit their strata, whether they be populated by shoemakers or professors or men or women or blacks or Europeans, to be sacrificed in the interests of another stratum. The same argument would exclude principles based on combinations of particular interests, for every such combine—however wide—would offend the duty of our agent for the very *lowest* social stratum. And, if it failed to exclude *any* interest in society, we would arrive at the proposition that we ought to maximize the reward given everyone, which can be interpreted either as a vacuity or as the basic demand of utilitarianism.

> *Proposal 2: Utilitarianism: Maximize the sum of rewards given to the members of society.*

This maxim would lead to a great many judgements which the agents could accept with alacrity. If, for example, a particular outcome benefits everyone in society, when compared to all the other alternatives considered, then unanimous consent should be expected. This would be so even if vast inequalities were required. But there is also the prospect of *predatory* utilitarianism, in which we sacrifice one interest to another. Since our agents are concerned for strata and not for particular groups, *some* such judgements would be accepted, as for example in this case:

Positions	Allocations	
	X	Y
Usurers	60	55
Debtors	50	70

It is true that agents for particular groups of positions would reject Y as an alternative to X (the usurers' agent says no). But our agents for *strata* would *approve* Y as an alternative to X, for each could advance the interests of his *stratum* by doing so. And moral intuition seems to point toward concurrence in their willingness to approve sacrifices for particular groups which can be objected to only by reference to those groups *in particular*. For such objections would demand obvious special pleading—a desire to require of others what will not be accepted for oneself. But utilitarianism cannot be the rule which describes the general interest, for imagine a case of predatory utilitarianism which takes its bite from the bottom, not from the top of society:

Positions	Allocations	
	X	Y
A	50	100
B	40	20

Utilitarianism leads to strict preference for the Y outcome here, for it is a profitable sacrifice of one position to the advantage of another. Yet for this reason, utilitarianism must not describe our court, since the agent for society's lowest stratum must refuse this departure from equality. The same reasoning would cover both classical and average utilitarianism. We can even more quickly dispatch a one-sided concern for equality.

> *Proposal 3: Equalitarianism: Minimize the average difference between the rewards given to the positions in society.*

Equality would, of course, account for the negative side of our court's activity. All those cases which fail of unanimity in favour of the less equal distribution will be resolved in favour of the more equal (or fully equal) result. But suppose it is proposed that some departure from equality which advantages every stratum be adopted:

Positions	Allocations	
	X	Y
A	30	100
B	30	70
C	30	60

It is obvious that the X outcome is perfectly equalitarian, but it is likewise clear that the agents of all three strata must judge Y superior, and equalitarianism cannot account for the judgements which they will reach. Next consider the general class of rules for which Rawls's maximin justice is a special case.

> *Proposal 4: Maximize the reward given to the ith stratum in society.*

Suppose, first of all, that the privileged stratum is not the lowest one. If this is so, then what works to its advantage may exact sacrifices from one or more lower strata, and agents for these strata must veto the relevant judgements. Since this would hold for all choices of inequality, the illustrations given against particularism may be repeated against all such proposals. And, for the same reasons given there, any conceivable combination of privileged strata must also be put aside. Any principle that favours any set of higher strata over any lower stratum or lower set of strata must imply results vetoed by some agent or agents for these low groups. Such principles would *all* favour Y here:

Positions	Allocations	
	X	Y
A	10	100
B	10	100
C	10	100
D . . .	10	100
M	10	9

Yet this sacrifice of the 'proletariat' must be vetoed by that stratum's agent and no principle of this type could account for this adoption of X. This brings us to Rawls's principle, for he alone proposes never to harm the lowest class:

> *Proposal 5: Maximin Justice: Maximize the rewards of the lowest stratum.*

and,

> *Lexical Proviso:*[1] *Maximize for the next higher stratum if two allocations are equally generous toward the lowest stratum, maximize for the next highest given equal generosity toward the two lowest stratum, and so forth and so forth.*

In fact, this second feature makes little difference. I include it so as not to overlook a nuance upon which Rawls seems to place some importance.

Consider first of all those cases where utterly perfect equality is among the feasible alternatives. Suppose that this perfect equality provides a given payoff, q, to each position. Then if we maximize the minimum, and achieve $q+e$ for the

---

[1] The term 'lexical proviso' is taken from Rawls's notion of the 'lexical difference principle' which provides that after the bottom stratum's share is maximized, the share of each successive stratum should be maximized, in turn. See *A Theory of Justice* (Cambridge, Mass.: Harvard University Press, 1971), pp. 82–83.

minimum stratum, we must have also achieved at least $q+e$
for all the other strata, and this is surely preferable to perfect
equality (hence only q) for each stratum. Thus, for example,
both maximin and our court must accept the inequality given
in Y below:

Positions	Allocations	
	X	Y
A	10	100
B	10	20
C	10	20

Moreover, both the court and Rawlsian justice must reject
any *predatory* departure from perfect equality. The victims
must include the lowest stratum and are protected by Rawls's
principle. For the court, some agents (always including the
agent for the bottom stratum) will certainly veto predatory
inequalities of this sort. Thus, for example, Rawls's principle
correctly accounts for the retention of equality (X) against
predation (Y):

Positions	Allocations	
	X	Y
A	50	100
B	50	100
C	50	10

This can indeed be generalized to the following proposition:
If *perfect* equality is an alternative, maximin is a valid
principle of simple justice.[2]

But suppose we are given a choice which denies us perfect
equality as an available alternative. For instance:

Positions	Allocations	
	X	Y
A	30	100
B	30	100
C	30	11
D	30	11
E	30	11
F	30	11
G	30	11
H	10	11

Since X displays less inequality, it is to be chosen unless

[2] A point proved formally in my paper, 'Maximin
Justice and an Alternative Principle of General Advantage',
American Political Science Review, vol. 69, no. 2 (June
1975): pp. 630–47.

unanimous agreement can be achieved in favour of Y. But agents for the 'middle class'—positions C through G—must find Y unacceptable, and must veto it so that X is imposed. Yet maximin justice would indicate a social preference for Y, and cannot, therefore, serve as the general maxim which we seek. Rawlsian justice is evidently the special case of our general rule which regulates choices involving *perfect* equality.

Notice how our court would have to be altered in order to conform with maximin for *all* cases. The delegates for all strata except the lowest would need to be expelled from the bench (or with the 'lexical' proviso would be permitted to cast votes only when delegates for all lower strata declared themselves indifferent between two outcomes.) In all those choices which involve differing returns to the lowest stratum, the agent for that stratum *alone* must monpolize all authority within the court if Rawls's principle is to be justified. If there are only two strata, this is essentially without consequence; if there are several strata, it is far from innocuous. In those instances, it leads to a one-sided view of justice. But this takes us beyond our present problem, which is to find a principle which *will* account for our court's behaviour.

Having come in Rawls's case to a near miss, I will quit arguing against particular principles. This is because I want to establish the unique claim of one principle and any string of rejected principles must always leave open some $n+1^{th}$ principle which might prove acceptable. Consider, instead, the following very general set of principles. This category includes all principles which would sometimes lead us to choose in either or both of the following ways:

(1) Choose a less equal allocation which diminishes the reward of some stratum or strata, even if other strata benefit from it,
(2) Choose a more equal allocation which diminishes the reward of some stratum or strata while increasing the reward of no stratum.

A principle belongs to this category if it would lead us to a decision of either sort for even a single case. All five of the principles so far considered belong in this category. Maximization of the utilitarian sort leads, for instance, to choices of the first kind. A principle of pure equality leads to choices of the second variety. A little reflection will show similar propensities for the other three principles considered. Moreover, all procedural principles—such as Marxian theories of social production or libertarian theories of entitlement—must sometimes produce results fitting either or both of these descriptions.

Notice next that this abstract set corresponds precisely to the range of case-by-case judgements which could *not* occur in our court. In cases of the first sort, we find augmentations of inequality which are detrimental to some strata: These must necessarily be vetoed by the agent(s) for these damaged strata, and cannot express simple justice. Since all 'divided decisions' are to be settled in favour of more rather than less equality, no such judgements can be imposed. Now consider the second category in which the outcome is, roughly speaking, 'destructive equality.' In cases of this sort, the more equal result is accomplished by diminishing the advantages of some strata without increasing the returns received by any others. Such judgements as these correspond, for example, to the destruction of wealth rather than to its redistribution. In our court, some agents must cast their ballots against all such levellings and none—not even the agent for the lowest stratum—will speak in their favour. Retaining the *in*-equalities in question involves no predation of lower strata, and corresponds to simple justice. The court will retain, not reject these inequalities since no agent will decide against them. The principle of simple justice we are looking for must never ask us to reach a judgement of either type, and only one principle has this property. It is, in awkwardly negative form, the principle that we should:

> *Never choose any outcome which either: (1) increases inequality while diminishing the rewards of some strata, or (2) diminishes the reward of some strata while increasing that of no strata (even if the effect is to increase equality).*

While this hardly gives the ring of a fighting slogan, it does describe the behaviour of our court. Its two operative clauses are tautologously equivalent to the two categories of judgement considered a moment ago, and we have already established that these are ruled out by the court. In other words, this principle rules out the same things ruled out by the court of allocation as I have conceived it. If a positive formulation can be achieved, we have finished our search. And such a formulation is quite simple:

> *Principle of Simple Justice: Choose only those augmentations of inequality which advantage some strata and disadvantage none.*

While perhaps less than a fighting slogan, this is at least a reasonably simple rule. It is, in two respects, a little simpler than it should be in strict logic. First, 'Choose only' must be understood to mean '*choose* and only choose.' Not only is one forbidden to choose predatory inequalities but he *must* choose those inequalities which advantage some strata at cost to no other strata. This is a minor point in logic but would lead us to troublesome misunderstandings if overlooked. Second, the principle is silent about the range of comparisons which must be made. If there happen to be only two feasible allocations the single comparison is obvious. If, however, there should be three or more alternatives, then any proposed augmentation of inequality must be compared with *all* more equal alternatives before it is justified by this principle. Saying that X advantages some strata while disadvantaging none when compared to *some* more equal allocation is not enough: all more equal prospects must have a hearing.

This principle of simple justice answers the question with which we began: When can inequality among *prima facie* equals be justified? It answers by saying that diminutions of equality are just when they serve some social strata without damaging others. I believe that this principle is properly justified by the analysis given, and that no rival principle can be justified in this way. Let me turn, then, to a partial *vindication* of the principle's implications. By 'vindication,' I have in mind arguments which rest on the logical or empirical consequences of a principle. Whereas justification tries to treat the principle as a result of other desiderata, vindication asks what logical or empirical results may issue in turn from adoption of the principle. I will confine my argument to one important problem.

I I I Vindication

The aim of simple justice is to account for each of two partly conflicting concerns. We are interested in equality among *prima facie* equals, but not only in this. For we must also take into account their generally shared interests. A good principle of simple justice will take both of these considerations into account. My proposed principle is justified with respect to a theory which gives consideration both to equality and to generally shared interests, and the argument of Part II commits us to choices which reflect at least one of these two undertakings—equality and generally shared interests. In this section, I will offer a modest (and very brief) vindication for simple justice. In doing this, I will show that every judgement required of us by simple justice must also be commended by:

	(1) equality,
or,	(2) maximization of average (or total) welfare,

or both at once. The first represents a consequence of the commitment to *prima facie* equality, and the second (crudely) represents an interpretation of shared interests. The requirement here is that the principle should, in *every* logically imaginable case, select an alternative that would also be selected by equality, maximalism, or both. Put negatively, *no principle of simple justice should ever require that we choose less, less evenly divided, when it would have been possible to choose more, more evenly divided.* This is a rigourous test only in the sense that it covers all logically possible cases, for it seems a modest demand that simple justice should correspond with at least *one* of these considerations. Momentarily, I will show that maximin justice does not satisfy this minimal test; here, I will show briefly that simple justice does so.

Of all logically imaginable choices, only a special subset provides any opportunity to violate this minimal test. If equality and the maximization of totals fall on opposing sides of a decision, no judgement under any principle could possibly violate both at once. Only where one alternative offers a greater total and greater equality, while another offers a lesser total and lesser equality, is it possible to violate the minimal test, viz., by choosing the latter. We need only show that simple justice can never lead us to choose an allocation such as Y instead of an allocation such as X when such a decision as this one presents itself:

X: A greater total divided with greater equality,
Y: A lesser total divided with less equality.

In expanded form, simple justice tells us to 'choose and only choose those augmentations of inequality which advantage some strata and disadvantage none.' If simple justice recommends an 'augmentation of inequality' this must add something to the total while subtracting nothing. If simple justice recommends a possible diminution of the total (when neither alternative advantages some while disadvantaging none), this must lead to greater equality. Outcome Y would, of necessity, disadvantage *some* stratum or strata, and could be commended by simple justice only if it also offered greater equality. But this is contrary to the description of Y, for it must also divide rewards less equally. It follows that simple justice meets the minimal test, and must therefore always lead to greater totals, or greater equality, or both. This is faint praise, and would be properly left out of account if other well-known principles also survived the same test: not all such principles do meet the minimal test.

Rawls's principle is *blind* to a great deal in its treatment of alternative plans for the allocation of social values. Save cases where two rival plans treat the minimum stratum with equal generosity, *only the treatment of that single stratum ever figures as a warrant for the judgement reached by maximin justice*. We do, of course, obtain a single and important additional piece of evidence: All other strata must receive at least as much as the one whose welfare we actually consider. By ignoring these other strata, we do not risk depressing their returns *below* those granted at the minimum. And this is no doubt enough to warrant the view that Rawls's principle gives a certain indirect attention to the interests of all. But is it enough?

Concepts like equality and maximization require us to compare the welfare of all strata, and all must be given full attention in deciding which of two allocations should be preferred under these principles. Simple justice also requires that we attend directly to all strata. Suppose, now, that we are given two possible allocations about which we know very little:

Strata	Allocations	
	X	Y
A	?	?
B...	?	?
M	10	11

Maximin justice would permit a final and conclusive judgement on the basis of this fragmentary evidence.

Principles of equality, or overall maximization, or simple justice would require us to learn more, indeed a great deal more, before arriving at a final conclusion. If this is so, might there not be cases in which these other principles converge on one conclusion while maximin requires another?

Since the minimal test requires that a principle *never* violate both equality and maximization together, a single example will serve our purpose. Imagine a society with three strata. At top and bottom are small groupings comprising, say, 5 per cent of the total population each. A large middle stratum accounts for the remaining 90 per cent of the overall population. Here are two possible allocations:

	X	Y
Top 5%	31	100
Middle 90%	30	20
Bottom 5%	10	11

Ignoring the relative treatment of those 95 per cent who do not find themselves at the minimum, maximin would conclude that allocation Y must be preferred. Notice, first, that this provides a lower average or total benefit (23·55 in Y versus 29·05 in X). Maximin has thus required us to violate one of two provisions. It is also evident that the rejected allocation (X) is more egalitarian overall. The overall range from top to bottom is merely 21 units as against 89 units. The mean deviation from the mean is about 7·6 units under Y and less thãn 2 units under X. And any intuitive examination of the figures confirms these inferences: Allocation Y offers less and divides it less equally, yet maximin justice compels us to override both of these considerations at once, rejecting X in favour of Y. What maximin justice ignores are the absolute and relative treatments of all strata save the lowest, and by ignoring so much it may require us to make judgements which violate even so minimal a test as the one adopted here. Attending to more of the relevant comparisons, equality, utilitarian maximization, and simple justice would all have us do something different and better.

While one may construct innumerable examples of this kind, it should be noticed that some important circumstances rule out such peculiar judgements under maximin justice. If there are only two strata, maximin justice must always satisfy the minimum test. Why? If we improve the lower stratum's position, then raising or leaving constant the higher stratum's entitlement must imply a greater total overall. If, instead, we lower the higher stratum's entitlement while increasing that of the lower stratum, this must serve equality (and may or may not raise the total). Moreover, Rawls's peculiar conception of 'chain connection' would function as an imaginative way of producing the two-class configuration which saves his principle. This is because maximin can endorse a lower-total-less-equality result only if two or more nonminimal strata can 'move' independently: chain connection would mean that more (or less) for any nonminimal stratum must imply more (or less) for all other nonminimal strata. In effect, two strata to worry about. There is, so far as I can see, no more reason to embrace this suggestion than to embrace the special features which so badly damage Rawls's social-contract argument. Rawls might put forward maximin justice as a partial principle of justice, saying in effect: 'For all societies whose strata are chain connected, maximize the minimum.' But he does not, and seems to expect that we should accept this peculiar doctrine on faith for all those societies in which justice might be sought.

Rawls is again saved from this difficulty if one of the alternative results provides *perfect* equality. If the other allocation raises all payoffs, Rawls will have us choose it and maximization of the total would also commend this. If some strata are pushed below their initial level of perfect equality, Rawls will have us reject this and so of course would equality. Rawls might, then, formulate maximin as a partial theory for those circumstances in which we ask whether or not to reject perfect equality. But simple justice will always lead to identical results with maximin where perfect equality is an alternative (Part II above), and will not require us to embrace those aberrant judgements which concern us in other instances.

IV Conclusion

I began with the aim of justifying and vindicating the following principle of simple justice: *Choose only those augmentations of inequality which advantage some strata and disadvantage none.* I have tried to justify this principle in accordance with a hypothetical 'court of allocation,' and this justification seems successful, at least in two particulars: (1) the interests of all strata are considered, while none are permitted to pass off their particular interests as the interests of all, and (2) all rival principles are shown to be unacceptable so that simple justice must be uniquely preferred. I have also given a very partial vindication of simple justice, since its exactions must always and under every circumstance be concurrent with equality, maximization overall, or both of these. The principle is justified only for the circumstances of *simple* justice as these were defined to begin with, and may not (even though the vindication is more general) be applied indiscriminately to all problems of justice. I do not suppose that the principle is without flaws, perhaps flaws more serious than those I attribute to Rawls. I hope nevertheless that the principle and my argument in its favour will be of enough interest to provoke the criticism which would reveal these flaws.

8 Is Democracy Special?[1]

Brian Barry

> *Martin* ... if government, in the sense of coercion, has hitherto been essential to society, that is because no society has yet been founded on equity. The laws have been made by one class for another; and there was no reason, other than fear, why that other class should obey them. But when we come to imagine an ideal society, would government, in this sense, be essential to it?
>
> *Stuart* I suppose there would always be recalcitrant people.
>
> *Martin* Why should there be? What makes people recalcitrant, save the fact that they are expected to obey rules of which they do not approve?
>
> *Stuart* But make your institutions as just as you like, and your people as public-spirited as you like, there must always be differences of opinion as to this or that law or regulation; and if those differences become acute there must be a point at which coercion comes in. ...[2]

I

The question to which this essay is addressed is the following: does the fact that a law was passed by a democratic procedure provide a special reason for obeying it? Let me begin by explaining what I mean by 'a special reason'.

If we look at any law we can say that there are usually reasons for obeying it such as fear of punishment, anxiety about the general effects of disobedience on social stability, and unwillingness to take advantage of the compliance of

[1] This essay was prepared during my tenure of a four-week Fellowship at the Australian National University, Canberra, in August/September 1977. I am grateful to the Department of Political Science in the School of Social Studies for facilities and for comments at a seminar at which it was presented. I also acknowledge with thanks comments from James Fishkin, Carole Pateman, Aristide Zolberg and the participants in a Yale Law School workshop.
[2] G. Lowes Dickinson, *Justice and Liberty: A Political Dialogue* (London: Allen and Unwin, 1908, repr. 1943), p. 125.

others (the essence of the Rawlsian sense of 'justice as fairness'). There are also often reasons for disobeying it, of which personal advantage is the most obvious. In addition it seems plausible that approval of the content of the law makes the case for obeying it stronger than it would otherwise be, while disapproval makes it weaker. 'Approval' and 'disapproval', however, are anodyne generic terms, which conceal a range of relevantly different responses. It seems on the face of it reasonable to say, for example, that equally strong disapproval of two laws, one on the basis of its imprudence or inefficiency, the other on the basis of its injustice or immorality, should have different implications.

Exactly how and why all these factors provide reasons in favour of obedience or reasons telling against it is by no means straightforward. Nor, I am sure, would everyone agree that all of them should be reckoned as reasons at all. For the purpose of this paper, however, I shall simply assume that at least some of these factors, and perhaps others like them, provide reasons for obeying or disobeying laws. My question then is whether an entirely different sort of consideration, namely the procedure by which the law was enacted, or, in the case of long-standing laws, the procedure by which it might have been repealed and has not been, should be a reason for obeying a law.

More specifically, the question I wish to raise is whether or not a law's having been enacted (or not repealed) by a democratic procedure adds a reason for obeying it to whatever reasons exist independently of that. By a democratic procedure I mean a method of determining the content of laws (and other legally binding decisions) such that the preferences of the citizens have some formal connection with the outcome in which each counts equally. Let me make four comments on this definition.

First, I follow here those who insist that 'democracy' is to be understood in procedural terms. That is to say, I reject the notion that one should build into 'democracy' any constraints on the content of the outcomes produced, such as substantive equality, respect for human rights, concern for the general welfare, personal liberty or the rule of law. The only exceptions (and these are significant) are those required by democracy itself as a procedure. Thus, some degree of freedom of communication and organization is a necessary condition of the formation, expression and aggregation of political preferences. And in a state (as against a small commune, say) the only preferences people can have are preferences for general lines of policy. There are not going to be widely-held preferences about whether or not Mr Jones should be fined £10 for speeding or Mrs Smith should get supplementary benefit payments of £3.65 per week. At most there can be preferences for a speeding tariff or for general rules about eligibility for supplementary benefit. If magistrates or civil servants are arbitrary or capricious, therefore, they make democracy impossible.

Second, I require that there should be a formal connection between the preferences of the citizens and the outcomes produced. My intention in specifying a formal connection is to rule out cases where the decision-making process is *de facto* affected by the preferences of the citizens but not in virtue of any constitutional rule. Thus, eighteenth century England has been described as 'oligarchy tempered by riot'.[3] But however efficacious the rioters might be I would not say that their ability to coerce the government constituted a democratic procedure. In the concluding words of the judge appointed to enquire into riots in West Pakistan in 1953: 'But if democracy means the subordination of law and order to political ends—then Allah knoweth best and we end the report.'[4]

Third, by 'some formal connection' I intend deliberately to leave open a variety of possible ways in which democratic procedures might be implemented. In particular, I wish to include both voting on laws by the citizens at large and voting for representatives who exercise the law-making function. I shall take either of these to constitute 'some formal connection with the outcome' in the sense required by the definition: in the first case the citizens choose the laws and in the second they choose the law-makers (in both cases, of course, within the limits of the choice presented to them).

Finally, the phrase 'each counts equally' has to be read in

[3] W. J. M. Mackenzie, *Power, Violence, Decision* (Harmondsworth: Penguin, 1975), p. 151.
[4] Quoted in Hugh Tinker, *Ballot Box and Bayonet: People and Government in Emergent Asian Countries* (Chatham House Essays, 5; London: Oxford University Press, 1964), p. 83.

conjunction with the preceding phrase 'some formal connection with the outcome'. That is to say, nothing is
suggested by the definition of democratic procedure about
equality of actual influence on outcomes. The equality is in
the formal aspect: each adult citizen is to have a vote (only
minor exceptions covering a tiny proportion of those
otherwise eligible being allowed) and there are to be no 'fancy
franchises' giving extra votes to some.

What about the notion that each vote should have an 'equal
value'? This is valid if we construe it as a formal requirement.
If there are two constituencies each of which returns one
representative, the value of a vote is obviously unequal if one
constituency contains more voters than another.[5] To talk
about 'equal value' except in this *a priori* sense is, in my view,
sheer muddle. In recent years, for example, supporters of
systems of proportional representation in Britain have
succeeded in scoring something of a propaganda victory by
pressing the idea that the vote for a candidate who comes
third (or lower) in a plurality system is 'wasted' and the
people who vote for the candidate are 'effectively disfranchised'. But then why stop there? The only way of making
sense of this argument is by postulating that anyone who
voted for a candidate other than the actual winner—even the
runner-up—was 'effectively disfranchised'; and it was not
long before some academics stumbled on this amazing
theoretical breakthrough.[6] I do not think that anyone of
ordinary intelligence would be found saying of an election
for, say, the post of president of a club: 'I didn't vote for the
winning candidate. In other words my vote didn't help elect
anybody. And that means I was effectively disfranchised'. It
is a little alarming that such palpably fallacious reasoning
should have the power to impose on people when the context
is a parliamentary election.

[5] This is, it may be noted, the line taken by the U.S.
Supreme Court in its decision requiring redistricting to
secure approximately equal constituencies. (The leading
case is Reynolds *v.* Sims, 377 U.S. 533 (1964).)
[6] An analysis with whose general line I concur is Paul E.
Meehl, 'The Selfish Voter Paradox and the Thrown-
Away Vote Argument', *The American Political Science
Review* LXXI (1977): pp. 11–30.

II

There is one simple, and, on the face of it, attractive, reason for giving special weight to laws arrived at by democratic procedures, namely that, on any given question about which opinion is divided, the decision must, as a matter of logic, accord with either the preferences of the majority or the preferences of the minority. And, by something akin to the rule of insufficient reason, it seems difficult to say why the decision should go in the way wanted by the minority rather than in the way wanted by the majority.

Obviously, even if the majority principle were accepted, there would still be a gap between the majority principle and democratic procedures as I have defined them. The implication of the majority principle is, fairly clearly, that the best form of democratic procedure is that which permits a vote on issues by referendum. There is no guarantee that elected representatives will on every issue vote in such a way that the outcome preferred by a majority of citizens will be the one chosen. However much we cry up the effects of electoral competition in keeping representatives in line, there is no theoretical reason for expecting that a party or coalition of parties with a majority will always do what a majority of voters want. (Persistent non-voters will in any case have their preferences disregarded by competitive parties—though it may be noted that this is equally so in a referendum.) Even a purely opportunistic party would not necessarily be well-advised to back the side on every issue that the majority supports, as Anthony Downs pointed out.[7] And in practice no party is purely opportunistic—indeed a purely opportunistic party would in most circumstances be an electoral failure because it would be too unpredictable. The party or parties with a legislative majority are therefore always liable to have a package of policies approved of by a majority and policies opposed by a majority. (On many other issues, there may be no single policy with majority support, but that is a complication in the specification of the majority principle that I shall discuss below.)

All this, however, is not as damaging for democratic

[7] A. Downs, *An Economic Theory of Democracy* (New York: Harper and Brothers, 1957), pp. 55–60.

procedures as might be supposed. For it may surely be said that no method for selecting law-makers and governments that was *not* democratic (in the sense defined) could provide a better long-run prospect of producing outcomes in accord with the majority principle. However disappointed an adherent of the majority principle might be in the actual working of democratic procedures, it is hard to see what he or she would stand to gain by helping to secure their overthrow. In principle, of course, this majoritarian might assist the rise to power of a group of dedicated majoritarians who would be committed to acting in accord with majority preferences as ascertained, say, by sophisticated opinion polling. But once in power what reason would there be for confidence in the good faith of these people, or, even more perhaps, of their successors?

I think, therefore, that an adherent of the majority principle would be prepared to disobey laws that were enacted (or not repealed) in the face of clear majority sentiment. But he or she would not take part in any activity either designed for or having the predictable consequence of bringing about the collapse of democratic procedures, because in the long run democratic procedures are more likely to produce majoritarian outcomes than are alternative procedures. Of course, it does not follow that a majoritarian who is satisfied that there is a clear majority against a piece of legislation is thereby committed to disobeying it. All the reasons for not breaking the law that I mentioned at the beginning of this paper may still apply. The only thing that the absence of majority support does for a majoritarian is to remove one (conclusive) reason for obedience.

Can an adherent of the majority principle break the law in an attempt to get the majority to change its mind? I think that this may be done consistently with the principle if it is formulated so that not just any majority counts but only one based on a serious and informed consideration of the issue. Thus, on the facts as stated by him, Bertrand Russell's campaign against nuclear weapons could be consistent with a majoritarian standpoint.[8] But it is essential to the honesty of

[8] 'Long and frustrated experience has proved, to those among us who have endeavoured to make unpleasant facts [about nuclear weapons] known, that orthodox methods, alone, are insufficient. By means of civil disobedience a

such a position that one must be prepared to specify what would constitute a fair test of 'real' majority opinion in a way that does not fall back on the proposition that 'No majority can *really* be in favour of X'.

I have suggested, then, that the majority principle provides fairly strong backing for democratic procedures. What now has to be asked, of course, is whether there is any reason for accepting the majority principle. The view that there is something natural and inevitable about it was expressed forcefully by John Locke in paragraphs 95–9 of the *Second Treatise*. The argument is tied up with Locke's consent theory of political authority but can, I think, be detached from it. The nub is that if there is going to be a body capable of making binding decisions then it 'must move one way' and 'it is necessary the Body should move that way whither the greater force carries it, which is the *consent of the majority*'. Locke adds that 'therefore we see that in Assemblies impowered to act by positive Laws where no number is set by that positive Law which impowers them, the *act of the Majority* passes for the act of the whole, and of course determines, as having by the Law of Nature and Reason, the power of the whole'.[9]

In my first book, *Political Argument,* I put forward the example of 'five people in a railway compartment which the railway operator has omitted to label either "smoking" or "no-smoking"' each of whom 'either wants to smoke or objects to others smoking in the vicinity'.[10] (I should have added that the carriage should be understood as one of the sort that does not have a corridor, so the option of changing

---

certain kind of publicity becomes possible.... Many people are roused into inquiry into questions which they had been willing to ignore.... It seems not unlikely that, in the end, an irresistible popular movement of protest will compel governments to allow their subjects to continue to exist.' Bertrand Russell, 'Civil Disobedience and the Threat of Nuclear Warfare', in Hugo Adam Bedau (ed.), *Civil Disobedience: Theory and Practice* (New York: Pegasus, 1969), pp. 153–9 at p. 157.

[9] John Locke, *Two Treatises of Government,* ed. Peter Laslett (New York: The New American Library, Mentor Book, 1965), pp. 375–6.

[10] B. M. Barry, *Political Argument* (London: Routledge and Kegan Paul, 1965), p. 312.

compartments is not open.) I still think that the example was a good one. Unless all five can reach agreement on some general substantive principle—that in the absence of positive regulation there is a 'natural right' to smoke or a 'natural right' for any one person to veto smoking—it is difficult to see any plausible alternative to saying that the outcome should correspond to majority preference.

The position of someone who is outvoted but refuses to accept the decision is difficult to maintain. As I have suggested, quite persuasive arguments can be made for saying that the decision should not simply reflect the number of people who want to smoke as against the number who dislike being in the presence of smokers. But, since opposing principles can be advanced, the existence of relevant principles does not seem to offer a sound basis for resistance to a majority decision. Or suppose that one of the travellers happens to be the Archbishop of Canterbury. He might claim the right to decide the smoking question on the basis either of his social position or on the basis of his presumptive expertise in casuistry. If his claim is accepted by all the other passengers, no decision-making problem arises because there is agreement. If not all the fellow-passengers accept his claim, however, it again seems difficult to see how the question can be settled except by a vote. And if he finds himself in the minority it must be because he has failed to convince the others (or more than one of them) of his claim to authority. He may continue to maintain that it should have been accepted, just as a believer in the natural right to smoke may continue to maintain that the others should have accepted that principle. But in the face of actual non-acceptance, the case for bowing to the majority decision looks strong.

On further analysis, however, we have to recognize that the 'naturalness' of the majority principle as a way of settling the dispute rests on several features of the particular example which are not commonly found together. I am therefore now inclined to say that it was a good example in the sense that it illustrated well the case for the majority principle but that it was in another sense a bad example because of its special features. I shall single out four, the first three of which make the majority principle determinate while the fourth makes it acceptable. First, we implicitly assume that the people in the compartment have to make only this one decision. Second, only two alternatives are envisaged: smoking or non-smoking. Third, the decision-making constituency is not open to doubt. And fourth, nothing has been said to suggest that the outcome on the issue is of vital importance for the long-term well-being of any of those involved.

To begin with, then, let us retain the feature from the original case that the decisions to be made are dichotomous (that is to say, there are only two alternatives to choose between) but now say that several different decisions have to be taken. In addition to the question whether to permit smoking the passengers also have to decide whether to allow the playing of transistor radios. Suppose that a vote is taken on each question and there is a majority against each. It may be that a majority of the passengers would nevertheless prefer permitting both to prohibiting both, if they were given a choice in those terms.

Let us assign the following symbols: W is no smoking, X is smoking allowed; Y is no playing of radios, Z is playing allowed. The preferences of the five passengers (A, B, C, D and E) are in descending order as in Table 8.1.[11]

Rank order	A	B	C	D	E
1	WZ	WZ	XY	WY	WY
2	XZ	XZ	XZ	WZ	XY
3	WY	WY	WY	XY	WZ
4	XY	XY	WZ	XZ	XZ

Table 8.1

In a straight vote A, B, D and E all prefer W to X, and C, D and E prefer Y to Z, so the outcome would be W and Y. But the pair WY is less well liked than the opposite pair XZ by A, B and C.

We now ask: what does the majority principle prescribe in a situation like this? Are we committed to the view that neither smoking nor playing radios should be allowed, because there is a majority against each? Or can we take account of the fact that there is a majority in favour of overturning the result of the two separate votes and substituting their opposites?

[11] Adapted from Appendix, Example 1 (p. 69) of Nicholas R. Miller, 'Logrolling, Vote Trading, and the Paradox of Voting: A Game-Theoretical Overview', *Public Choice* 30 (1977): pp. 49–75.

The case just presented is consistent with each person's preferences on smoking being independent of what is decided about radio playing, and vice versa. But, in most political matters, this assumption of 'separability' does not hold. What we favour on one issue depends on how other issues are settled. Some things are complementary: we don't want to vote for buying the land unless there is going to be a majority for spending money on the building that is proposed to go on the land. Others are competitive: if expensive project X is going to be funded, we don't want to vote for expensive project Y as well, but if project X is going to be defeated, we would favour project Y. In such a case, the whole concept of a majority on a single issue becomes indeterminate, because each person's preference depends on his or her expectations about the way the other relevant issues are going to be decided. And the outcome if issues are packaged together depends on the way the packaging is done.

A further difficulty is that as soon as we aggregate two or more dichotomous decisions we get a choice between more than two outcomes, and there is then the possibility that no one is capable of getting a majority over each of the others in a pair-wise vote. (In the jargon of collective choice theory, there is no Condorcet winner among the alternatives.) Thus, in the example I set out, I pointed out that A, B and C prefer XZ to WY. But I could have gone on to say that C, D and E prefer XY to XZ, that A, B and D prefer WZ to XY, and that C, D and E prefer WY to WZ. Since, as we already know, A, B and C prefer XZ to WY, it is clear that we have here a cycle including all four possible combinations. No outcome is capable of getting a majority over each of the others and so the majority principle offers no guidance.

The simplest way of generating a situation in which there are cyclical majorities is to have a choice between three possible outcomes. Suppose that our passengers consider three candidates for a binding rule about smoking: X (no smoking), Y (smoking but only of cigarettes) and Z (smoking of pipes and cigars as well as cigarettes). There may, of course, be an outright majority for one outcome. And, even if there is not, there may be a majority for some outcome over each of the others. Thus, suppose the preferences lie as in Table 8.2. Then Y gets a majority over X (C, D and E prefer it) and also a majority over Z (A, B and C prefer it).

Preference ranking	A,B	C	D,E
I	X	Y	Z
2	Y	Z	Y
3	Z	X	X

Table 8.2

A sufficient (though not necessary) condition of there being an outcome that is preferred by a majority to any other is that preferences should be what is called 'single peaked'.[12] All this means is that it should be possible to arrange the alternative outcomes along a single line in such a way that, when we draw for each of the people involved a curve whose height represents their relative preference for each outcome, we get a curve with a single peak for each. Thus, in the present case we can easily see that the preferences satisfy the condition of single-peakedness. (C's preferences could instead have the order YXZ and still be consistent with single-peakedness).

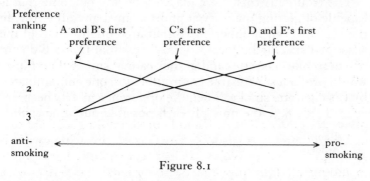

Figure 8.1

When preferences take a single-peaked form, as in Figure 8.1, it is normally possible to discern an underlying dimension from which the orderings derive. (I have here labelled it pro-smoking/anti-smoking.) But the existence of a majority winner is established if we can arrange the outcomes on a line so as to be compatible with single-peaked preferences—even if we as analysts have trouble assigning a label to the line.

When preferences are single-peaked we know not only that a majority winner exists but we also know how to find it easily. The simple rule is that the outcome that is most preferred by

---

[12] The *locus classicus* is Duncan Black, *The Theory of Committees and Elections* (Cambridge: Cambridge University Press, 1963).

the median person is the outcome that is preferred by a majority to any other. The median person is the one (for an odd number of participants) who has exactly as many others on one side as on the other. If there are n people (n being an odd number) whose preferences are to be taken into account, we should start counting at one end (it doesn't matter which since the answer will be the same) and stop when we get to $1/2(n + 1)$. This will be the median person. In our example of five people $1/2(n + 1) = 3$ and it will be seen that we get to C's most preferred position by counting to three from either end. Where there is an even number of people, there is no unique median but the people at $1/2\,n$ and $(1/2\,n) + 1$ (again counting from either end) occupy positions each of which is capable of gaining a majority against any other position. These two positions have an equal number of supporters when matched against each other so on the majority principle they may be regarded as equally good.

The trouble is that there may not be any outcome that is capable of getting majority support against any other (or, in the case of even numbers, two that are equally good in the sense just specified). Thus, suppose now that D and E do not like to smoke cigarettes and, if they cannot smoke their pipes, would prefer a smoke-free environment to one contaminated by C's cigarette smoke. Then the preference matrix becomes as in Table 8.3. We now pit each possible outcome against

Rank order	A and B	C	D and E
1	X	Y	Z
2	Y	Z	X
3	Z	X	Y

Table 8.3

each other in a series of three pairwise comparisons and get the result that X beats Y (A, B, D and E prefer it), Z beats X (C, D and E prefer it) and Y beats Z (A, B and C prefer it). Thus, a quite plausible distribution of preferences generates a 'paradox of voting' in which the majorities arising from pairwise comparisons form a cycle.

The two sources of indeterminacy in the majority principle that I have so far been pointing out may be considered rather dull and technical, incapable of arousing political passions. This is by no means true. Consider, for example, the importance that both sympathizers of President Allende and apologists for the coup that overthrew him and the regime have attached in their polemics to the question whether or not he had majority support for his policies. Given a political set-up with three blocs, Allende was able to come into power as President on a bare plurality; and the Popular Unity Coalition that supported him never achieved a majority of votes cast. It was on the basis of these facts that the junta claimed legitimacy in terms of the majority principle for overthrowing the constitutional government. On the other side, however, it may be argued that 'one cannot infer that those who opposed Allende necessarily supported a military coup, especially the bloody one that ensued following his overthrow. Thus there is little evidence that a majority of Chileans wanted Allende overthrown by the military'.[13]

It is not my intention to join in this debate, merely to point out that, where the majority principle is indeterminate, generals find it worth appealing to it and scholars find it worth rebutting that appeal. However, if we measure the importance of a question by the blood spilt over it (and I find it hard to think of a better criterion) the importance of the third reason for the indeterminacy of the majority principle can hardly be denied. The question is the deceptively innocent one: majority of *what?*

In the railway carriage example this is not a problem. If the decision about permitting or prohibiting smoking is to be made according to majority preference there can be no doubt that the people whose preferences should be taken into account are the five people in the railway carriage who will be affected by the decision. But when the question is the boundaries of political entities—empires, supranational organizations, federations, nation states, provinces or other sub-divisions—and their respective decision-making powers, the question 'who is included?' is an explosive one.

There is no need to labour the point. The briefest survey is enough. In Western Europe, after centuries of wars between states, civil wars, and heavy-handed centralizing government, Northern Ireland is paralyzed by conflict, Scottish nationalism is a powerful force, the centralized Belgian state

---

[13] James Petras and Morris Morley, 'Chilean Destabilisation and Its Aftermath', *Politics* XI (1976): pp. 140–8 at p. 145.

has been virtually partitioned, unfinished business from the nineteenth century still hangs over the Swiss Jura and the Alto Adige, while in Spain Basque and Catalan separatism are stirring again after the long freeze. In Eastern Europe almost every state has claims on the territory of at least one other. Order, of a kind, is maintained by the Soviet Union, which is itself a patchwork of nationalities held together by coercion. And nobody is taking bets on the existence of Yugoslavia in ten years time. In North America, Quebec has a separatist government, and the unity of the country is in question. In the Middle East three wars have been fought over the boundaries of Israel and no end is in sight. In Africa, the boundaries bequeathed by the colonial powers, after a period of surprising stability (interrupted only by the Biafran and Katagan secessions) are coming under pressure in the Horn of Africa, and the trouble looks as if it may well spread further in coming years. The Indian subcontinent has seen first the convulsion of the creation of Pakistan and then the almost equally bloody process of its splitting into two; while in India the states have had to be reconstituted, amid a good deal of disorder, in an attempt to satisfy the aspirations of linguistic groups. There are few parts of the world where boundaries are not a potential source of serious conflict, and where we do not hear that they are (e.g. China) this is as likely to reflect our ignorance as the absence of potential conflict.

The only thing that has to be established, beyond the existence of conflicts over boundaries, is that the majority principle has no way of solving them, either in practice or in theory. In practice, the majority principle, so far from alleviating conflicts over boundaries, greatly exacerbates them. It may be tolerable to be ruled over by a cosmopolitan autocracy, like the Austrian empire, or a more or less even-handed colonial power like the British in India. But to be subject to a majority of different language, religion or national identity is far more threatening. In an area where nationalities are intermingled, like the Balkans, every move to satisfy majority aspirations leaves the remaining minorities even more vulnerable.

On a theoretical level, any use of the majority principle in order to establish boundaries must involve begging the question. Locke, to do him credit, saw that the majority principle could come into play only after the constituency has been identified, but he finessed the problem by resorting to the fiction that those who are to form 'one body' all individually agree to do so. This approach obviously fails to provide any guidance in any situation where it is actually needed, that is to say where people are disagreeing about the 'body' they want to be members of.

The so-called 'principle of national self-determination' espoused by the Versailles Treaty of 1919 says, in effect, that if a minority within a state wishes to secede and the majority does not wish them to secede the minority should win— provided the minority is a 'nation'. As it stands, this is both question-begging (since the crucial judgement is packed into the question whether the would-be secessionists constitute a 'nation') and contrary to the majority principle. But the attempt to reformulate it so as to derive it from the majority principle simply begs the question in a different way.

Suppose we say: the majority in any given territorial area should decide on the political status of that area. Then the question is thrown back one stage further. What is the relevant territorial area within which to count preferences? Consider, for example, the Irish question as it stood between 1918 and 1922. Simplifying somewhat, there was (probably) a majority in the U.K. as a whole (i.e. the British Isles) for the maintenance of the union; within Ireland (i.e. the whole island) there was a majority in favour of independence for the whole of Ireland; within the six provinces that became Northern Ireland there was a majority for partition as a second best to union; but within two of those six counties there was a majority for unification with the south as a second best to independence for the whole of Ireland. But why stop at counties? Counties could have been further divided and some areas within them would have had one sort of majority and others other sorts.

A contemporary puzzle of the same sort is offered by Gibraltar: 'London insists that it will respect the wishes of the 25,000 Gibraltarians, a mixture of people who, for the most part, tend to favour retaining their colonial connection with Britain. Madrid insists on regaining sovereignty over what a broad spectrum of Spanish opinion considers a usurped segment of national territory'.[14] Is the majority of

[14] James M. Markham, 'Talks on Gibraltar Due in October', *The New York Times*, Sept. 25, 1977, p. 4.

Gibraltarians the relevant one, or the majority of people in Spain plus Gibraltar?

It seems clear that the majority principle can offer no guidance. If we feel that (within limits of contiguity and feasibility) the right answer is to try to satisfy the wishes of as many people as possible to form a polity with those they wish to have in it and only those, we are moving beyond the majority principle to another, and in my view more defensible, notion. This is that what matters is not to satisfy the preferences of a majority but to respect the interests of all. I shall argue in the next section that democratic procedures, can, under some conditions, be defended in terms of that conception.

Meanwhile, it should be noted that the upshot of the discussion is that any attempt to justify boundaries by appealing to the majority principle must be void. You can have as many referenda as you like, and show every time that over half of the people within the existing boundaries approve of them, but you cannot use that to prove to a minority that wants to secede that they ought to acquiesce in the *status quo*. If their loyalty is to be awakened, other and better arguments—backed by deeds rather than votes—are needed.

Suppose, however, that the composition of the group that is to be subject to a common policy is not at issue, and that the two more technical sources of indeterminacy are absent, does that make the majority principle unassailable? Of course not. The fourth and last of the special features of the railway carriage case that I singled out was that, as the story had been told, we had no reason to suppose that the question of smoking or not smoking was of vital importance to any of the people involved. (It might be said that smoking is inherently a vital interest in that being smoked at lowers one's expectation of life; but, if we put it as a question of interests, is a few minutes more life a greater interest than the freedom of the addict from withdrawal symptoms?) Suppose, however, that one of the passengers suffers from severe asthma or emphysema, and that being subjected to tobacco smoke is liable to precipitate a dangerous attack. No doubt one would hope that this fact, when explained, would lead the others to agree not to smoke, however many of them would like to. But say that it does not. It seems clear to me that the person at risk would be behaving with an almost insane disregard for his or her interests in accepting a majority decision to allow smoking. The obvious recourse would be, I presume, to pull the communication cord and bring the train to a grinding halt.

It might be argued that nothing said here shows that the majority principle lacks universality: it still applies but in some cases the reason it provides for obedience is overridden by a more pressing consideration, such as self-protection against a risk of substantial harm. However, it does not seem to me that this is a correct representation of the position. Where the decision is sufficiently threatening to the vital interests of (some of) those affected by it, its pedigree is neither here nor there.

Take for example a group of youths like those in *The Clockwork Orange* who beat up strangers for fun. Would we be inclined to say 'Well, at least there's one redeeming feature: they choose their victims by majority vote'? I think not. This example of course raises the question of constituency, since the victim is outside the decision-making group. But if we modify it so that the members of a group decide by majority vote to beat up one of their own number I still do not think that the chosen victim has less reason to resist or escape than he would if the decision were taken by a strong-arm leader. I do not see any significant respect in which my modified example of the railway passengers differs from that. I suppose that someone might adduce the difference between deliberately causing harm and doing something whose known but unintended consequences are harmful, but that is not in my view a morally relevant distinction.

The political parallels hardly need to be filled in. No minority can be, or should be, expected to acquiesce in the majority's trampling on its vital interests. Unfortunately the parallel to pulling the communication cord—bringing the state, or that part of its policy that is objectionable, to a grinding halt—is a much more messy business and carries the risk of incurring costs much higher than a £25 fine. But the principle is clear enough. Nobody but a moral imbecile would really be prepared to deliver himself over body and soul to the majority principle.

This is not to say that no reason can be found for giving weight to the fact that a law arose from a democratic procedure. But it is to say that the majority principle is a broken reed. The attraction of the majority principle lies in the claim that the majority 'naturally' is entitled to act for the whole. If it turns out that this 'naturalness' is contingent on the presence of a number of highly restrictive conditions, we must press our enquiries further and ask whether we can identify some more fundamental basis for saying that democratic procedures matter.

III

At several points in the preceding section, I gestured towards the lines on which an alternative defence of democratic procedures might be mounted. In arguing that the majority principle is helpless in the face of boundary disputes, I suggested that we might adopt the principle not of satisfying the preferences of the majority but safeguarding the interests of everyone; and, in making the point that the majority principle cannot be regarded as sacrosanct even where it is perfectly determinate, I suggested that no minority should respect laws that disregard its vital interests. I now want to follow up those ideas and lay out systematically if sketchily the theory from which they can be derived.

It should be emphasized that the framework within which I am operating is not the familiar one of asking what is the 'best' decision-making system. Rather, I am concerned with the question that each person must ask: 'Given the procedure and the outcome, am I to obey this law?' The advantage of focusing on this practical question can be seen by reflecting on the discussion of the majority principle in the previous section. Social choice theorists often write as if all our problems would be over if *(per impossible)* we could crack the Arrow General Possibility Theorem. Yet for a single dichotomous choice, the majority principle satisfies all of Arrow's conditions for a satisfactory system of aggregating preferences into a 'social decision' and other stronger conditions as well. For all this, as we have seen, it is perfectly possible for a single dichotomous decision to be one that nobody with any elementary regard for self-preservation would voluntarily submit to. We thus get much deeper into the real problems of politics by asking not what is the best procedure but what one should do about actual decisions, taking account (among other things) of the procedures by which they were reached.

In order to offer any general statements we have to be able to imagine ourselves in all the possible positions that a person might get into, and ask what for someone in this position would be the right thing to do. A dramatic though not essential way of setting up the problem is to say that we are to imagine ourselves behind a Rawlsian veil of ignorance.[15] A person behind a veil of ignorance does not know his or her talents, aspirations, race, sex etc., but must choose principles that will be binding on whoever he or she turns out to be. Unlike Rawls I shall posit (and not suggest that I can derive it from the specification of the choice situation and the notion of rationality) that someone who is looking at all the possible positions he or she might turn up in will be particularly concerned with the protection of vital interests.

The first question to be asked is whether to have laws at all, and, if so, what is to be their status. One possibility is that there should be no rules of any kind. Another is that there should be rules but that they should have only the status of suggestions to aid interpersonal co-ordination. Alternatively, there might be a society in which laws carried sanctions but nobody ever considered anything except the sanction in deciding whether or not to obey the law (just as in our society we buy a bottle of Scotch if it is worth it to us after paying a large sum to the government); or there might be one in which the existence of a law was taken as a reason for obeying it but no sanction was attached to disobedience. Finally, the existence of a law might be taken as a reason for doing what it requires but there might be sanctions against disobedience too.

The question has been set up in classical 'social contract' terms, and the classical 'social contract' answer is that the last of these possibilities is preferable to any of the others: we need stable expectations that certain rules will be generally followed, we want there to be sanctions underwriting the rules, but we don't want people to keep the rules only when the sanctions are sufficiently probable to make obedience the course of action that pays on a prudential calculation. I think in general this is a good answer.

[15] John Rawls, *A Theory of Justice* (Cambridge, Mass.: Harvard University Press, 1971), pp. 136–42.

But it is one thing to say that one would wish the standard situation to be one in which people accept the existence of a law as a reason for obeying it. That still leaves open the question whether or not something's being a law should always be taken as a decisive reason for obeying it. And, if the answer to that question is negative, it leaves open the question of particular concern here, whether or not the law's origin in a democratic procedure should make a difference.

The first of these questions does not seem too difficult. Looking at the matter impartially, taking account of all the contingencies in which he or she could be exposed, it is surely apparent that our person choosing principles and institutions would not wish to be committed to unconditional obedience to law. In some cases, open disobedience or rebellion may be right. I shall discuss these later. But I should like to say a word here for ordinary non-heroic disobedience, in other words crime, that is to say law-breaking undertaken for private rather than public ends and with the intention of avoiding detection if possible.

A typical reaction among political philosophers is that 'the ordinary criminal may be viewed as acting primarily out of motives of self-interest—motives which render him morally blameworthy and socially dangerous'.[16] Presumably it is not simply the self-interested motive that makes for a presumption against the moral acceptability of ordinary criminal law-breaking. Most market behaviour is motivated by self-interest but is not normally taken to be *ipso facto* reprehensible. I think that the basic reasons for condemning ordinary law-breaking are that breaking the law causes harm to the victim(s) and that it is unfair to take advantage of the forbearance of others to secure a private advantage. The

[16] Jeffrie G. Murphy, in his Introduction to a book of readings on *Civil Disobedience and Violence* (Belmont, Calif.: Wadsworth, 1971), p. 2. Similarly, H. B. Acton, in 'Political Justification', reprinted in Hugo Adam Bedau (ed.), *Civil Disobedience: Theory and Practice* (New York: Pegasus, 1969), pp. 220–39, having said that 'disobedience... may take a variety of forms', dismissed that of 'not obeying and of endeavouring to escape the legal consequences' as 'of no interest to us in this paper, since either it is nothing but a sort of unprincipled subterfuge or else it leads to [rebellion, i.e. the attempt to overthrow the government by force]' (p. 222).

criminal is, in Rawlsian terms, a 'free rider' on the scheme of social co-operation from which he or she benefits. This rationale, however, fails to apply in two kinds of cases: where nobody is benefited by the actor's forbearance and where the whole scheme of social co-operation is not on balance beneficial to the actor.

We must, as Dr Johnson exhorted, clear the mind of cant. Will anyone seriously maintain that he or she has ever stopped drinking in a pub at exactly 10:40 p.m. (assuming that the landlord is prepared to go on serving) out of respect for the licensing laws rather than out of fear of possible unpleasantness with the police? There are a whole range of laws whose observance benefits nobody—laws against Sunday entertainment, laws prohibiting off-course betting, laws against contraception and abortion, laws regulating the sexual relations of consenting adults, and so on. There can be no unfairness to others in disobeying such laws, and it is surely significant that people break them on a massive scale without guilt feelings. The 'what if everybody did that?' argument against breaking the law has no force in such a case, as long as 'that' is understood as 'breaking the same law'.[17] For *ex hypothesi* the case is one where disobedience has no ill-effects whatever the scale. And inasfar as mass disobedience has a tendency to bring about the demise of the law as a by-product, that is a plus factor in the reckoning. As Christian Bay has pointed out, the massive evasion of Prohibition in the USA had no high-minded motives 'for the Volstead act was usually evaded in secret, even if Clarence Darrow is said to have referred to bootleggers as fighters for American liberties and predicted the erection of statues to Al Capone in many a public park'.[18] But it still made repeal virtually unavoidable.

These are cases where nobody benefits from forbearance. The other cases are those where there are indeed beneficiaries from forbearance, but there is no mutual benefit. Thus, let us say that the system of *apartheid* in South Africa benefits (at least in the short run) the white minority. It clearly does not

[17] Compare Richard A. Wasserstrom, 'The Obligation to Obey the Law', reprinted in Bedau, *Civil Disobedience,* pp. 256–62.
[18] Christian Bay, 'Civil Disobedience: Prerequisite for Democracy in Mass Society', reprinted in Murphy, *Civil Disobedience and Violence,* pp. 73–92 at p. 85.

benefit the rest of the population and I can conceive of no reason other than concern for his or her own safety why anyone subject to this apparatus of legal oppression should pay it any respect. Published reports suggest that the hundreds of pass-law violators who are processed by the courts each day regard the inevitable fine as an incident of life in an unjust society rather than as the expiation of personal wrongdoing.[19] Turning T. H. Green on his head (the time-honoured treatment for idealists) one may say that force, not will, is the basis of the State, at any rate in its discriminatory aspects.

We now need to face the question whether a law's having been passed by a democratic procedure should provide a special reason for obeying it. A common argument for accepting an outcome reached by a democratic procedure even when you dislike it is that you should take the rough with the smooth: you can't win them all, but in the long run you can expect to win more than half the time because on each issue the majority principle ensures that more people win than lose. I want in the rest of this section to take this popular idea, see what it presupposes in order to be persuasive, and then ask what should be done where it breaks down.

As we have already seen, the majority principle cannot be equated with democratic procedures (as I equated it in presenting the view to be discussed) so it will make for clarity to split the analysis into two parts. First, I shall show that the application of the majority principle produces satisfactory results so long as the preferences to be taken into account are distributed in certain ways. Following that I shall try to establish a connection for such cases between the outcome required by the majority principle and the general tendency to be expected of democratic procedures.

Consider, then, a country in which issues are always dichotomous and in which the following characteristics hold: (1) on each issue, each of those who are in the majority stands on the average to gain as much satisfaction from the law as each of those in the minority stands to lose from it; and (2) on each issue there is an independent probability for each person of being in the majority that is equal to the proportion of the

[19] For a recent account, see Larry Garbus, 'South Africa: The Death of Justice', *The New York Review of Books*, August 4, 1977.

total number in the majority on that issue. The first condition says in effect that the stakes of each person are the same on any given issue (though they may not be the same on different issues). The second says in effect that, whatever we know of a person's previous voting record, we cannot do better than predict he or she has a .6 probability of being in the majority if the majority is 60%, a .7 probability of being in the majority if the majority is 70% and so on.

The second condition entails that, over a period sufficient for a number of issues to come up, decisions made in accordance with the majority principle can be expected to yield approximately equal satisfaction to each person. Adding the first condition we can go further: if we count getting the outcome you want as $+1$ and getting the outcome you don't want as -1, then each person can expect $(x - .5) \times 2$ units of satisfaction, where x is the average majority. (E.g. if the average majority is .7 each person can expect .4 units of satisfaction.) But in addition the first condition alone tells us that the majority principle maximizes average satisfaction, for it can never increase average satisfaction to please fewer people rather than more, given that the average gain of each winner is the same as the average loss of each loser.

If the person choosing from behind the veil of ignorance were seeking to maximize the average of the levels of satisfaction of all the people he or she might turn out to be, the first condition alone indicates that the majority principle is the one to pick. But suppose instead that the person behind the veil of ignorance were to follow Rawls's recommendation and choose a rule for aggregating preferences with the object of making the lot of the worst off of all those that one might turn out to be as desirable as possible. Then, because in the special case stated in the second condition everyone has the same expectation of satisfaction, it would still be best to pick the majority principle. For any other principle lowers the average, and, since everyone's expectations are the same, that means that on any other principle each of the people he or she might turn out to be would be worse off.

Let us take this idea and cash it out into the choice of sanctions for breaking the law and principles about obedience to the law. Obviously, when we say that people get satisfaction from getting a law they want or lose satisfaction from getting a law they don't want, we are speaking in shorthand. What people gain or lose satisfaction from is not the enactment itself but the operation of the law. If those who are in the minority on any law ignore it with impunity, they do not suffer the loss associated with it; but those in the majority do not experience the gain associated with it either, at any rate if the minority is large enough for its disobedience to undermine the law. But in the case as specified there is a net gain from each law (that is, from the operation of each law) and each person stands in the long run to share equally in these gains. Therefore, from behind the veil of ignorance it is advantageous both to support sanctions and to adopt the principle as binding on all that laws which have majority approval ought to be obeyed even in the absence of prudential motives.

Now, by contrast, suppose that the second condition does not hold, though the first still does. It still maximizes the average satisfaction of all the people one might turn out to be to endorse the majority principle. But if one is concerned to avoid the worst threats to one's interests, the majority principle is no longer so attractive. Take the opposite extreme from the atomistic society in which there is no association between one person's vote and any other's and consider a society permanently divided into two rigid groups. Each group always has monolithic preferences, so the same people are always in the majority and minority. The average of all the people one might be is still $(x - .5) \times 2$, though here x is simply the proportion of the whole constituted by the majority group. But the expectation of each member of the minority group is -1, since on every issue they lose.

If in addition we give up the first condition, we can no longer even be confident that the average satisfaction will be maximized by adopting that side on every issue that corresponds with the majority preference. If (as William Riker assumes in his theory)[20] politics is a zero-sum game, so that on every issue the amount gained by those who are on the winning side is exactly equal to the amount lost by those on the losing side (which entails, of course, under the majority principle, that winners always win less per head than losers lose) it would obviously be better to have no procedure for making laws. Anyone who wants gratuitous risks can always

20 W. Riker, *A Theory of Political Coalitions* (New Haven: Yale University Press, 1962).

gamble privately—there is no point in forcing risks on everyone. And of course if politics is a negative-sum game (as some even more gloomy theorists seem to believe) the case for having no government at all is overwhelming. In practice however, even the worst state is one in which some laws are positive-sum: in South Africa, for example, it is clearly to the mutual interest of non-whites to respect the law against murder—all the more so because the police take little interest in enforcing it.

The upshot of this very crude analysis is that, from behind the veil of ignorance, a person of reasonable prudence would accept outcomes produced in accordance with the majority principle for an atomistic society or a pluralistic society, which we may take as the closest real-life approximation: that is to say, a society in which there are many groups and the relations between them are fluid. In such a society, the majority principle gives each group a good chance of being in the majority over half the time. This description of the pluralistic society is, of course, recognizable as the picture of the USA drawn by the celebrants of the nineteen-fifties. It is probably a fair description of the way the system works for the best-placed sixty or seventy per cent of the adult population. Conversely, the more closely a society approximates to the model of a monolithic majority bloc facing a minority which is always on the losing side, the more a reasonably prudent person would refuse to accept that, if he or she found himself in such a society and in the minority group, he or she would be bound to respect the laws that had been passed by the majority over minority opposition.

The assumption that all issues are dichotomous is a very restrictive and unrealistic one. Let me extend the analysis just one step, to the simplest case beyond: that where all preferences lie on one dimension. I have already, in Section II, pointed out that in such a case the majority principle picks out one point as the unique one that is capable of gaining a majority in a pairwise comparison with any other. This is the point corresponding to the preference of the median person, in other words the person with exactly as many others on each side. In investigating the properties of the majority principle, then, all we need to do is examine the properties of the median.

Consider first a case in which these three things are true: (1)

on any issue, each person experiences the same loss of satisfaction for any given distance between the most preferred outcome and the actual outcome; (2) for each person the loss of satisfaction is linear with distance, in other words it is always true that an outcome twice as far away represents twice as much loss of satisfaction; and (3) on each issue, each person has an independent probability of being in any position that is equal to the proportion of the total number of people in that position.

(1) and (2) here replace the first stipulation for the dichotomous case, that winners and losers gain and lose equal amounts: they say that the same increase in distance away from one's most preferred position results in an equal loss for everyone. (3) is a strict analogue of the second condition. And we get analogous results. Condition (3) guarantees that in the long run everyone can expect to lose the same amount (i.e. be on the average the same distance away from the median), and (1) and (2) guarantee that the overall average loss on each issue is always minimized by choosing the median. What this is really saying (given the first two conditions) is that the total distance from all the points on a line to the median is less than the total distance to any other point. This can be seen intuitively by imagining the people standing along an actual line. You start by standing in front of the median person and then moving away: in whichever direction you move you are adding an equal amount to your distance from some people and decreasing your distance from others by the same amount, but you are going away from more people than you are going towards. It is important to recognize that this is true regardless of the way the people are distributed along the line. Even if most are bunched at one end with a few stragglers out in the distance you still minimize total distance by taking up the median position.

We can therefore say, strictly analogously with our conclusions in the dichotomous case, that someone who was concerned only with maximizing the average satisfaction (or in this case minimizing the average loss of satisfaction) of all the people he or she might be would choose the majority principle (i.e. the median position) purely on the strength of the first two conditions; while adding the third condition (which provides everyone with an equal expectation) would make the majority principle the choice either of a maximizer or of someone concerned to minimize the losses of the person losing the most.

At this point, however, the analogy with the dichotomous case breaks down. In dropping the second condition for the dichotomous case—the atomistic assumption—we went to the opposite extreme and imagined a society with no changing of places at all, and decided that a person of reasonable prudence would not endorse the majority principle for such a society. In the one-dimensional case, however, a similar total lack of fluidity in relative positions does not necessarily have such disturbing implications for the majority principle.

Consider the most neutral assumption about the way preferences are distributed: that they are evenly distributed along the dimension. If we plot the density of preferences on the vertical dimension, a distribution of this kind looks as in Figure 8.2. Now the interesting thing about this distribution

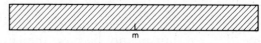

Figure 8.2

is that the median position (marked m) not only minimizes average loss (as does the median with any distribution, given the first two assumptions) but also minimizes the maximum loss of any person. For if we move away from it in either direction, the people at the far end are made worse off than they were when the outcome was at the median.

As may be apparent, a rectangular distribution is not needed to generate this result. Any distribution such that the median point lies half way between the extremes will do it. Therefore all symmetrical distributions—that is to say distributions such that one half of the line is a mirror-image of the other half—satisfy the requirement. Examples are Figures 8.3 and 8.4. Of course, the average loss of satisfaction differs between the three distributions: it is greatest in Figure

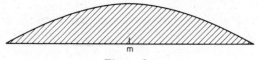

Figure 8.3

8.4, least in Figure 8.3 and intermediate in Figure 8.2. The society depicted in Figure 8.3 has more ability to satisfy its average member than the society in Figure 8.2, and that in Figure 8.2 more than that in Figure 8.4. Failing some realignment of preferences—the rise of a different issue, perhaps—it might be as well for the two groups in the last society to split off into separate polities, or form a federation allowing each the maximum autonomy; or if they are too geographically mingled for that they might at least try *verzuiling* (functional decentralization). But if there *is* going to be one set of policies binding on all of them, the median is the one that anybody choosing from behind a veil of ignorance will have to go for.

The natural reaction to Figure 8.4 is, I think, to dispute the

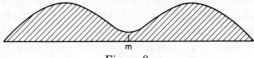

Figure 8.4

analysis and suggest that the median position is unlikely to be the outcome. I agree, but mainly because the situation as depicted is so finely balanced. The tension between the two groups would be extreme because so much was at stake: changes in the birthrates or the migration rates, or a little gerrymandering, could so easily swing the outcome a long way to one side or the other. The reasonably prudent person choosing from behind a veil of ignorance would not, I concede, give unqualified allegiance to the majority principle for a society so evenly balanced between two blocs, with so few people in the region of the median, as in Figure 8.4. The logic of the situation is illustrated by Figure 8.5. This shows how once we move off symmetry with a bimodal distribution like that in Figure 8.4, the median position leaves those in the minority group out in the cold. The average loss is still minimized but the maximum loss is great.

Notice in passing that moving the unimodal distribution of

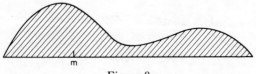

Figure 8.5

Figure 8.3. away from symmetry does not have the same kind of drastic results. Figure 8.6 illustrates the way in which the median shifts a little away from the centre, but not dramatically. A distribution of this kind may be thought of as a rough sketch of a politics of economic interest in an otherwise homogeneous society, where income and status follow a pattern of continuous graduation (as against dichotomous classes) but where the distribution of income and status is in the traditional 'squashed diamond' shape.

How do these results relate to those we obtained for the dichotomous case? We can establish two fairly direct parallels. The atomistic society, in which people distribute themselves randomly on dichotomous issues, is, I suggested, a rose-tinted model of the USA in the 1950s. It might approximate other societies with a fluid social structure, perhaps the USA and other settler societies at a certain stage of development. The one-dimensional model with random placement may be thought of as a somewhat more complex version of the same thing, in which we allow that groups may have a variety of different positions on any given issue. The alternative model of two rigid groups facing one another on successive dichotomous issues approximates the condition of a society with a deep structural cleavage running through it: a division based on ethnicity, language, race, or possibly (where there is a sharp gulf between landlords and peasants or owners and workers) on class. The one-dimensional model with a bimodal distribution refines on this by allowing for a certain range of position within the groups and the possibility of some people holding intermediate positions. But the general implications are much the same as in the dichotomous case: outcomes in accordance with the majority principle may be highly injurious to the interests of the minority group.

Where we get something distinctively new from the one-dimensional analysis is in the case of a unimodal distribution. For we can see here how fixed positions may be compatible with acceptable outcomes. Admittedly the people on the two

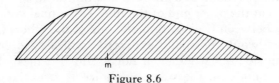

Figure 8.6

tails of the distribution will be dissatisfied with the outcomes that the majority principle calls for, that is to say the outcomes preferred by the person in the median position. But what alternative can they seriously propose? Those in the minority group have a good cause for complaint when there is a bimodal distribution and the median person is in the majority group. But with a unimodal distribution any move towards one set of extremists leaves the extremists at the other end even more dissatisfied than they were in the first place. From behind the veil of ignorance it would be inconsistent to say that if one found oneself on one tail of a unimodal distribution one should resist outcomes corresponding to the median position without acknowledging that those at the other extreme should also resist them, for there is no way of distinguishing the two. 'The end I happen to be at' will not do.

Although we started from a defence of the majority principle that was expressed in terms of winning and losing, we have finished up with a case where the majority principle can be defended even though the line-up is the same on each question that comes up for decision. That is to say, on each question the same single dimension defines the positions of each of the actors and they find themselves in the same places. We got here by transforming the winning and losing in the dichotomous case into a value of getting the outcome you want and a (negative) value of getting the outcome other than the one you want. We then made a natural extension of that way of thinking so as to accommodate the analysis in one dimension by assuming that the distance between the preferred outcome and the actual outcome provides a measure of dissatisfaction with that outcome. We are thus able to evaluate the median position as an outcome in terms of the distribution of loss of satisfaction that it produces, without any need to refer to winning and losing.

To see that winning and losing is irrelevant, go back for a moment to the set-up depicted in Figure 8.1, where A and B take one position, C a middle position and D and E the position at the other end of the line. If the final vote on each issue is between C's position and one of the others (which is what we would normally expect) C will always be on the winning side but whether or not A and B 'win' or D and E 'win' depends on the way the choice is structured. If the choice is between the outcome preferred by A and B and the outcome preferred by C, then C, D and E will vote together and A and B will go down to defeat. If the position preferred by D and E is set against that preferred by C, we will get the result that A, B and C combine against D and E. Yet in both cases the outcome is the same: the outcome preferred by C is the one that gets a majority. This simple example illustrates the fallacy of counting up 'wins' and 'losses' where there are more than two possible positions. The only sound procedure is to compare the position preferred by each actor with the actual outcome.

The unimodal model of preference-distribution fits reasonably well the Scandinavian countries, England, New Zealand and Australia. Other countries are not adequately represented by this unimodal model, in which political differences reflect the socioeconomic stratification of an otherwise relatively homogeneous population. Yet at the same time they do not exhibit the radical pluralism of societies such as Guyana, the Lebanon, Indonesia, Nigeria, Cyprus or Malaysia, in which different groups live side by side sharing no common institutions except those of the state. These other societies, of which the Netherlands and Belgium are paradigmatic, have a division between 'spiritual families' (and, in the Belgian case, an ethnic cleavage) but are at the same time sufficiently integrated to have the potential for a politics of socioeconomic interest cutting across these ascriptive lines. An adequate model of preference-distribution in such societies requires two or even three dimensions. However, except for special cases, there is no longer a unique point picked out by the majority principle once we move away from one dimension. There is in general no Condorcet winner, no point capable of gaining a majority over all others. The problem of circularity rears its head once more. I cannot afford here the space to follow up the complexities that arise in analysing spaces of two or more dimensions, since I still have not made the connection, even for the one-dimensional cases, between the majority principle and democratic procedures. Having established that connection, however, I shall be in a position to take some short-cuts in the analysis of the politics of plural societies.

So far, then, I have been operating with the majority principle as the object of analysis. But if this analysis is to tie up with democratic procedures, I have to argue that democratic procedures have a tendency to produce the outcomes called for by the majority principle. This I believe to be true in general, and I think that theoretical arguments can be offered to show why it is not accidental that it happens, but I can do no more than sketch the argument here.

In the dichotomous case, I have already suggested in Section II that democratic procedures are more likely to produce the outcomes desired by a majority than any alternative procedure. All that needs to be added here is that the case in which a purely opportunistic party would sometimes support minority policies is ruled out for any case where the per capita gains and losses of majority and minority are equal.

The one-dimensional case requires a little more analysis. With direct voting between all pairs of positions, we know that the median position can obtain a majority over all rivals. But even in a committee cruder devices are used. In a referendum, only two choices are commonly offered: to accept the proposal or reject it. This leaves a good deal of scope for manipulation open to whoever is able to set the terms of the referendum. For, if preferences are one-dimensional, the option closer to the median will win; but, if both the options are some way off the median, the result will obviously not have the desirable properties attributed here to the median. This suggests that referenda are dubious unless either (a) the topic 'naturally' creates a dichotomy or (b) it is open to any group of fair size to place an alternative on the ballot and some form of preferential voting is employed.

Voting for representatives is not subject to the same difficulties because the parties in effect do the work of sifting issues and putting together a majority. Very crudely, let me divide the types of party-system to be analysed into two-party and multi-party systems. In two-party systems, the parties will tend to converge toward the median voter's position if they are concerned with winning elections. This is because, if each voter votes for the party whose position is nearer his own, the party nearer the median voter must get the most votes.[21] The argument is, in my view, compelling, and can be extended by observing that even if parties are not trying to

[21] Downs, *op. cit.*, Chapter 8.

win elections (or have other aims as well) it is still true that the party nearer the median voter will win. So the tendency for the party that gets a majority to be somewhere in the neighbourhood of the median voter does not depend on strong assumptions about party motivation, only on the assumption that, for whatever reason, at least one party will usually be fairly near the median voter at an election.

The multi-party case is more controversial. Downs argues in effect that with multi-party systems no systematic relationship between voter preferences and the policies pursued by governments can be expected.[22] In my view this is false to experience and also contrary to the logic of parliamentary tactics. Downs assumed that if several parties formed a coalition government the policy of the government would be some sort of average of the positions of the parties making it up. But his assumption has no rational foundation. The same logic that leaves the median voter with the whip-hand in a direct vote leaves the party containing the median legislator (call it the median party) with the whip-hand. Give me the minimum assumption that, other things being equal, parties prefer to be in governments that pursue their own programmes to being in governments that pursue other parties' programmes, and I can show that for any majority coalition with a policy other than that of the median party there is another majority coalition (which must contain some overlapping members) with the policy of the median party all of whose members prefer it to the first one. Qualifications are of course needed, and cannot be given here, to deal with anti-system parties, cartels and so on. But I believe that the basic tendency of multi-party systems that fall along one dimension is towards implementing the policies desired by the median party.

It still has to be shown that the median party's position can be anticipated to be in the region of the median voter, but this can be done fairly easily. As in the two-party case, we can say immediately that, if each voter votes for the nearest party, the median party will have been voted for by the median voter. But, in a multi-party system, the median party is normally quite closely hemmed in by other parties, so the range within which it is closer to an elector than any other party is likely to

[22] Ibid., Chapter 9.

be quite small. So there is good reason for expecting the median party and the median voter to be near one another.

The upshot of this analysis is that the earlier discussion of the strengths and weaknesses of the outcomes corresponding to the majority principle can be transferred to the outcomes that we can expect democratic procedures to produce. (To the extent that party competition and coalition formation do not operate in the way I have postulated, our confidence in the reliability of this coincidence must of course be weakened.) Thus, the tendency of democratic procedures in societies with a bimodal distribution of preferences will be to produce outcomes that are highly prejudicial to the interests of the minority group. And in the less extremely fragmented societies of Western Europe we can say that democratic procedures have the same tendency when the political parties draw their support on the basis of ethnic, religious, racial or other ascriptive criteria rather than competing by offering alternative positions on the dimension of party preferences related to location in the system of socioeconomic stratification.

What would be a sensible attitude to adopt towards obedience to law? Although we do not observe people choosing from behind a veil of ignorance, we do see the way they choose in real life and from that we can infer the relative strength of different motives—information that would be needed before an intelligent choice could be made from behind the veil of ignorance. And if we look at the empirical evidence we find that people do in fact tend to deny the legitimacy of a regime—however much it may bolster itself up by appeals to the majority principle—if they find the group to which they belong systematically discriminated against, treated as second class citizens, denied cultural expression or communal organization and generally not dealt with in terms of equal partnership.

It does not follow from that, however, that disobedience should be prescribed from behind the veil of ignorance. We need to examine the evidence. It seems clear that resistance to the majority has in some instances produced a more acceptable outcome, especially where it was backed up by the threat that disunity within the country might result in its loss of independence. If we look at instances where majorities have drawn back from pressing their maximum claims and accepted minorities as equal partners in what has been called 'consociational democracy',[23] we find that they come about when the minority has established (given the background of the international situation) a capacity to cause trouble to the majority. These conditions can be seen in the stock examples of the conciliation of a minority: the Swiss settlement in 1848 following the Sonderbund war, the Dutch 'pacification' of 1917, the complex Lebanese balancing act and the Austrian compromise between 'black' and 'red' in 1945. In two cases (Switzerland and Austria) the minority lost a civil war, and in the Lebanese case the possibility of a civil war was (as recent events have tragically proved) too clear to miss. At the same time, in all of them, the international situation was threatening. Switzerland's integrity was threatened by the growing idea that state boundaries should correspond to 'nationalities', with the prospect that Switzerland might be dismembered and the parts absorbed into national states. The risk to the survival of the Netherlands of harbouring a discontented minority predominantly located on its border with Germany are too clear to need spelling out. The position of the Lebanon has always meant that internal disturbances risked outside intervention—as in the recent civil war. And in Austria the country was under four-power occupation in the post-war period, the withdrawal of the Russians could not be taken for granted, and the country was bordered by states under Russian influence.

There are, it need hardly be said, other situations that are far less favourable to the minority, where the only effect of resistance is to increase the degree of injustice and repression. In such cases, the minority has prudential reasons (though no others) for refraining from resistance, and hoping that some new turn of the wheel of international politics will bring about a more propitious situation, in which the ability to create a disturbance will be a stronger bargaining counter.

[23] For a critical discussion of the concept, see my 'Review Article: Political Accommodation and Consociational Democracy', *The British Journal of Political Science*, 5 (1975): pp. 477–505.

IV

The premise of the previous section was ruthlessly instrumental: it assumed that people were concerned to get the outcomes they wanted, and were interested in procedures only as a means to that end. The content of the laws, not the way in which they were brought into existence, was all that mattered. The case for democratic procedures was simply that, under favourable circumstances, they were likely to produce acceptable outcomes. But any other procedure that produced the same outcomes would be equally acceptable. I am convinced that there is more to be said for that view, both morally and as a way of predicting how people will actually behave, than there is for the 'majority principle'. And yet— wasn't there *something* in the idea mooted in Section II, that there is a certain naturalness about majorities as a basis for settling matters that are in dispute? I think there is and in this final section I shall try to say what I think it is.

Come back for a moment to the notion of consociational democracy. The essence of it is that the elites may be able to prevent democratic procedures from exacerbating conflict if they co-operate (maybe but not necessarily in a formal 'grand coalition') to find an agreed solution to the divisive issues and then sell it to (or impose it on) the electorate. Arendt Lijphart, who was responsible for introducing the term into contemporary political science, remarked that 'consociational democracy violates the principle of majority rule, but it does not deviate much from normative democratic theory'.[24] But the whole idea of consociational democracy is clearly at odds with any notion that the point of democratic procedures is that the parties are forced by the exigencies of competition to articulate the preferences for public policies of their supporters. The defining characteristic of 'consociational democracy' is that the party leaders do *not* press for the interests of their supporters (as those supporters see them)

[24] Arend Lijphart, 'Consociational Democracy', reprinted in Kenneth McRae (ed.), *Consociational Democracy: Political Accommodation in Segmented Societies* (Toronto: McClelland and Stewart, 1974), pp. 70–89 at p. 77. See also Lijphart, *Democracy in Plural Societies: A Comparative Exploration* (New Haven: Yale University Press, 1977).

but rather somehow manage to carry their followers along a path of compromise.

Obviously, if peace and stability can be achieved only by preventing the electoral pressure from deflecting the party leaders from compromise, it is natural to ask why they should have to put up with electoral sanctions at all. Why not just have 'consociation' and drop 'democracy'? In practice, it might be said, this is what does happen in some states: where representative institutions produce a clash between ethnic groups, a non-representative system permits controlled 'consociation' from the top in the shape of participation of members of different groups in the government. (Nigeria and Kenya could both be cited as examples.) But if there is in the literature of consociational democracy an implicit value judgement that, other things being (approximately) equal, it is better to have representative institutions, on what is that judgement based? Clearly, not on the majority principle, since the essence of 'consociational democracy' is to avoid finishing up with what the majority wants. The answer would, I think, have to be on the lines that, *if* the trick can be brought off, the combination in divided societies of elections and elite collusion is superior to either elections without collusion or collusion without elections, because it satisfies both the value of peace and stability and the value of freedom of speech and organization.

How would this claim be made out? I think the key is the following assertion: once a society reaches a level of development in which there is widespread education and where the bulk of the population enjoys independence from grinding poverty and continuous toil, the choice can *only* be between repression (including arbitrary action against citizens, making political prisoners out of critics and tight restraints on freedom of publication, assembly, etc.) and a system of representative government. This may appear a quite banal generalization and yet if it is true (and it seems to stand up well empirically) it is surely a remarkable fact.

In principle, after all, any kind of regime might be able to establish itself with sufficient acceptance to allow freedom to its critics. One would gather, for example, from Michael Oakeshott's *On Human Conduct* that there is no particularly favoured basis for the legitimacy of regimes. Their authority simply rests on the fact of recognition. He offers as an 'analogue' the case of the Marylebone Cricket Club's having acquired over time recognition as the arbiter of the rules of cricket. Its authority 'has nothing to do with the recognition of the desirability of the rules or with the constitution of the committee'.[25] I am inclined to think that this analogue tells us more about Oakeshott's view of the world than about the world. Who cares, to put it bluntly, what the rules of cricket are? Certain modifications of, say, the l.b.w. rule may provide special opportunities for bowlers with a particular technique to cramp the style of certain batsmen, but on the whole any rule leaves teams as well placed in relation to one another as they were before. It is in the nature of rules of a game (and therefore makes them highly tendentious paradigms of political decisions in general) that any rule, so long as it is simply applied impartially, defines a fair procedure for determining who wins. It is therefore less important what the rules are than that everyone plays by the same ones. I venture to suggest that if the MCC claimed jurisdiction over any matter that has anything in common with the normal stuff of politics—if, for example, it were able to levy a royalty on every game of first-class cricket played in the world and the question arose how the money raised were to be spent—it would not be long before the demand would arise for the body charged with disbursing the funds to be put upon some kind of representative basis.

Why is this? It would be easy to say that 'democratic ideology' is triumphant and therefore provides the only basis for general consent. But it would be so easy as to be worth very little. The use of 'ideology' in this context is an essentially irrationalist one and implies that some other basis of legitimacy with a different content altogether might just as well have become established in the world. It seems to me that such a view would be misguided and would ignore the very real advantages of competitive election as a rationale for placing the government in one set of hands rather than another.

The point I am driving at was put more effectively than by anyone else I have come across by Sydney Smith in one of his 'Four Speeches on the Reform Bill'. The Reform Bill in question was that of 1832 and it was of course (considered in relation to universal suffrage) a very limited measure. But the

[25] Oxford: Clarendon Press, 1975, p. 154 fn.

logic of his argument shows how difficult it is to find any
determinate stopping-place short of universal suffrage.

> It is not enough that a political institution works well
> practically: it must be defensible; it must be such as will bear
> discussion, and not excite ridicule and contempt. It might
> work well for aught I know, if, like the savages of Onelashka,
> we sent out to catch a king: but who could defend a
> coronation by chase? Who can defend the payment of
> £40,000, for the three-hundredth part of the power of
> Parliament, and the resale of this power to Government for
> places to the Lord Williams and Lord Charles's, and others
> of the Anglophagi? Teach a million of the common people to
> read—and such a government (work it ever so well) must
> perish in twenty years. It is impossible to persuade the mass
> of mankind that there are not other and better methods of
> governing a country.[26]

The most important point about a system of election for
representatives is that it provides an intelligible and
determinate answer to the question why these particular
people, rather than others perhaps equally well or better
qualified, should run the country. If people can be induced to
believe in the divine right of kings or the natural superiority
of a hereditary ruling caste, it may be possible to gain general
acceptance for rule based on the appropriate ascribed
characteristics. But once the idea of the natural equality of all
men has got about, claims to rule cannot be based on natural
superiority. Winning an election is a basis for rule that does
not conflict with natural equality. Indeed, it might be said to
flow from it. For if quality is equal (or, as Hobbes more
exactly put it, quality must be taken to be equal as a condition
of peace) the only differentiating factor left is quantity. Once
we supply the premise of natural equality, we can see why it
seemed obvious to Locke that the majority 'necessarily'
constitutes the 'greater force'. Justification for rule in terms
of the specific achievements of the government lacks this
essential feature of determinateness. Others can always claim
that their performance would be superior, and who is to say it
would not be?

To express any confidence in the possibility of democratic
institutions continuing to rest on a basis of mass acceptance
is, of course, highly unfashionable. Theorists of the left and

[26] Sydney Smith, *The Selected Writings of Sydney Smith,*
ed. W. H. Auden (London: Faber and Faber, 1957),
p. 346.

the right agree that the jig is up. There is a 'legitimacy crisis' in the advanced capitalist societies, they have become 'ungovernable', governments are 'overloaded' by popular demands, and the 'economic contradictions of democracy' are revealing themselves ever more starkly.[27] Events may indeed prove these Cassandras right, but my own view is that they are grotesquely over-reacting to the disequilibriating effects of a sudden fourfold increase in the price of crude oil.

It seems to me that the only perspective from which things could be said to look sticky now for democratic institutions would be one from which the nineteen-fifties and the first half of the 'sixties constituted the norm. But that period of prosperity and peace among all the advanced capitalist economies was historically unique. (I am not denying that favourable objective conditions help.) A simple exercise is to run back decade by decade to the beginnings of universal suffrage in each of the major countries and ask in how many of these periods (except the 1950s) democratic institutions looked more firmly established in popular sentiment than they are today.

It is of course true that there is a tension between the formal political equality of one-man-one-vote and the inequalities of wealth, status and actual power over the lives of others (especially their working lives) generated by the other institutions of these societies. But this is hardly a new thought: it was a commonplace to Victorian conservatives and was elaborated by ideologues of the privileged strata like Maine and Lecky. The tension is still there but I see no sign that the forces that have kept it within bounds until now are losing their efficacy.

[27] As a representative sample, see: Jürgen Habermas, *Legitimacy Crisis* (Boston: Beacon Press, 1975); Alan Wolfe, *The Limits of Legitimacy: Political Contradictions of Contemporary Capitalism* (New York: The Free Press, 1977); Michel Crozier, Samuel P. Huntington and Joji Watanuki, *The Governability of Democracies* (New York: Trilateral Commission, 1975); Anthony King, 'Overload: Problems of Government in the 1970s', *Political Studies* 23 (1975): pp. 290–5; Samuel Brittan, 'The Economic Contradictions of Democracy', *British Journal of Political Science* 5 (1975): pp. 129–59; James O'Connor, *The Fiscal Crisis of the State* (New York: St. Martin's Press, 1973); and G. Rogers and R. Rose, *Can Governments Go Bankrupt?* (forthcoming).

I conclude, therefore, that there is a case for democratic procedures over and above the instrumental one developed in Section III. It is related to the majority principle in one way: it makes use of the idea that decision by majority has a natural attractiveness about it. But it really differs quite fundamentally. The majority principle, as I defined it following a whole body of 'social choice' literature, is that outcomes are legitimate if they correspond to majority preference and illegitimate if they run counter to majority preference. Democratic procedures are justified (to the extent that they can be) in terms of their tendency to bring about outcomes that correspond to majority preference. In contrast, the argument in this section has been that elections are a way of picking out, without reference to inherently arguable claims to superior competence, a unique set of rulers.

The implication is, I think, that a qualification has to be added to the results arrived at in Section III. Laws that systematically violate the vital interests of a minority are still devoid of any claims to obedience except prudential ones. But we must expand the sphere of prudential reasons beyond sanctions to long-term consequences. If the price of successfully changing the laws is the collapse of a democratic system, that is a heavy price to pay because, if I am right, it will include the suppression of freedom of publication and political organization. In non-democratic systems, the choice between trying to prevent the government from implementing unjust policies and trying to overthrow the government is a purely tactical one: the only question is which route has the better chance of success and the lower expected cost. In democratic regimes, however, the choice is not purely tactical. There are strong reasons for aiming at a result that leaves the government resting on election but accommodating the interests of the minority as the recognized price of gaining their co-operation.

The course of the argument in this chapter is rather tortuous. I have found, when presenting these ideas in academic gatherings, that many people find difficulty in grasping the distinction between the first argument in favour of democratic procedures, which I reject, and the third, which I accept. Let me therefore juxtapose the two in the hope of making the contrast more apparent.

The first argument relates in the first instance to the

relation of preferences to policies and only secondarily to institutions such as voting. The notion here criticized is that there is something natural, obvious or almost inevitable in the principle that the policy put into effect ought to be that corresponding to the majority preference. I accepted the correctness of that claim for the special case of the five people in the railway carriage but went on to suggest that the obviousness of the principle was an artifact of a number of special features either specified or implied in the description of the case. If anything, I was perhaps too lenient to the principle, since one could imagine other alternatives than the majority principle to agreement on a substantive meta-principle (such as the right to breathe uncontaminated air) or some principle of authority (like the one that the Archbishop's decision should be binding). For example, the participants might agree in a more 'consociational' spirit to divide up the estimated length of the journey into five equal periods and give each passenger control of one segment.[28]

What I wish to emphasize is, in any case, the difference between this majority principle and the rationale of voting for representatives put forward in Section IV. The argument here does, like the first one, invoke the claim that a certain procedure appears natural or obvious. But the assertion in the second case is not that naturalness is in itself a justification for the procedure. Rather it is that, if voting for representatives settles the question of who should rule in a way that claims to superior competence or claims to inherent personal superiority do not, it permits freedom of speech and organization as no other regime does.

> The friends of democracy too often speak loosely and carelessly in its favour, seeming to make impossible claims for it. If these claims are taken literally, what democracy is in fact falls so far short of what it is in theory supposed to be that it looks like a fraud.[29]

[28] I am grateful to my colleague Jane J. Mansbridge for impressing this point upon me.
[29] John Plamenatz, *On Alien Rule and Self-Government* (London: Longmans, 1960), p. 74.

9 Tyranny and Democratic Theory[1]

James Fishkin

By what ethical criteria should we evaluate alternative forms of government? What kinds of regimes, in other words, should we regard as more legitimate than others? Principles offered in answer to such questions will be referred to here as legitimacy criteria.

In this essay I will propose a minimum condition for acceptable legitimacy criteria. This minimum condition can be argued for as a principle in its own right, and it can also be derived from an account of rational choice under conditions of fairness.

I The Problem of Tyranny

I will first define this minimum condition—which I will call the principle of nontyranny—and then I will go on to show that it has important substantive implications. These can be seen from the fact that it is violated by *any* instance of the two general kinds of legitimacy criteria which dominate contemporary discussions—or at least those contemporary discussions which are broadly compatible with the democratic tradition. These two kinds of criteria are those which are *procedural* and those which are *structural* in character. According to the first, a regime is legitimate because of its conformity to some procedure or decision-rule; according to the second, a regime is legitimate because of its maintenance of some structure of distribution (of goods or welfare). Prominent examples of procedural criteria include consent, unanimity and majority rule; prominent examples of

[1] I would like to thank Douglas Rae, Robert Dahl, Charles E. Lindblom, Peter Laslett, Bernard Williams, John Rawls, Brian Barry, Adina Schwartz, Lawrence Kohlberg and Susan Rose-Ackerman for discussions which greatly enriched various parts of this essay. I would also like to thank members of the Project on American Democratic Institutions at Yale's Institution for Social and Policy Studies for comments on an earlier version.

structural criteria include equality, utilitarianism and Rawlsian maximin justice.

I will argue in this essay that both of these general kinds of criteria are misconceived. By this I mean that *any* principle of that general kind is subject to the objection that it would legitimate tyranny. Contemporary theorists, I will argue, are thus offering us criteria of the wrong general kinds.

As a first formulation requiring further specification, I will define tyranny as the choice of a policy, A, which imposes severe deprivations, when an alternative policy, B, would impose no severe deprivations on anyone. The availability of the B alternative must be specified because the justification of objectionable consequences, under some possible circumstances, cannot, by itself, constitute a decisive objection to a principle. For a principle might justify the choice of policy A only when every other alternative policy is at least as bad. It is possible, in other words, that no matter how bad the consequences of A, there are *some* conditions under which it would be justifiable.

The question for theory construction is thus whether a principle justifies an alternative involving objectionable consequences when some *other* alternative, involving less objectionable consequences, could have been prescribed instead. It is only the choice of A when such a B is available that I will take as offering a decisive counterexample.

Thus far, I have said little about the notion of 'severe deprivations'. Its definition is the main task of this section. I take the phrase 'severe deprivations' from Dahl, who reconstructs the 'Madisonian' notion of 'tyranny' as 'every severe deprivation of a natural right'.[2] However, Dahl argues, convincingly, that this definition of tyranny is unworkable in this form:

> Nearly all governmental actions deprive some individuals of legal rights they had previously possessed, and nearly all political groups seek some kind of governmental action that will deprive some individuals of certain existing legal rights. Hence rights must be read to mean natural rights; but as we have shown, consensus is lacking on what kinds of behavior are included in natural rights, particularly in concrete instances.[3]

[2] Robert A. Dahl, *A Preface to Democratic Theory* (Chicago: University of Chicago Press, 1956), p. 6.
[3] Ibid., p. 26.

Instead of relying on an explicit definition of natural rights, Dahl suggests a different strategy for defining the 'severe deprivations' involved in tyranny. With some substantial modifications, it is his strategy which will be developed here. Dahl gives an argument, 'essentially ethical in character', for considering 'intensities' of preference in a definition of tyranny:

> Supposes that A prefers x to y, B prefers y to x and the choice of one excludes the other. Many of us would like to know whether A prefers x to y more than B prefers y to x. All other things being the same, many of us would want A to have his alternative if his preferences were considerably more intense.[4]

Dahl's notion is that in our ethical judgements (if not in our institutional mechanisms) we should account for the intensities as well as the numbers on each side of an issue. For example, if an apathetic majority were to override a sufficiently intense minority, that would constitute 'the modern analogue to Madison's implicit concept of tyranny'.[5]
He explains the parallel:

> ... as one can readily see, intensity is almost a modern psychological version of natural rights. For just as Madison believed that government should be constructed so as to prevent majorities from invading the natural rights of minorities, so a modern Madison might argue that government should be designed to inhibit a relatively apathetic majority from cramming its policy down the throats of a relatively intense minority.[6]

The implication, of course, is that the numbers and intensity of the minority in this case counterbalance the greater numbers but lesser intensity of the majority. Hence the contrast between what Dahl calls the 'symmetrical' and the 'asymmetrical' cases of disagreement. When an apathetic majority is confronted with an intense minority, the disagreement is 'asymmetrical' (one side feels intensely while the other does not). On the other hand, when *both* the

---

[4] Ibid., p. 92. This discussion concerns Dahl's views at the time of the *Preface* (1956). I understand that his position on these issues has changed.
[5] Ibid., p. 99.
[6] Ibid., p.90.

majority and minority are intense, then the disagreement is 'symmetrical' (both sides feel intensely).

Let me begin my discussion of tyranny by suggesting: (i) why I think that this distinction between the symmetrical and asymmetrical cases is *not* useful for defining tyranny, and (ii) why I think Dahl's introduction of the notion of the intensity of the opposition to a policy is, on the contrary, of great value in the attempt to define the severe deprivations which involve tyranny.

Turning to (i), I will argue that the distinction between asymmetrical and symmetrical cases does not usefully distinguish tyrannous from nontyrannous cases. It leads to the misclassification of some tyrannous cases as nontyrannous, and of some nontyrannous cases as tyrannous. I will offer, in other words, asymmetrical cases of nontyranny and symmetrical cases of tyranny.

First, let us begin with a central and obvious case of tyranny (in the general Madisonian sense summarized by Dahl as 'severe deprivation of a natural right'). Let us imagine a minority group (say Jews in a state like Nazi Germany) whose extermination is voted by majority rule in a procedurally fair election (my example has been made intentionally hypothetical). Let us imagine, to begin with, that only a few of the majority feel strongly about this issue (the rest being quite apathetic), but that that minority, of course, feel extraordinary intensity about the issue. This would, of course, appear to offer the classic example of Dahl's severe asymmetrical disagreement as a model for tyranny.

Suppose, however, that the example is altered slightly. Suppose that the majority is not so apathetic. Suppose that the issue and the distribution of preferences are precisely as before except that the Nazis in the majority are simply *more enthusiastic*. I submit that whatever normative reasons we would have for classifying as tyrannous the acts upon the minority in the first example, we would also have good reason for applying, as well, to the second example. The majority extermination of the minority would seem tyrannous in *either* case: the distinction between the severe asymmetrical and the severe symmetrical cases does not properly mark the dividing line.

Consider now another (less dramatic) example. Suppose there is an ongoing policy of Prohibition. Suppose, further, that there is a minority of extremely zealous supporters of the policy and that, over time, there also develops a largely apathetic majority who favour repeal (my example is, again, deliberately hypothetical). Would it be *tyrannous* for the less intense majority to overrule such a minority? The minority feel intensely about whether *others* should be permitted to drink (*they* will, of course, continue to abstain). I believe that if the issues are this simple, it could not be tyrannous to overrule such a minority. One way of explaining this conclusion is to return to the fundamental (but vague) Madisonian view cited by Dahl: There is no way in which that minority could claim 'a severe deprivation of *its* natural rights'. It is their preferences concerning the behaviour of others which is at issue.

If I am right in these inferences, the prohibition case is asymmetrical nontyranny and the Nazi case (as modified) is symmetrical tyranny. But then does 'intensity' have anything to do with tyranny? I believe it does. I propose to incorporate the intensity of opposition to a policy as a necessary but not sufficient condition for that policy being tyrannical. The rationale here is that if those who lose do not themselves 'care,' then the imposition cannot be tyrannical. Roughly, if they do not care, why should we?

One caveat to this last inference is required. It presupposes conditions concerning freedom of information and the *formation* of preferences (which cannot be specified fully here). If, for example, the minority were brainwashed so as not to care, then the result might still be tyrannical (and for that very reason). In other words a certain degree of freedom is required before the preferences of a person X (whose intensity is accounted for by the principle) should be truly regarded as X's own preferences. To return to the extreme case just mentioned, if X is brainwashed, we would not want *those* preferences to be decisive in our account of X's interests. While the issue is clear enough in the extreme case, the task of specifying workable criteria for more ordinary cases would make this essay unmanageable. Hence, I will set aside the issue of criteria for evaluating the background conditions under which preferences are formed.

I believe that a first step towards a definition of tyranny which more closely approximates 'a severe deprivation of a natural right' (Dahl's formulation of the basic Madisonian notion) can be reached if a classification of the kinds of consequences and issues involved is added to this notion of intensity. In another context, Barry distinguishes between wants which are 'privately-oriented' and those which are 'publicly-oriented'. While he does not define these systematically, the distinction in its rough form can be put to use here:

> By 'privately-oriented' I mean having one's self (or at most one's family) as the reference group; or, more precisely, affecting oneself or one's family. When I speak of 'being affected' here I mean having one's life materially impinged upon by some change in opportunities or routine. I do not mean being made to feel, as in the phrase 'an affecting sight.' Thus, in the sense of 'being affected' relevant here a Swiss hotel-keeper, asked if he was affected by the war might reply that it decreased his trade but he could not reply that he was upset by the thought of cities being bombed. Or again, a Northern Negro in the U.S.A. is affected by discrimination which prevents him from getting certain jobs or houses, etc.; but he is not affected by what happens in the South.[7]

A similar distinction can be seen in the debate over 'interdependence effects.' Should a person's 'resentment or envy of the achievements of others' be included in his utility? Is each person's utility, in part, a function of the real incomes of others, or are utilities not 'interdependent' but 'independent' ('the utility of each person depending on his own goods only')?[8] Such independent utilities would be restricted to privately oriented wants in Barry's sense, while interdependent utilities would include publicly oriented wants in Barry's sense.

While there are important questions about the precise dividing line between private and public-regarding wants, a rough form of the distinction can be put to use here. I will say that a want is private-regarding for X when it concerns those wants and actions of X which are not conceived by X in terms of the wants or actions of anyone else. Hence X's want for Y's happiness is public-regarding; X's want for X's own happiness is private-regarding. But X's want to be made happy by Y's happiness (because X is altruistic) must be

[7] Brian Barry, *Political Argument* (London: Routledge and Kegan Paul, 1965), p. 63.
[8] E. J. Mishan, *Welfare Economics: An Assessment* (Amsterdam: North-Holland Publishing Co., 1969), pp. 34–35.

public-regarding because it is a want of X conceived by X in terms of the wants of someone else (Y).

I propose to employ this distinction in a definition of severe deprivations as follows: I will say that *X suffers a severe deprivation when (i) he experiences consequences which negatively affect his private-regarding wants and aims and (ii) he intensely opposes those consequences.*

Hence the Nazi case clearly would involve severe deprivations because (a) there are, obviously, consequences affecting private-regarding wants and aims, and (b) those consequences are intensely opposed. If tyranny is the imposition of such severe deprivations by the choice of a policy A when there is an alternative policy B which involves no such deprivations, then the Nazi case clearly involves tyranny.

By contrast the imposition of non-Prohibition upon a similarly intense minority could not be tyranny in this sense. For it would not, in the first place, involve a severe deprivation. No matter how intensely that minority might feel about the issue, it does not affect their private-regarding wants and aims. It involves, rather, their intense *public*-regarding wants—their wants concerning the behaviour of others (whether others should be permitted to drink).

Something more should be said about the notion of intensity employed by this criterion. It might be objected that interpersonal comparisons of this kind are problematical. It is true that the problem could be avoided if we restricted ourselves to the narrow range of judgements supported by the Pareto principle. For that principle would have us adopt a change if it benefits some persons so long as it harms no one. When a change would make some people worse-off, the principle says nothing about what is to be done. A principle conforming to these limits requires no *inter*personal comparisons—only the intrapersonal judgement of each person about whether he is benefited or harmed.

But as Little notes, with only mild hyperbole, 'No change of any significance in the real world could ever be made without harming some people.'[9] If interpersonal comparisons are avoided by adopting the limited range of the Pareto principle, it is at the price of silence on almost all choices of social importance.

[9] I. M. D. Little, *A Critique of Welfare Economics* (Oxford: Oxford University Press, 1957), p. 120.

Any principal for social choice which moves beyond these limits and which also takes account of the interests which it affects, must be committed to the possibility of interpersonal comparisons. For any such principle will evaluate choices which make some people worse-off and some better-off.

Now these interpersonal comparisons may be made in terms of the actual preferences of the people involved or in a way which abstracts from those preferences. The former strategy is illustrated by cost-benefit analysis and the latter is illustrated by Rawls's theory of primary goods. In the former case, a person X can only be interpreted as better (or worse) off when X himself thinks he is better (or worse) off. In the latter case, this condition does not hold (an agent in the original position is to assume that he will be better off with more primary goods, in the hypothesized order, regardless of what his actual preferences turn out to be). According to either strategy, interpersonal comparisons are required if the theory is to be employed beyond the narrow limits of the Pareto principle.

The problem is thus a general one and not special to the line of argument adopted here. It is not, in any case, as intractable as it might seem, for few would deny that some interpersonal comparisons can be made. These comparisons become problematical only when great precision is claimed.

Here the judgement about whether a person X is better or worse-off is in terms of his actual preferences of a private-regarding kind. But what, precisely, is meant when X is said to be 'intense' in his private-regarding preferences about a given issue? The terminology here is ambiguous between various views.[10] I will adopt one of them for the purpose of my definition here. In claiming that X has intense private-regarding preferences about certain consequences, I will *not* mean that X's emotions have been aroused to a fever pitch (although that might also be the case), nor will I mean that X is experiencing extreme 'sensate intensity' in thinking about those consequences (although that also might be the case).[11]

[10] See Douglas Rae and Michael Taylor, 'Some Ambiguities in the Concept of Intensity,' *Polity* 1 (1969): pp. 297–308.
[11] Dahl, however, sometimes discusses intensity in a way which implies that the fundamental phenomenon is 'sensate intensity.' See *Preface,* pp. 121–3.

Rather, I will mean that X himself attaches great *importance* to the effects of those consequences upon his private-regarding wants and aims. He regards those consequences as seriously affecting his own plan of life.[12] It is not, in other words, the extent to which those consequences arouse or excite him, but rather the importance which he attaches to them which determines whether his preferences about them are 'intense.'

These comments are meant to clarify the notion of severe deprivations involved in my proposed condition of non-tyranny. Let us now turn to the question of whether this principle can be justified or supported.

I I Fairness and Non-tyranny

Rawls describes the fair way to cut a cake as follows:

> Consider the simplest case of fair division. A number of men are to divide a cake: assuming that the fair division is an equal one, which procedure, if any, will give this outcome? Technicalities aside, the obvious solution is to have one man divide the cake and get the last piece, the others being allowed their pick before him. He will divide the cake equally, since in this way he assures for himself the largest share possible.[13]

This method is offered to us as a model of procedural justice analogous to the original position: self-interest (of the cake cutter) is harnessed under conditions of fairness to produce a morally appropriate outcome (equality). It is worth adding that if there were 'incentive effects' such that making some shares larger would increase the size of the smallest share, the cake cutter would choose a maximin rather than an equal distribution—for he is only concerned with the size of the last piece.

[12] I mean 'plan of life' in the Rawlsian sense with one caveat: I am interested only in a person's actual plan of life and not also in the plan which he would choose under hypothetical rational conditions, i.e., the plan he would choose with what Rawls calls 'full deliberative rationality' (see John Rawls, *A Theory of Justice* [Cambridge, Mass.: Harvard University Press, 1971], p. 408).

[13] Ibid., p. 85. There are more complex variations of this 'cut and choose' procedure which are invulnerable to collusion and deception. But these safeguards are not necessary for the thought experiment explored here.

This cake-cutting procedure is, of course, designed for the problem of fair division. I wish to devise an analogous procedure for the problem of choice among alternative social policies. Suppose that we can identify alternative policies A_1, $A_2, \ldots A_N$ for a given social choice. And suppose we can identify alternative positions P_1, $P_2, \ldots P_N$. By positions I mean identifiable roles or locations within which persons experience the consequences resulting from a given policy. Suppose further that there are individuals I_1, $I_2, \ldots I_N$, each of whom will occupy some position under each policy.

I propose the following thought experiment for evaluating the choice among alternative policies: Imagine a rational chooser (I_1) who chooses among policies A_1, $A_2, \ldots A_N$ under the hypothesis that everyone else ($I_2 \ldots I_N$) *will select their positions under the policy and he will be left with whatever position is remaining.*[14] Just as the cake cutter designs the slices under the hypothesis that he will have whatever share is left after the others select theirs, our rational chooser selects policies under the hypothesis that he will have whatever position is left after the others select theirs.

There are, of course, complexities involved in the notion that a person is to imagine himself in the position of another. For included in the 'position' must be whatever preferences of the person (who will actually experience that position under the policy) are crucial to understanding his reaction to the policy. Consider, for example, Sen's problem of distributing beef and pork to devout Hindus and Moslems.[15] Since the Hindus will not eat beef and the Moslems will not eat pork, the preferences of the persons receiving any particular allotment must be included in the description of how the meat was distributed if we are to evaluate the policy.

In the procedure described above, each alternative policy A_1, $A_2, \ldots A_N$ would be described by specifying consequences to positions P_1, $P_2, \ldots P_N$. The description of these positions must include mention, for example, of whether each recipient of beef or pork is Hindu or Moslem under that particular

[14] The order of choice before I_1 may be specified, for these purposes, as random or determined by lot. A similar specification should be supplied for the division of the cake.

[15] A. K. Sen, *Collective Choice and Social Welfare* (San Francisco: Holden Day, 1970), p. 149.

policy. Hence, the individuals I_1, I_2, ... I_N who are imagined to choose positions must imagine themselves in a position which includes a preference which may be different from their own actual one. This act of imaginatively putting one's self in the position of another, however, is involved in all universalizable moral reasoning and is even embodied in the Golden Rule. Hence it is not an unusual requirement for a moral decision procedure.

I wish to argue that, on the basis of a minimal assumption about how these positions are to be evaluated, our rational chooser would select policies according to the principle of nontyranny defined in the last section.

I offer only a minimal assumption because of the difficulties facing a more complete basis for choice. What is required for any individual to choose a position (in the fair decision procedure above) is some theory of interests. He must compare the desirability of different positions under a given policy. This raises, of course, the general problem of interpersonal comparisons mentioned in the last section. For this reason I have based my argument on a very limited account of interests which seems noncontroversial. For the cases it resolves it would be difficult to argue against, but it leaves many cases entirely unresolved. It is sufficient, however, to support my proposed principle of nontyranny. Any adequate, more complete account of interests would, I believe, include my minimum assumption.

Suppose that individuals I_1, I_2, ... I_N are imagined to choose positions according to this minimal assumption: Suffering severe deprivations (as defined in the last section) is worse than not suffering severe deprivations. Our rational chooser would then select a policy which imposed no severe deprivations on anyone as opposed to any policy which imposed severe deprivations on someone. Our chooser (I_1) would select policies in this way because everyone else (I_2, I_3, ... I_N) would select any nondepriving positions which were available; hence if a position involved severe deprivations, it would be left for him (I_1). The rule of choice which thus results is identical to the principle of nontyranny defined in the last section: do not choose a policy which imposes severe deprivations when an alternative policy imposes no severe deprivations on anyone; in such cases, of course, choose the nondepriving alternative.

To return for a moment to Sen's problem, suppose there is one distribution of beef and pork which gives beef only to Moslems and pork only to Hindus. Let us call that policy A_1. The other policies ($A_2 \ldots A_N$), let us suppose, all involve some allotments of beef or pork going to persons with the wrong religion. Let us ignore, furthermore, obvious ways out of the problem by assuming that, for some reason, it is impossible for Hindus and Moslems to trade their shares (perhaps they are physically separated in some way). If the issue is of sufficient importance to them (we might imagine them all on the verge of starvation), any policy other than A_1 would be tyrannous. Furthermore, only policy A_1 would be selected by our rational chooser. For that policy imposes no severe deprivations on anyone. Any other policy would leave our rational chooser, according to the thought experiment, imagining himself in the position either of a starving Hindu stuck with beef or a starving Moselm stuck with pork. Our rational chooser would select A_1—which rules out such severe deprivations for everyone. Hence the rationality (under the hypothetical conditions of fairness) of the principle of nontyranny.

This principle of nontyranny, however, says nothing about cases where every alternative would impose severe deprivations on someone. But note that our fair decision procedure would leave those cases similarly indeterminate. For our rational chooser would have no basis for choosing between policies in such a case. By hypothesis, he has only distinguished between positions according to whether or not they involve severe deprivations. If *every* alternative policy would impose a severe deprivation on someone, then the position which he would envisage as remaining for him would involve severe deprivations—no matter which policy he chooses.

In this sense, of course, the principle of nontyranny is a radically incomplete principle. It says nothing about many of the most important social choices. For this reason I am arguing for it, not as a complete theory of legitimacy but rather as a minimum condition for acceptable principles. As such a minimum condition it is far from trivial. In the sections below, I will argue that *any* procedural principle and *any* structural principle must violate this minimum condition by legitimating tyranny. In other words, any such principle would prescribe choices conflicting with the minimum condition of nontyranny for some of the cases where the condition would, in fact, prescribe choices. It is in this sense that the minimum condition just proposed has important substantive implications.

It might be objected to the above analysis that this fair decision procedure has less moral interest than Rawls's original position. It would take us beyond the scope of this essay to attempt to resolve that question here. I would, however, like to note three points in response.

First, Rawls cites the cake-cutter's analogy upon which this method is based as a model of procedural fairness. Furthermore, he never justifies his adoption of the original position rather than the cake-cutter's analogy—even though the cake-cutter's analogy would yield his proposed principle (maximin) if his other assumptions about the theory of primary goods and about incentive effects were applied to it.[15]

A second point is that the actual implications of the original position, as contrasted with my proposal, are far from clear. As I have argued elsewhere, the original position with the additional 'features' which Rawls believes to imply maximin, acutally implies a guaranteed minimum. On the other hand, without the special 'features' thought to imply maximin, the argument can plausibly be interpreted as yielding average utility. Hence, unlike my proposal, the actual implications of the original position are problematical.[16]

The third point is that this adaptation of the cake cutter shares a fundamental conception of fairness with the original position. One formulation of the Golden Rule is 'Do as you would be done by.' For the multi-person case this might be generalized to this notion of fairness:

> *General Notion of Fairness:* A should decide on a policy affecting B, C, D, etc., only after taking account of how he would wish to be treated were he in the place of B, C, D, etc.

This is an incomplete definition so long as it lacks specification of how A is to 'take account' of his reactions in the place of B, C, D, etc. The original position can be seen as

---

[15] See James Fishkin, 'Justice and Rationality: Some Objections to the Central Argument in Rawls's Theory,' *American Political Science Review* 69 (1975): pp. 615–29.
[16] Ibid.

one particular version which completes the definition: the agent in the original position does not know which position is to be his; hence he has to take seriously the possibility that he will turn out to occupy the representative position of any stratum. Rawls then argues that it is rational, because of the special stakes involved, to take with greatest seriousness the possibility of being at the bottom. In the original position an agent ends up making the selection 'a person would choose for the design of a society in which his enemy is to assign him his place.'[17]

The Rawlsian original position thus offers one version of fairness; my adaptation of the cake cutter offers another. Both methods—the original position and the one proposed here— constitute procedural expressions of the general notion of fairness just specified—a notion which makes a deep appeal to reciprocity reminiscent of the Golden Rule.

This fair decision procedure is proposed here as a way of dramatizing the ethical claim of my minimum principle. It is not meant as a rationally inescapable argument. It is hoped, in any case, that the principle which results from it is appealing in its own right. Now I would like to turn to certain of its implications.

In the sections which follow I will show that all procedural and all structural principles are vulnerable to the objection that they can legitimate tyranny in the sense defined above. My objection to each principle, in other words, will be that it would legitimate the choice of a policy A, which would impose severe deprivations when there is an alternative policy B, which would impose severe deprivations on no one.

My argument is thus directed against all possible procedural principles and all possible structural principles. However, these objections are meant to be decisive only against the use of these principles as ultimate criteria for political legitimacy. I intend to rebut the claim, in other words, that any one of these principles could, by itself, adequately prescribe choices among alternative political (or political-economic) arrangements. Principles become subject to my argument only if they claim the status that Rawls, for example, claims for his proposed principles, i.e., that they resolve the 'priority problem.'

A principle which resolves the priority problem is one

[17] Rawls, *Theory of Justice*, p. 152.

which does not have to be balanced or weighed 'intuitionisti-cally' against any other moral principle.[18] It is an absolute or ultimate principle and not a weak or *prima facie* one. It is a principle which purports to resolve the question at issue without any need to appeal to any other possible con-siderations which might have to be balanced against it. In this sense, it purports to be conclusive.

While my argument attempts to rule out the use of procedural principles and structural principles as ultimate conceptions, it does not rule out a *prima facie* claim for any of those considerations. As criteria which may sometimes be overridden, they may each make valid points. But as ultimate, self-sufficient conceptions they would legitimate wrongs which are both egregious and avoidable.

Now in considering whether principles of a given kind have this implication I will sometimes envisage circumstances which seem unlikely to occur with great frequency. However, the frequency with which such choices would follow is not the issue. For my argument is meant to demonstrate a theoretical defect in the principle, i.e., that it justifies the choice of A (which imposes severe deprivations) rather than B (which imposes no severe deprivations). The principle would have us legitimate the choice of A rather than B *were* that choice to present itself. So long as the choice of A rather than B is both (1) possible and (2) explicitly justified by the principle, it constitutes a relevant implication of the principle.

Such a defect is theoretically relevant regardless of how frequently the principles would, in practice, produce the results discussed. A common objection to utilitarianism, for example, is that under certain empirical conditions, it would justify slavery. If the utilities of those benefiting from slavery outweighed the disutilities of those suffering from it, utilitarianism would have this result. The fact that utili-tarianism would justify slavery were such conditions to obtain is taken to reveal a theoretical defect in the principle—regardless of the frequency with which these conditions actually occur. It is this general kind of theoretical defect which I hope to reveal in all procedural and structural principles.

It is important to distinguish in this argument (i) cases where a principle either prefers such an unacceptable A to an

[18] See Rawls, *Theory of Justice*, pp. 40–5.

acceptable B (or says they are equally good), and (ii) cases where a principle says nothing about whether A or B is better or worse than the other. I will take it as a necessary condition for a decisive counterexample to a principle that it have an implication of type (i). A principle which says that A is better than (or at least as good as) B would legitimate and justify what is, by hypothesis, a dreadful wrong. On the other hand, a principle which says nothing about the comparison between A and B (which leaves the choice entirely indeterminate) would *not* legitimate the transition from A to B. Some additional principle would be required for that transition to be justified.

It is also worth emphasizing that each of these decisive counter-examples is meant to be general in its implications. It is not meant to apply merely to particular principles, but rather, to all principles of a given kind. It is in this sense that my argument is diagnostic: I wish to claim that in recent writings, political theorists and philosophers have been offering criteria of the wrong general kinds. Whether this argument is persuasive will depend upon the normative force of the notion of tyranny just defined.

III   Procedural Principles

By a procedural principle I mean a principle which specifies a rule of decision but which specifies nothing about the content of those decisions—apart from possible requirements that the rule of decision be maintained in the future.[19] By a rule of decision I mean a specification that support (i.e., agreement,

[19] This last clause would permit procedural principles to include guarantees of participation which cannot be abridged even if a procedurally valid decision is taken to abridge them. A majority might, for example, attempt to deny some minority the right to vote. According to this provision a procedural principle might be designed to prevent such actions. It might, for example, be rigidly inclusive. By this I mean that it might require universal opportunities for participation by all (minimally competent) members of the regime. I believe, however, that even rigidly inclusive procedural principles are subject to the argument against all procedural principles to be presented below.

concurrence or actions of assent) from certain combinations of persons (i.e., certain numbers, proportions or particular groups of persons, perhaps in some specified order) is necessary and sufficient to produce authoritative (i.e., legitimate) actions by the regime.

This specificiation may be a decision rule in the ordinary sense, e.g., a criterion (such as unanimity or majority rule) that support from some stated proportion of members (100 percent, say, or 50 percent plus one) will be required for winning coalitions. But it might also specify support from any other combination of individuals. It might, for example, specify that the King (or the Party Central Committee) should decide, or that a person chosen by lot should decide.

So long as a criterion leaves open the possibility that *anything* may be done—provided that it has support from the persons or groups specified by the decision rule—it is procedural in the proposed sense. Criteria which would define legitimate political regimes as those preserving consent, or unanimity, or majority rule or political equality (conjoined with a specific decision rule) offer examples of procedural criteria.

Precisely because my argument is meant to apply generally to all procedural principles I will not be able to do justice to the enormous differences among procedural principles. I will only be able to discuss difficulties which result from an important feature which they have in common.

I will first consider procedural principles which have nonunanimous rules of decision, i.e., rules of decision which do not require the support or agreement of everyone.[20] I will then turn to the case of unanimous decision rules.

My argument in this section can be regarded as a generalization to *all* procedural principles of Schumpeter's famous argument against majoritarian democracy as an ethical 'end in itself'. Schumpeter invites us to participate in 'a mental experiment':

[20] Or everyone with at least minimal competence. See footnote 19 above. I will set aside interesting boundary questions involving children, aliens and criminals. For an illuminating account of the problem of who is to be included in the polity see Robert Dahl's essay in this volume.

> Suppose that a community, in a way which satisfies the reader's criteria of democracy, reached the decision to persecute religious dissent. The instance is not fanciful. Communities which most of us would readily recognize as democracies have burned heretics at the stake—the republic of Geneva did in Calvin's time—or otherwise persecuted them in a manner repulsive to our moral standards—colonial Massachussetts may serve as an example....
>
> Now for our experiment. Let us transport ourselves into a hypothetical country that, in a democratic way, practices the persecution of Christians, the burning of witches, the slaughtering of Jews. We should certainly not approve of these practices on the ground that they have been decided on according to the rules of democratic procedure.[21]

Schumpeter's conclusion is that: 'There are ultimate ideals and interests which the most ardent democrat will put above democracy ...' 'Democracy,' he argues, 'is a political method.' Although it has instrumental value it is 'incapable of being an end in itself, irrespective of what decisions it will produce under given historical conditions'.[22]

His point is that if such persecutions were passed by democratic procedures the mere fact that they were passed in that way would not legitimate them. We would have to overrule the procedural principle in order to condemn them. As an ultimate ethical criterion ('end in itself') democracy has this theoretical defect.

In our definition of tyranny, the imposition of these severe deprivations on a losing coalition defines the tyrannous (A) alternative. Furthermore, the nonimposition of such deprivations defines a (B) alternative which, by itself, imposes no severe deprivations on anyone. For no matter how strongly the winning coalition may feel about the imposition of such deprivations, that preference is a public-regarding, and not a private-regarding one. Hence its denial cannot constitute a severe deprivation.

Of course the argument need not be confined to religious persecution. The argument can be generalized to any severe deprivation imposed, in a procedurally correct manner, on any losing coalition. A losing coalition (perhaps defined on religious, racial or ethnic grounds) might be deprived of all its

[21] Joseph Schumpeter, *Capitalism, Socialism and Democracy,* 3rd ed. (New York: Harper and Row, 1950), pp. 240, 242.
[22] Ibid., p. 242.

property, or it might be deprived of equal opportunity in employment or in education (by, for example, laws of a segregationist kind).

The vulnerability of all purely procedural principles, other than those requiring unanimity, is that all such principles would legitimate the adoption of a policy imposing any such deprivation—provided only that it has support from those specified by the decision rule. Any procedural principle would *require* that the deprivation be imposed so long as it has the specified support. This consequence follows from the fact that procedural principles were defined as those which would legitimate any action of a regime decided on in the required manner.

It should be noted that some of these deprivations might be ruled out by a rigidly inclusive procedural principle in that such a principle might be formulated so as to specify universal voting (or other participation). Killing a minority group would, of course, interfere with that participation. However, many of the other deprivations mentioned (removal of property, interference with freedom of religion, discrimination in the job market or in education) would not be affected by such a provision. I will assume that whatever participation is required by a principle, it is possible for a member to continue the specified participation in the political process and still be subject to serious deprivations in other spheres of life. In order to protect everyone from such deprivations, a principle which is not merely procedural would be required.

Now it will be useful for us to distinguish two ways in which the imposition of such deprivations may be brought about. They may result from the adoption of a new policy or from the failure to adopt a new policy; they may result, in other words, from a regime's commissions or from its omissions.

More precisely, by a commission, I mean a *change* in policy and by an omission, I mean a *continuation* of existing policies. Hence some 'commissions' will actually be changes in policy which produce a failure to act, e.g., a cancellation of programmes previously adopted, while some 'omissions' will actually be retentions in policies which produce a continuation of action, e.g., the noncancellation of programmes previously adopted. Hence objections to policy omission include objections to the nonenactment of new policies as well as to the continuation of old ones; objections to policy commission include objections to the enactment of new policies as well as to the cancellation of old ones.

The status quo has no privileged position in this analysis although retention of the status quo should never be left out if it is a possible policy. It should be emphasized that retaining the status quo can involve severe deprivations through policy omission just as changes in policy may involve severe deprivations through policy commission. For example, if P will starve or suffer severe consequences if his share of food or medical resources is not increased, the maintenance of the status quo distribution can impose a severe deprivation upon him. If severe deprivations brought about by both omissions and commisions are taken into account, no decision rule is immune from the legitimation of tyranny.

Dealing with commission first, it should be obvious that any nonunanimous decision rule can impose severe deprivations—by commission—on the subset of its members whose support is not required for adoption of a new policy. Depending on the precise decision rule, this losing coalition must be at least equal to 1 and must be less than the total number of members (a nonunanimous decision rule can require support from any proportion or group of members who number less than 100 percent and at least 1).

If we consider possible decision rules, as the number required for approval of a new policy approaches unanimity, the maximum size of a coalition which can unsuccessfully oppose a new policy shrinks to zero. If unanimity is the decision rule then, by definition, a new policy cannot be adopted if it is opposed even by one member. But we must distinguish groups which lose by policy commission from groups which lose by policy omission. For once severe deprivations resulting from *omissions* are taken into account, there is no guarantee that the numbers affected will be small. Consider the limiting case when unanimity is the decision rule. Under that rule even one person can always avoid losing by policy commission. But, of course, *everyone* except one person can then lose by omission.

How may deprivations be imposed by omission? Imagine only that some group requires food to avoid starvation (perhaps there has been a famine) or some group requires emergency assistance or medical care (perhaps there has been a flood or other natural disaster) and such events pose a new policy problem. If there is not an already extant policy, the veto of any new policy could have consequences as dreadful (for all of those apart from the blocking coalition) as any acts of commission discussed above. Or, suppose the issue is not a new one but merely an old one about which agreement has never been reached. Perhaps there is mass poverty and a small wealthy elite who are just sufficiently numerous to block any redistribution. The continuing absence of any redistributive measures (unemployment compensation, medical care, food assistance) could deny the satisfaction of basic human needs to the bulk of the population.

Once omissions are taken into account, it should be obvious that unanimity is no more successful than any other decision rule in preventing a regime from imposing severe deprivations. Severe deprivations which a regime fails to prevent can be as terrible as those which it decides to impose.

In my discussion of unanimity thus far, I have assumed that if no agreement is reached, existing policies (previously agreed to) continue to be in effect. In terms of the regime's policies, the status quo constitutes the point of no agreement. The unanimity rule has also sometimes been interpreted to imply that if no agreement is reached the government simply ceases to exist.[23] On this interpretation, anarchy constitutes the no-agreement point. But, of course, there is no reason to suppose that the choice of anarchy (i.e., a state of affairs where there is no longer a state) will not have worse consequences than the continuation of the status quo (i.e., the continuing governance of the regime without the new policy about which there was disagreement). Individuals who will suffer from the government failing to intervene when unanimous agreement is not reached, may suffer in the same way under anarchy (since there is no government to intervene). They are, furthermore, rendered subject to the consequences of a host

[23] Robert Paul Wolff, in his argument for unanimity, suggests this no-agreement point: 'Since by the rule of unanimity a single negative vote defeats any motion, the slightest disagreement over significant questions will bring the operations of society to a halt. It will cease to function as a political community and fall into a condition of anarchy. . .' See *In Defense of Anarchism* (New York: Harper and Row, 1970), p. 24.

of other cessations of policy—the lack of police protection, fire protection and whatever other essential services the state may have provided before its dissolution. It should be evident that this alternative interpretation of the unanimity rule will not save it from its vulnerability to the legitimation of severe deprivations.[24]

The argument encounters an additional complication if the decision rule specified by the procedural principle applies at the level of constitutional choice rather than at the level of policy choice. Suppose there is, for example, unanimous consent to a particular constitution. Should not individuals, if they have actually and explicitly consented to such an arrangement, be bound by whatever results from it?

While it might be granted that there is a *prima facie* case for X's being obligated because he (and perhaps everyone else) actually consented to a constitutional arrangement,[25] would not this obligation be overrideable depending on the content of later actions and decisions by the regime? Consider Hanna Pitkin's example of the minor official in Nazi Germany who continues to carry out his oath of office. Is his explicit consent to the regime enough to obligate him regardless of what policies it later implements? She argues:

> ... sometimes past promises and oaths are not enough to determine present obligations. Sometimes a man who cites even express oath to obedience, is being not admirable but hypocritical, refusing to recognize where his real duty lies.

'While we would not want to say that past oaths and promises count for nothing,' she adds, 'they cannot be allowed to settle the question.'[26]

But the distinctive feature of all procedural principles (universal consent included) is that reference to the procedure would, by definition, settle the question. If the decision rule conferring legitimacy is universal consent to the

[24] Douglas Rae makes this point forcefully in his essay, 'The Limits of Consensual Decision,' *American Political Science Review* 69 (1975): pp 1270–94. See pages 1280–2.
[25] When consent is defined so that it can be applied universally it may also become vacuous in content. See Pitkin's criticisms of Tussman in 'Obligation and Consent,' *Philosophy, Politics and Society*, Fourth Series, pp. 44–85.
[26] Pitkin, 'Obligation and Consent', p. 66.

regime, then that decision rule must settle the question of one's obligations to it, regardless of what the regime's later policies turn out to be (the decision rule defines the necessary and sufficient conditions for legitimate actions by the regime). If the regime changes in conformity with the constitutional arrangement or if the constitutional arrangement itself changes in accordance with the stated procedural principle, the result must be legitimate—because it corresponds to agreement reached under the decision rule. Hence if the constitution were changed so as to deny basic rights to certain groups—so long as the stated constitutional procedures were satisfied—the result would be legitimated. Thus it should be obvious that the strategy of locating the decision rule at the level of constitutional choice does not obviate the possibility that regimes legitimated by the procedure will impose severe deprivations.

Thus, for both unanimous and nonunanimous decision rules, it should be evident that all procedural principles—all principles that would legitimate *any* action of a regime provided that it has the support specified by the stated decision rule—can sanction the imposition by the regime of severe deprivations on some losing coalition. The imposition of such deprivations (via commission or omission) can be *required* by such principles—even when the alternative is a state of affairs which involves no severe deprivations whatsoever.[27] In this way all such principles can legitimate tyranny in the sense defined here.

The implications of Schumpeter's 'mental experiment' are thus not limited to majority rule (and other procedural interpretations of democracy). For we may substitute *any* (nonunanimous) procedural principle for the 'reader's criteria of democracy' in his argument and reach the same conclusions with respect to commissions (new policies). Furthermore, once deprivations resulting from omissions are taken into account, the argument applies to unanimous procedural principles as well.[28]

[27] See the discussion of Schumpeter's mental experiment above.
[28] We have only to substitute the words 'failed to prohibit persecution' for 'reached the decision to persecute' and the argument can be applied directly to unanimous principles.

Whether they are nonunanimous or unanimous, whether they are for policy choice or for constitutional choice, and whether they are rigidly inclusive or variable in their inclusiveness—all procedural principles can legitimate a policy of severe deprivations to losing coalitions. And they would do this when the alternative is a policy of severe deprivations to no one. This is their decisive theoretical defect.

IV   Structural Principles

By a structural principle I mean a principle which will judge any state of affairs X to be better, worse, or equal to any state of affairs Y based on the information available from an account of payoffs to positions under X and under Y. By payoffs I mean goods or welfare in a sense specified by the principle; by positions I mean either individuals listed in order of their shares of goods or welfare or groupings of individuals (n-titles), each consisting of $\frac{1}{n}$th of the population listed in order of their shares of goods or welfare. Such a purely structural principle of distribution can provide a criterion of legitimacy if it is held that an ethically acceptable political-economic arrangement is one which achieves the prescribed distributions.

Rawlsian maximin justice (his 'general conception') is a structural principle in this sense for it will prescribe a choice of X or Y based on whichever has the greater share of primary goods at the minimum position. Classical and average utilitarianism are also structural principles for they will prescribe X or Y based on the total or average welfare under the two states (information easily calculated from payoffs to positions). A principle of equality (in, say, primary goods) would similarly be structural since the more equal of two distributions can be determined from a listing of payoffs to positions.

It is important in order for a principle to be structural, that the positions be identified anonymously in terms of a ranking of goods or welfare: it is not particular individuals whose payoffs are compared under X and Y but, rather, ranked positions. Structural positions say nothing, in other words, about how particular persons match up to positions under X as compared to how they match up under Y. So long as the structure of the distribution (as judged by payoffs to positions) is improved, principles of this kind will prefer a distribution—regardless of how persons are moved around from one position to another in order to achieve the prescribed structure. This is a characteristic of purely structural principles—such as maximin, utilitarianism and equality—to which we shall return.

Structural principles presume interpersonal comparisons for these are necessary for an identification of the ranked positions. Principles vary, however, in whether the account of payoffs required is ordinal or cardinal.

Prominent principles which are structural in this sense include: equality (as measured, for example, by the mean of the deviations from the mean of the payoffs to positions), maximin (maximize the minimum payoff), and utilitarianism (maximize the total payoffs).

Consider the situation X below. Under that situation we can rank the positions P_1, P_2, etc., to the Nth position P_N. To each position there corresponds a payoff or share represented by S_1, S_2, etc., to S_N. The payoffs determine a ranking of positions from highest (P_1) to lowest (P_N). Corresponding to each position are persons (I_1, I_2, etc., to I_N) who occupy those positions under X.

	X			Y	
Positions	Payoffs	Persons	Positions	Payoffs	Persons
P_1	S_1	I_1	P_1	S_1	I_1
P_2	S_2	I_2	P_2	S_2	I_3
P_3	S_3	I_3	P_3	S_3	I_4
...	...	...	...	...	...
P_{N-1}	S_{N-1}	I_{N-1}	P_{N-1}	S_{N-1}	I_N
P_N	S_N	I_N	P_N	S_N	I_2

Now consider an alternative state of affairs Y. Y is structurally identical to X in that the payoffs to positions are precisely the same as in X (P_1 has S_1, P_2 has S_2, etc.). Y differs from X only in that the assignment of persons to positions is different. Under Y, I_2 has been moved from the second highest position to the lowest one while I_3 has been moved up to P_2 and each individual below I_3 has been moved up one position. In other words, I_2 has been moved to the bottom and each individual below I_2 has been moved up one notch.

I will assume in this example that the differences between

adjacent positions are minimal while the differences, of course, between positions which are not adjacent may be substantial. Hence each individual who is moved up only a single position under Y is not significantly benefited. However, I_2, who is moved from P_2 down to P_N, has experienced a very substantial change in his position.

Let us apply any structural principle to the problem of choosing between two alternative policies: (a) retention of X as a status quo, and (b) shift to Y from X.

Now the essential point about this example is that *any* structural principle must be *indifferent* between these two alternatives. For a structural principle was defined as a principle which will evaluate any X as better than, equal to, or worse than any Y, based *merely* on an account of payoffs to positions under X and Y. Because X and Y are structurally *identical*, any such principle—whether it be equality, utilitarianism, maximin or something else—must be indifferent between them. For within the limitations imposed, by definition, on structural principles, they are the same case. They have precisely the same degree of equality, the same total, the same minimum. Because there are no structural considerations at issue in the choice between X and Y, they must be rated equal by any structural principle.

But because they are rated equally by any such principle, such a structural principle would legitimate the choice of (b) the shift to Y as an alternative to (a) the retention of X. It would legitimate such a choice because there would be, by hypothesis, no grounds for a moral objection to the change. One alterntive is fully as good as the other.

But the alternative which is rated equally good (b) would move I_2 from P_2 to P_N. Assuming that this substantial change in his distributional share is important to I_2, this would involve the imposition of a severe deprivation upon him. Furthermore, this is a deprivation which is accompanied by no substantial benefits to anyone else (since the differences between adjacent positions were assumed to be insignificant) and no improvement on structural grounds—no improvement, that is, in the degree of equality, the total goods or welfare, the level at the bottom, etc.

Because *any* structural principle would, by definition, have to be indifferent between these two policies, any structural principle would, in this case, legitimate tyranny: the choice of a policy (b) which imposes severe deprivations as opposed to a policy (a) which imposes no severe deprivations on anyone.

It should be added that there is nothing special about this particular example. Innumerable instances could be adduced where structural principles would legitimate tyranny in the sense proposed here because of their unique focus on the payoffs to positions without any sensitivity to the way persons are assigned to those positions. I_2 in this example could as easily be a group as an individual. Any number of similar examples could obviously be devised where severe deprivations result from changes in assignment to structurally identical positions.

This is the special property of structural principles: they are entirely indifferent to such effects on persons independent of effects on positions. Structural principles have no place for the information that we have introduced by the third columns under X and Y: the information that persons in particular positions under Y are different from the persons in those positions under X. Yet it is persons and not positions who would experience these moves; it is the life history of particular individuals that would be affected, positively or negatively. Ranked positions, by themselves, are only abstractions from those life histories. My point, in other words, is that an account of payoffs to positions under X and Y may mask the imposition of severe deprivations to persons resulting from changes in the way persons are assigned to positions under X and Y. It is these severe deprivations which render all structural principles vulnerable to tyrannous counterexamples.

It must be emphasized that the avoidance of tyranny, defined in this way, does not necessarily lead us to ratify the status quo whatever it may be. For there are, commonly, conditions in which the maintenance of a status quo distribution will impose actual worsenings which constitute severe deprivations. As emphasized above, there are some distributions whose very continuation imposes further deprivations. Such distributions will not be legitimated by a principle designed to avoid tyranny in the sense defined here.

If this possibility is not made explicit a mistaken objection could be directed at the whole analysis. Consider this example and my reply to it: X′ is a distributional status quo, Y′ is an alternative which would require substantial redistribution. But Y′ would also heavily tax the rich, hence imposing severe deprivations (let us suppose). On the other hand, merely maintaining the distributional status quo does not appear to impose any severe deprivations with respect to that status quo. Hence, the argument would go, maintaining X′ would be required if tyranny in my sense is to be avoided. But this result would rationalize the continuation of an unjust distribution which merely continues the poor in their misery and the rich in their luxury. Consider this example (the numbers correspond to some index of primary goods):

X'	Y'
15	6
15	6
3	6
3	6
3	6

It is arguable that Y′ would represent an improvement if the lowest level under X′ represents a sufficiently severe level of degradation. But continuation of X′ would appear to be required by my notion of tyranny (assuming that the avoidance of tyranny is valued).

But this objection ignores the possibility, emphasized above, that the continuation of a distributional status quo may, by itself, impose severe deprivations. The continuation of the X′ distribution may, over time, make the persons at the bottom (with the meagre distribution of only '3' primary goods) even worse off—by preventing the satisfaction of important human needs. The denial to those at the bottom of enough food to feed their families, or of necessary medical care, or of educational opportunities (without which they must sooner or later become unemployed) may constitute severe deprivations.

Hence maintaining the X′ distribution would, under these conditions, produce severe deprivations for those at the bottom just as redistributing to Y′ would produce severe deprivations for those at the top. *Both* X′ and Y′ impose severe deprivations in this example. If these are the only two alternatives, then neither is tyrannous. For tyranny was defined as the imposition by a policy A of severe deprivations when there was an alternative policy B which imposes severe deprivations on no one. There is no such B policy in this case.

Nothing we have said so far settles the question of what

should be done when *all* of the policies considered impose severe deprivations. Neither alternative would be tyranny on these assumptions; which alternative is better is not a question which will be settled here.

The point to be emphasized is that, in this case, the avoidance of tyranny would not require the maintenance of the status quo. The maintenance of a status quo may, over time, produce severe deprivations just like those of any other policy.

V   A Minimum Proposal

In the preceding sections, I have argued that all procedural principles and all structural principles are subject to this objection: They will all legitimate the choice of a policy which would impose severe deprivations when an alternative policy would impose severe deprivations on no one.

A central question to be raised about this objection is whether or not it is avoidable. It could hardly count as an argument against these principles that they were subject to a given difficulty if any alternative principle would share that difficulty as well. However, tyranny as I have defined it clearly is, in fact, avoidable.

My definition only yields the judgement that a policy is tyrannous when there is an alternative policy which imposes no severe deprivations. It says nothing about the imposition of severe deprivations when every alternative policy would also impose severe deprivations. The definition in this form is, thus, radically incomplete.

I will not attempt to complete the definition in this paper. For it is sufficient, in this incomplete form, for our purposes here. In this form it may be interpreted as proposing a necessary condition for an acceptable, complete theory of legitimacy. In other words, a complete principle conforming to this proposal would include the limited judgements it supports—and others besides.

In its incompleteness, this notion of tyranny might be compared to the Pareto principle. The Pareto principle singles out certain changes as improvements, but says nothing about the rest. The changes which the Pareto principle actually prescribes are not controversial; it is difficult, in fact, to argue against a change which makes some better-off and no one worse-off. However, when no Pareto-superior alternative is available, the Pareto principle offers no prescription whatsoever. To decide such cases, some additional principle would be required.

Similarly, the notion of tyranny proposed here would offer a prescription in only a limited range of cases. The resolution of other cases must be left to other principles. The point to be emphasized, however, is that *any* principle which ruled out tyranny in the sense just defined would, by definition, avoid the counterexamples posed above. It is in this way that the objection I have directed against procedural and structural principles may be avoided. Any complete theory which incorporates nontyranny as a necessary condition for legitimacy must avoid the preceding counterexamples. Any such principle must avoid legitimating the choice of a policy imposing severe deprivations when an alternative policy imposes severe deprivations on no one.

How a more complete theory should decide other cases lies outside the scope of this paper. It should be apparent, however, that such a more complete theory would have two general kinds of additional cases to resolve: (1) cases where every policy involves a severe deprivation, and (2) cases where no policy involves a severe deprivation. How deprivating alternatives should be compared for cases of the first kind and how nondeprivating alternatives should be compared for cases of the second kind raises questions about the interpersonal comparison of interests which, as we have noted, involve profound problems. My minimum proposal is only that were these to be satisfactorily resolved, the resulting more complete principle would rule out tyranny in the sense defined here.

10 Political Obligation and Conceptual Analysis[1]

Carole Pateman

It has been argued in some recent discussions that it is meaningless to raise general questions about political obligation. Questions can only properly be asked about specific cases where our obligation to obey particular laws might seem in doubt; to suppose otherwise is to reveal oneself as conceptually confused. Margaret Macdonald argued along these lines in her well-known and influential essay on *The Language of Political Theory*,[2] and she has been followed more recently by, for example, Hanna Pitkin in her discussion of *Obligation and Consent*,[3] and Thomas McPherson in his monograph, *Political Obligation*.[4] Such an argument is not new, and nor would all writers on political obligation agree with it, but it deserves attention because it raises a series of important and complex issues, not least that of the nature of the task on which the political philosopher is engaged.

In the first part of this Chapter I shall argue that the writers considered draw unacceptable conclusions from their central argument, an appeal to the conceptual link between the idea of social life and concepts like obligation (for convenience I shall refer to this as the conceptual argument). Acceptance of the conceptual argument, and I shall suggest that the version offered in these discussions of political obligation is an unduly narrow one, does not show that general questions about political obligation are meaningless; nothing follows

[1] Reprinted with minor changes from *Political Studies 21*, 2 (1973): pp. 199–218. I owe thanks to Steven Lukes and Haim Marantz for their critical comments, and to Trevor Pateman for allowing me to read his unpublished paper, *In Defence of a Question*.
[2] Reprinted in (ed.) A. Flew, *Logic and Language*, Oxford, 1960.
[3] H. Pitkin, 'Obligation and Consent,' in *Philosophy, Politics and Society*, Fourth Series, Oxford, 1972.
[4] T. McPherson, *Political Obligation*, London, 1967. To keep the discussion within reasonable bounds I shall confine myself to these three examples.

from such an acceptance about general political obligation to specific forms of political institutions, especially those of the liberal democratic state. I shall argue that empirical as well as conceptual matters are crucial to arguments about political obligation, and that it is possible to accept the conceptual argument, yet, depending upon an assessment of the evidence relating to the empirical feasibility of realizing participatory forms of democratic institutions, reject the claim that political obligation in a liberal democratic state is justified.

Some complex problems, central to political philosophy, are raised by these arguments; problems relating to two familiar models of political relations (called by McPherson the 'individualist' and the 'collectivist'), to the idea of consent to government in a democracy, and to the frequent comparisons made between consenting, promising and political obligation. Perhaps because of the frequency of this comparison, the similarities and differences between the obligation incurred by a promise and political obligation are often assumed to be more obvious than they are. This Chapter begins a more detailed exploration of the similarities and differences, and also their consequences for arguments about political obligation in liberal democratic political systems.

In the second part of this Chapter I draw on these arguments to examine McPherson's objections, in *Political Obligation,* to what he calls the 'moralising' of politics, and his claim that 'we may well feel justified in dispensing with the concept of political obligation'.[5] Given the wide range, and great complexity, of the issues raised by the arguments of Macdonald, Pitkin and McPherson, the discussion in this paper is necessarily limited. My aim is less to offer solutions to problems than to show that the 'traditional', general problems of political philosophy are more than symptoms of conceptual disorder, and to bring to the surface some of the assumptions that remain implicit in much contemporary political philosophy.

[5] McPherson, p. 84.

I

1   In their discussions of political obligation, the writers with whom I am concerned here all stress the point, a familiar one, that theorists who argue that our political obligation rests on consent offer a different model of political relationships than writers who argue for different grounds of obligation. Macdonald, for example, contrasts the two 'images' or 'pictures' to be found in 'contractual' and 'organic' theories; in the one political relations are 'like undertaking to provide goods or services in return for certain payment', in the other political relations are 'not determined by free choice'.[6] Pitkin refers to 'the peculiar picture of man and society' of the consent theorist, where each individual is a 'separate, self-contained unit'.[7] McPherson presents a more radical distinction between 'individualistic' and 'collectivist' theories, claiming that it is *only* in theories of an individualistic kind, the product of philosophers 'who regard society as artificial rather than natural', that the concept of political obligation is needed at all. In collectivist theories, in which government is seen as 'the community in a certain aspect of itself ', the concept is unimportant, or absent, and the question of why ought I to obey the government is an unreal one.[8]

I shall say more about these two models of political relationships later. At this stage a brief comment is required on McPherson's discussion. He takes Locke as his example of an individualistic philosopher, but Locke is not an individualist in that he regards *society* as artificial. Commentators on Locke stress that his state of nature is a social state, it includes private property and the use of money.[9] What is 'artificial' for Locke is precisely men setting up separate *political* societies, i.e. societies with government in the sense that each individual voluntarily gives up his natural right of interpretation and execution of the law of

---

[6] Macdonald, pp. 172–4.
[7] Pitkin, p. 74.
[8] McPherson, pp. 42–3.
[9] Wolin in *Politics and Vision* (London, 1961) in an illuminating discussion of Locke, argues that it was from the writings of Locke that the concept of society began its rise to prominence in modern social and political thought.

230   *Carole Pateman*

nature and places this right in the hands of a few men, the government, whose decisions (always providing they do not infringe the law of nature) he is then under an obligation to obey. In Locke's theory what makes government legitimate is the consent of the individual, this provides a general justification for political obligation to government. But what of 'collectivist' theories?

McPherson doesn't explicitly offer an example here, but he does mention Rousseau's 'insights into the importance of community'[10] so I shall consider Rousseau. In *The Social Contract* we read that

> the strongest man is never strong enough to be master all the time, unless he transforms force into right and obedience into duty. ... Surely it must be admitted ... that the duty of obedience is owed only to legitimate powers'[11]

The reason that it might seem that the question of why I ought to obey the government is 'unreal' for Rousseau, or that he makes no use of the concept of political obligation, is that in *The Social Contract* he presents us with an account of the truly legitimate government, the ideal political system. But it still *makes sense,* in terms of Rousseau's theory, to ask why I am obliged to obey the government; a general justification for government can be offered and the grounds for its legitimacy spelled out.

However, the writers I am discussing in this paper are denying that this question is a sensible one, and I shall now turn to the major argument underlying this claim.

II   This argument is that general questions about political obligation are based on conceptual confusion. Macdonald writes that

> to ask why I should obey any laws is to ask whether there might be a political society without political obligations, which is absurd. For we mean by political society, groups of people organized according to rules enforced by some of their number.[12]

Pitkin argues that, like general doubts about promise-keeping, general questions about political obligation are a

[10] McPherson, p. 42.
[11] J. J. Rousseau, *The Social Contract*, trns. M. Cranston, Penguin Books, 1968, Book 1, Chapter 3.
[12] Macdonald, p. 184.

'symptom of philosophical disorder, the product of a philosophical paradox'. This would disappear if it could be shown 'why anyone should so much as suppose that political obligation in general needs (or can have) a general justification'. In the case of both promises and political obligation the answer lies in a failure to appreciate the way our language works; 'it is part of the concept, the meaning of "law", that those to whom it is applicable are obligated to obey it'.[13]

In *Political Obligation*, McPherson argues more strongly that the 'individualistic' philosopher is in the position of a man who does not see that belonging to a club involves him in taking on obligations, and who therefore does not understand what 'being a member' means. Similarly, he misunderstands what it means to be a member of society.

> That social man has obligations is an analytic, not a synthetic, proposition.... 'Why should I (a member) accept the rules of the club?' is an absurd question. Accepting the rules is part of what it *means* to be a member. Similarly, 'Why should I obey the government?' is an absurd question. We have not understood what it *means* to be a member of political society if we suppose that political obligation is something that we might not have had and that therefore needs to be *justified*.[14]

The conclusion drawn from this conceptual argument by these three writers is that, properly, we can only raise questions, or have doubts about, our obligation in the case of specific laws or demands of government. To attempt to go further and ask general questions about political obligation is to fall into absurdity and to reveal oneself as conceptually confused.

III   The basis of the argument I am considering here is a simple one; the argument rests on the point that it is conceptually incoherent to try to detach the concepts of 'society' and 'political society' from those of 'obligation' and 'political obligation'. So to ask the very general question whether there could be a political society without political obligation is to ask a meaningless question. However, if this point can be accepted, the conclusion drawn from it by some political philosophers cannot. The claim being advanced by Macdonald, Pitkin and McPherson is not just about the broad

---

[13] Pitkin, p. 75 and p. 78.
[14] McPherson, p. 64 (McPherson's emphasis).

conceptual implications of notions like 'political society', it is also a claim about political obligation to *particular* forms of government. What is being argued is that it is meaningless to ask general questions about political obligation in relation to specific forms of political institutions, especially those of the liberal democratic state.

The general terms of the conceptual argument—political society, government, law—say nothing about the actual form of political institutions. Yet the conceptual argument is held to be relevant to our political situation, today, in Britain or the United States. The absurdity of supposing that political obligation 'is something we might not have had' is held to refer to the obligation to an historically specific form of political institutions, namely the liberal democratic state. McPherson writes in his introduction to *Political Obligation* that his arguments are 'intended to apply to modern liberal democracies', and Macdonald's examples are drawn from our own political system.[15] An illustration of how deep-seated the assumption can be that there are no general questions to be raised about the legitimacy of liberal democratic government is provided by Pitkin's dismissal of this idea as flying in the face of common sense: 'surely, one feels, if the present government of the United States is not a legitimate authority, no government ever has been'.[16] But the philosopher's common-sense feelings are not enough to justify political obligation, and nor is the conceptual argument alone enough to justify, or show there is no need for justification of, political obligation in the liberal democratic state.

This use of the conceptual argument gains its plausibility because it rests on some assumptions that political philosophers too rarely seriously question.

A political anthropologist has recently remarked upon 'the spell' that the state has long exerted over political theorists.[17] The spell cast by the liberal democratic state, and the theory of that state, on English speaking political philosophers is

---

[15] Macdonald, pp. 184–5.
[16] Pitkin, p. 53. Pitkin herself adds that she has let this statement stand as originally written in 1964 as 'a historical relic'.
[17] G. Balandier, *Political Anthropology*, Penguin Books, 1972, p. 187.

particularly relevant to the conclusions drawn from the conceptual argument about political obligation.

The extent to which a certain interpretation of 'government' and 'political society' can be assumed, can be seen from Macdonald's claim that the philosophers who see a genuine, general problem about political obligation want 'an answer which is always and infallibly right.' She goes on to compare this to the man who persists, senselessly, in wondering whether all his perceptions of the world are delusory, thus robbing the word 'deluded' of all meaning.[18] However, this is not a valid comparison; at least, it is not an analogous philosophical mistake to have general doubts about the legitimacy of the (liberal democratic) state. While it may be the case that 'government', in a very broad sense of that term, only retains meaning so long as doubts about political obligation are confined to particular cases, to query whether a *specific* form of government, the liberal democratic state, really obliges is not to rob the term of significance. Here it is Macdonald who is demanding the 'right answer'—that we are, in fact, right now, under a political obligation. What is being claimed, on the basis of the conceptual argument, is that any given discussion of political obligation (especially discussions of political obligation in the liberal democratic state), if it is to be meaningful, must start from the assumption that we do have political obligation. Given this starting point, then a specific form of political institution does appear unproblematical; it ceases to be something that requires a general justification and becomes a fact about the world, a fact that we have to accept in any discussion of political obligation.

Any argument that moves straight from the conceptual connection between 'being a member of political society' and 'political obligation' to conclusions about our obligation to specific political institutions is stretching purely conceptual analysis beyond its proper limits. To argue from 'being a member of political society' directly to 'having political obligation to the (liberal democratic) state' is to make the implict assumption that 'political society', 'government' and 'the state' all imply each other, and that there is a logical, not just an empirical connection between the notions of a political

[18] Macdonald, p. 184.

society and the state. It is strange that philosophers who place so much weight on conceptual analysis should uncritically accept the popular identification of politics, government and the institution of the modern liberal democratic state; there is no logical objection to government being conceived in terms of institutional arrangements for taking decisions that relate to communal, public or political affairs, but that are very different in form from those of the modern state. For example, consider the political systems of the so-called primitive societies,[19] or the council system that has been a feature of much revolutionary theory and practice for at least a century now. Moreover, this use of the conceptual argument ignores the different wide characterizations of politics and political systems now being offered that do not link politics to the state: for example, 'a political system is any persistent pattern of human relationships that involves, to a significant extent, power, rule or authority'.[20] If general questions about political obligation are meaningless, then much of the discussion about, say, the difference between liberal democratic and council forms of political institutions is meaningless too.

IV   There are some very interesting parallels to be found with the arguments of writers being considered in this paper in the work of an earlier political philosopher, namely Hegel. The *Philosophy of Right* can be read as an extended, and extremely elaborate working out of what I have called the conceptual argument, and my criticisms of the conclusions drawn from this argument about political obligation in the liberal democratic state also parallel some of the criticisms that Marx made of Hegel's political theory.

Hegel's attack on philosophers who saw society as an aggregation of 'atomic units' or 'abstract individuals' is an aspect of his political philosophy emphasized by recent commentators. This emphasis is not surprising given the influence of sociological theory, because the argument that there is a conceptual link between 'society', 'being a member

[19] For arguments that these are 'political societies' see, for example, Balandier.
[20] R. A. Dahl, *Modern Political Analysis*, New Jersey, 1963, p. 6.

of society' and notions like obligation has formed the basis for sociological theory from, for example, Durkheim's stress on the non-contractual elements in contract, through to the attack of a contemporary theorist, Talcott Parsons, on 'utilitarian' theories of social action.[21] In his discussion of the three spheres of family, civil society and the state in the *Philosophy of Right*, Hegel is making exactly the point that the idea of social life is conceptually incoherent unless conceived of as a maturity of inter-relationships, which presupposes concepts like obligations, rights and so on.[22]

Hegel argues that the pursuit and fulfilment of private ends by each individual takes place in a context, in civil society, where the pursuit of those ends necessarily involves him in relationships with others, others who are pursuing their ends. The recognition of this interdependence in social life implies that each individual will recognize that just as he, if he is to be able to obtain his goals, must have certain rights and obligations, so must all other individuals. That is, the very notion of an individual pursuing his private ends presupposes, and is presupposed by, a system of universal (ethical) rules, a system of rights and obligations. The whole idea of the individual 'abstracted' from the context of this system of rules is conceptually incoherent. It is this mutually recognized and accepted system of universal rights and obligations, this 'ethical framework' or what philosophers now might call a system of social practices, that Hegel, in one of the senses in which he uses the term, calls the state.

If, put into this terminology, Hegel's argument seems familiar, what is less well appreciated are the implications of Marx's criticisms of the use which Hegel makes of his argument—the same use which is being made of the

---

[21] See, for example, the discussion of Hegel in J. Plamenatz, *Man and Society*, London, 1963. It has been stated that the *Philosophy of Right* is 'the work which, above any other single piece of writing in early nineteenth-century German philosophy, created the effective setting within which German sociology was later to arise'. R. A. Nisbet, *The Sociological Tradition*, London, 1970, p. 54.

[22] These remarks on Hegel owe a debt to C. Bentz, *Hegel on Civil Society and the State*, unpublished paper, Oxford 1971.

conceptual argument by contemporary political philosophers. Implicit in the *Philosophy of Right* is the claim that
once a proper conceptual understanding is reached of social
and political relations, then general questions (and perhaps
for Hegel, all questions) about political obligation to the state
are completely meaningless. This is the import of his
criticisms of Rousseau, who had seen that will was the
principle of the state, for making use of the idea of contract,
thus reducing 'the union of individuals in the state ... to
something based on ... their capriciously given express
consent'. This destroyed the divine principle of the state and
its absolute authority; it reduced membership of the state to
something optional.[23]

Similar criticisms to those that I made in the previous
section, of the conclusions drawn from the conceptual
argument by Macdonald, Pitkin and McPherson, can be
made of Hegel's arguments. First, that Hegel illegitimately
assumes that a purely conceptual point, that 'social life'
implies 'obligations and rights', means that particular,
existing obligations and rights have to be accepted, whereas,
in fact it leaves completely open the question of the form and
content that actual obligations and rights should have.
Second, and this makes Hegel's theory doubly confusing, he
assumes that for obligations and rights to exist it is logically
and empirically necessary for a state to exist; a state, that is, in
the second of the senses in which he uses the term, namely to
refer to the actual institutions of the modern constitutional
state. Hegel remarks that 'the private judgement and private
will of the sphere called "civil society" in this book—comes
into existence integrally related to the state'[24]: but the state in
which sense? If it is the state in the second sense the remark is
historically and theoretically illuminating. But Hegel's
political philosophy is based on the assumption that for
(modern) social and political life it is logically and empirically
necessary for the state to exist in both of his senses. However,
while an 'ethical framework' may be logically necessary for a
coherent conception of social life, and may be empirically
required (although not necessarily in its existing form) for

[23] Hegel, *Philosophy of Right*, trans. T. M. Knox, Oxford
University Press, 1952, §258, pp. 156–7.
[24] Hegel, §301, pp. 196–7.

social life to exist, one of Marx's main criticisms of Hegel was precisely that the state in the second sense, i.e. the actual institutions of the modern state, was neither logically nor empirically required. And the conclusion to be drawn from this is that general questions about political obligation in the constitutional or liberal democratic state cannot be disposed of by conceptual arguments alone.

V   If there is a general problem about political obligation in a liberal democratic state, why is this? Surprisingly, this question is rarely posed in this way. Political philosophers who assume that political obligation is genuinely problematical usually seem to regard it as obvious why this is so. They tend to begin by asking 'why ought I to obey the (liberal democratic) state?', i.e. by asking what is the justification of our obligation rather than by explaining why there is a general problem about obligation in the first place (which is exactly what the writers I am discussing here are denying). That is, political philosophers tend to assume that the citizens of a liberal democracy do have a political obligation to their government, even though this needs justifying, and this, perhaps, helps account for the lack of attention paid to the reasons why political obligation should be regarded as problematical at all.[25]

Another reason might be that it is far from easy to find a satisfactory explanation; it is not even immediately obvious where one should start to look for such an explanation. However, I would suggest (and what follows is meant to be no more than a sketch for an argument) that the reason that it can be argued that there is a real general problem about political obligation centres round the model of the social and political actor, and the conception of obligation, on which liberal democratic theory rests.

It is a familiar argument that one of the most central features of the development of 'modern', Western society is

[25]   To take the example of a recent textbook, D. D. Raphael in *Problems of Political Philosophy* (London, 1970), chap. IV while disagreeing that 'a statement of the formal implications of the terms "law" and "legal obligation"' offers a satisfactory solution to the problem of political obligation (cf. McPherson, p. 60) discusses the reasons for accepting the legal jurisdiction of the state.

the development of the concept of the free individual. Consider Hegel's remark quoted in the last section that 'the private judgement and private will of the sphere called "civil society" ... comes into existence integrally related to the state'. Liberal democratic theory is not the only political theory in which the concept of the free individual is of importance, but that theory lays particular stress on the individual social actor as an actor who judges for himself, makes his own choices and decisions, looks only to his own conscience, pursues his own, private interests, and enters into his own, voluntary contracts and exchanges. The question can be asked what conception of obligation is appropriate to such an actor; could he, for example, consistently be said to have obligations that he has not explicitly taken upon himself? The answer given here will partly depend how seriously the individual actor's own judgement, choice and decision is treated. Given that contracting, or, more generally, promising, tends to be taken as paradigmatic of obligation in liberal democratic political philosophy, it seems reasonable to suggest that part of the free choice of the actor is precisely when to take an obligation upon himself—he has a free choice when to commit himself by a promise, or enter into a contract. That is to say, the conception of obligation is that of self-assumed obligation. The central role played in liberal democratic theory by the idea of the individual citizen's consent to government, and the frequency of comparisons of this consent to the making of a promise is of significance here.[26]

But to point this out is to raise the crucial question whether political obligation is not different from obligations outside the political sphere. And it is this question that is central to the general problem of political obligation in liberal democratic theory. Whereas certain liberal writers may have taken extremely seriously the idea of *all* obligations as self-

[26] My only aim here is to suggest that this general conception of how obligation arises is central to the theory of liberal democracy and to argue that its implications should be treated more seriously in discussions of political obligation in the liberal democratic state. A great deal more can be said about the conception of self-assumed obligation; I am currently looking in more detail at self-assumed obligation in a book on the problem of political obligation.

assumed obligations,[27] liberal democratic philosophers have assumed that political obligation is an exception, for the following reason. If it is considered what form political institutions would have to take if political obligation is to be self-assumed obligation, the answer would seem to be that the form must be such as to allow each individual citizen actually to take part in making the political decisions through which his political obligation arises. This would be the only way in which the individual could be said to take his political obligation upon himself in a manner at all comparable to the self-assumption of his other obligations. However, it is a central assumption of liberal democratic theory that political institutions of such a directly democratic type are not empirically feasible, and hence that political obligation differs from other obligations. Although liberal democratic theory has as its central value the free choice and decision of the individual social actor, a distinction is made in the theory between the political and non-political or private sphere concerning the decision to assume an obligation; only outside the political sphere can the individual himself assume his obligations.

To make this point slightly differently; liberal democratic theory is the theory of the democratic election of a representative government. The job of the elected representative is precisely to take political decisions for, to impose political obligations upon, the community as a whole. Thus political obligation is an exception to the general conception of obligation as self-assumed obligation; the individual actor decides when to make a promise (oblige himself), the (few) representatives decide when political obligations will be incurred. That political obligation is, in general, problematical in the liberal democratic state, is because the question can always be asked, from within the assumptions of liberal democratic theory itself, why the individual actor's political obligation should differ from his other obligations.

---

[27] For example, Godwin, taking the independent producer as the paradigm of the social actor (an actor who makes his own choices and decisions, enters his own contracts) saw the whole of social and political life as a series of discrete, equal, voluntary exhanges between independent individuals, exercising their own 'private judgement'.

The answer given to that question, if my argument is plausible, concerns the possibility of alternative democratic forms. If alternative, directly participatory, forms of democratic political institutions are empirically feasible, then political obligation could reasonably be held to be analogous to other self-assumed obligations. If this is so, then the justification for political obligation in the liberal democratic state (i.e. the justification of non-self-assumed obligation) rests to a greater extent than is usually allowed for on the answers to questions about the empirical feasibility of realising different forms of democratic political institutions; in large part it rests on the reasonableness of the widely held assumption that the representative government of liberal democracy is the only feasible form of democratic government in large-scale, industrialized societies.

V I Political philosophers have often suggested that political obligation in a liberal democratic state is justified because it is grounded in the consent of the citizens to their government. Consenting to government is often compared to promising; just as I am obliged if I have promised, so I am politically obliged because I have consented to government. If liberal democratic government is based on consent, and if consenting to government can validly be compared to promising, then our political obligation would also seem to be self-assumed.

I noted earlier that Hanna Pitkin compares promising and political obligation as cases where a similar conceptual confusion leads to meaningless general doubts about obligation, and I now want to look more closely at some of her arguments. Pitkin points out how easy it is to confuse the fact that promises are self-assumed with the idea that the obligation to keep promises must also be self-assumed, thus leading to the query whether one is ever *really* obliged to keep any promise at all. This is an absurd question, she argues, because promising is something that we learn to do, and what we learn during the socialization process is that to say 'I promise' *is* to take on an obligation; that is to say, the making of any one promise presupposes the social practice of promising. So if it is asked why promises oblige, what is being asked is why self-assumed obligations oblige, 'and to the question why obligations oblige the only possible answer would seem to be that this is what the words mean'.[28] Or, to look at it slightly differently, this argument about promising—that for one individual freely to make a promise and so put himself under an obligation presupposes and is presupposed by the mutual recognition by the actors in the social system that this is what promising 'means'—follows the account of Hegel's arguments sketched in Section V, that individual 'private judgement' and promises (contracts) presupposes and is presupposed by an 'ethical framework' (or social institution or social practice) of obligations and rights.

However, even if one accepts this argument about promising, the comparison with political obligation is much more complicated than Pitkin's account suggests.[29] One difference is that promising involves the social practice of promising, 'promising in general', and individual acts of promise-making, whereas political obligation involves three, not two, 'levels'; the general concept of political society, particular political systems, and particular laws. The conclusion drawn from the conceptual argument by the writers discussed in this paper is unacceptable because it assumes that political obligation can be assimilated to the 'two-level' promising model, that a move can be made directly from the first to the third 'level'.

Few, if any, contemporary political philosophers would wish to argue for unconditional political obligation, or that individual promises oblige unconditionally. However, as Pitkin notes, to recognize that a particular promise might be outweighed by other considerations is not the same as asking whether any of my individual promises *really* oblige me. That is senseless—because ... I have promised, i.e. I have performed an identifiable act the 'meaning' of which is clear and understood by all actors. Now, if my obligation, in a given political system, to obey a particular law might sometimes be outweighed, it does not also follow, as it does in the case of promising, that it is senseless to ask, in the context of the liberal democratic state, 'am I *really* politically obliged at all?' The crucial question is what is the equivalent answer to 'because I promised', what is the equivalent act, in the political context, to making a promise? Another difference

[28] Pitkin, p. 77.
[29] I am grateful to Steven Lukes for drawing my attention to the problem of 'levels'.

between political obligation and promising is that, in a liberal democratic state, there is no clear answer to this question. The obvious suggestion, of course, and one that is frequently offered in discussions of consent theory, is 'because I voted'.[30] But if the 'meaning' of 'I promise' is perfectly clear and understood by all socialized actors, the 'meaning' of the individual's vote in a democratic election is far from obvious. The difficulty is well known of finding a sense in which the individual citizen can be said clearly and unambiguously to have consented to anything in a democratic election. Moreover, democratic voting has been interpreted, by Edelman for example, as primarily a ritualistic or symbolic activity[31]; yet if this interpretation makes perfectly good sense, the idea of promising as a symbolic activity is extremely curious. On the other hand, and importantly for the analogy with promising and the assumptions of liberal democratic theory, the individual citizen has undoubtedly made a voluntary decision and choice when he marks his ballot paper (or abstains from voting).[32]

At this point it might be argued that all that this shows is not something about the general argument about political obligation but that political obligation is really quite different from promising, that is why there are so many difficulties associated with the notion of consent in the liberal democratic state, and why it is necessary to reformulate, if not to give up, 'traditional' consent theory. In fact, despite Pitkin's comparison between political obligation and promising, this is her position; it is the differences that are crucial. I shall discuss this part of her argument in the next section, here I want to look at her reformulation of consent theory as a theory of 'hypothetical consent'.

Pitkin's theory of hypothetical consent in *Obligation and Consent* is that 'a legitimate government, ... one whose

[30] See, e.g., the discussion in J. Plamenatz, *Man and Society*, London, 1963, Vol. 1, pp. 238–41.

[31] M. Edelman, *The Symbolic Uses of Politics,* Chicago, 1964.

[32] When an actor abstains from making a promise he remains uncommitted; is the voter uncommitted when he abstains from voting, or is he (in a liberal democratic system) indirectly consenting to the system as a whole as Plamenatz suggests? (p. 240). There is wide disagreement how electoral abstention should be interpreted.

subjects are obligated to obey it, ... (is) one to which they ought to consent'.[33] She recognizes that this formulation rests on a 'point of grammar', that it still leaves open the question of the criteria of legitimacy, and that this purely formal, conceptual point, on its own, admits *any* criterion: as she says, for someone arguing that a legitimate government is one which promoted the evolution of a master race 'the doctrine of hypothetical consent holds ...; even for him, a legitimate government would be the one that deserves consent'.[34] Surely, what this shows is not something about consent (on the contrary that idea appears to have been robbed of any content at all) but something about the limitations of conceptual analysis. The whole point about consent theory is that it offers a possible criterion by which a legitimate form of government can be recognized, namely one to which actual consent has been given and continues to be given; and a criterion which can be argued for in the face of competing criteria and reasonably accepted or rejected. The theory of hypothetical consent means that *any* criterion whatever could always be relevant for someone, or some body of persons, so that a claim to legitimacy could never be defeated. But if, on the basis of the conceptual argument, *general* questions about political obligation are dismissed as meaningless, then such a conclusion is inevitable, for those general questions are bound up with the problem of which criteria of legitimacy may properly be admitted and accepted, and which specific forms of political institutions give practical expression to those criteria.

VII Pitkin's discussion notes two differences between promising and political obligation. First, that if the social institution of promising seems indispensable to social life, this is not so obvious in the case of government. She goes on to ask 'but can we conceive society without any such thing as authority?'[35] Again the points already made must be repeated: even if one accepts that analytically and empirically 'social life' requires 'authority', and even if 'government' is interpreted in the broadest way as the exercise of authority, it does not follow from this that government in the *specific* form

[33] Pitkin, p. 62.
[34] Ibid., p. 71.
[35] Ibid., p. 79.

of the liberal democratic state is legitimate or that there are no general questions to be raised about political obligation. Second, and importantly, Pitkin argues that promising and political obligation differ because the *content* of political obligation, unlike the obligation that arises from a promise, 'seems to be a subordination to the judgement of others'. Earlier she suggests that political obligation, unlike a promise, need not be 'explicitly taken on oneself '.[36] But perhaps it might be. If this possibility is to be treated seriously then the differences between promising and political obligation have to be explored further and a closely related question must be considered; that is, the problem of the two models of political relationships, the 'individualist' and 'collectivist' (for convenience I shall follow McPherson's terminology).

A crucial difference between promising and political obligation is that the paradigm case of a self-assumed obligation, a promise, is that of the interaction of two individual actors, as individuals, in their private, everyday life. Political obligations, on the other hand, paradigmatically arise from some form of collective decision making and apply communally, that is, the obligations and rights imposed by collective decision apply to everyone. A basic difference between the two models of political relations, the individualist and the collectivist, and a major reason why political philosophers find both, as alternatives, unsatisfactory, is that each model draws on one of these two aspects of social life; the individualistic model rests on the paradigm of individual interaction in everyday life, and the collectivist model draws on the communal nature of political life. Taken as alternatives there is always something missing; in each case precisely the aspect of social life basic to the other model.

There are various approaches that can be taken to these two models. For example, one or other might be rejected completely; both, or elements of both, might be combined in some way; or the whole idea of regarding them as alternatives might be rejected.

Hegel provides an example of a political philosopher who took the first course. I have already referred to his attack on the notions of abstract individuals and consent, but Hegel also rejected universal suffrage and one major reason for this

[36] Pitkin, p. 8o and p. 84.

would seem to be that he regarded it as, so to speak, an empirical manifestation of conceptual wrongheadedness, as the individualistic model, or a central feature of it, put into practice. One way of looking at the recent discussions of political obligation in the liberal democratic state that centre round the conceptual argument is as an attempt at com-bination, as an example of the second approach. This might seem misleading in that McPherson, for instance, rejects the individualistic model on the grounds that it involves 'a faulty analysis of the concept of society'.[37] On the other hand, none of the political philosophers I am considering wish to argue for unconditional political obligation, but the example of Hegel shows that rejection of the individualistic model on the basis of the conceptual argument could easily lead to that position. Although Macdonald, Pitkin and McPherson wish to insist that we are politically obliged, they also wish to combine this, in the context of the liberal democratic state, with an emphasis on individual voluntary choice and compliance—it is not absurd to have doubts about obligation to obey specific laws, the individual can make a choice (consent) by exercising his suffrage in a democratic election— an emphasis that is central to the individualistic model. Through this combination of elements it is hoped that full account can be taken of the fact that men are, at one and the same time both subject to and superior to their government, political institutions and political obligations; that they are both bound by them and can question them. Pitkin suggests that it is this seemingly paradoxical fact, which is a fact about all our obligations, not only our political obligations, that has driven political philosophers to ask meaningless general questions about political obligation (and promising).

In her discussion of this apparent paradox, Pitkin says that the purpose of the 'consent theorist', as Locke's theory illustrates, is to show what is true, that 'men are normally bound to obey governments' yet are also sometimes justified in disobeying'.[38] If 'government' here means the repre-sentative government of the liberal democratic state, then, as Pitkin's own discussion of Locke shows very clearly, this is Locke's purpose. He did not wish to question the general legitimacy of representative government; quite the contrary,

[37] McPherson, p. 65.
[38] Pitkin, pp. 80–81.

and contemporary political philosophers tend to follow Locke here. Basing his theory on individual consent allowed Locke room for disobedience; but consent in a direct, really meaningful sense is extremely difficult, as I argued earlier, to reconcile with representative government. Hence Locke's transformation of consent into tacit consent. Retaining the idea of consent at all, however, seems to solve the problem of keeping a link with the free individual choice and decision which is a central value for liberal democrats, and allows comparisons to be made with promising. Yet, given the existence of (democratically elected) representative government, political obligation seems crucially to differ from promises in exactly the way stated by Pitkin, namely that its *content* seems to be subordination to the judgement of others, to the judgement of the representatives (cf. my remarks in Section V).

A 'consent theorist' however need not necessarily follow Locke, nor base his theory on the 'individualistic' model. There is another possibility open to a non-Lockean consent theorist and this involves the third approach to the two models of political relationships; the rejection of the models as alternatives. And the basis of this alternative is an extended version of the conceptual argument.

In the discussion of promising in Section VI, the argument was that there could be no proper understanding of promising if individual acts of promise-making were treated as conceptually separable from the social practice of promising. Similarly, it can be argued that there can be no proper understanding of social life (and what it means to be a member of society) if its two conceptually inseparable aspects, the private and the public, communal or political spheres, are treated as if they are conceptually separable. And this separation has to be made if the two models of political relations are to be offered as alternatives. That is to say, this version of the conceptual argument suggests that social life, seen as a whole or as a complex totality, is socio-political life. Pitkin, as noted earlier, argued that 'society' is inconceivable without 'authority'; but what is the significance of this? In the light of wide definitions of the political in terms of social relations involving power or authority it implies that all societies are political societies. It is at *this* level of analysis that the conceptual link between 'being a member of society', 'being a member of a political society' and 'having political obligations' is relevant. If social life can only be properly understood conceived of as socio-political life then, as the three writers discussed in this paper argue, it *is* conceptually incoherent to suggest that political obligation *as such* is dispensable. But, it must be emphasized again, this does not mean that it is meaningless to ask for a general justification of *specific forms* of political institutions and the political obligations associated with them.

A closer consideration is also required of the idea of the 'ethical framework' or system of social practices presupposed by the conception of individual self-assumption of obligations. Not all of the 'framework' is of the same status as the social practice that forms the necessary background to an individual promise. For example, in Section 52 of *A Theory of Justice,* Rawls argues that the 'rule of promising', which is constitutive of the social practice of promising, is 'on a par with legal rules and statutes, and rules of games'. To argue in this fashion is to ignore the different 'levels' at which the rules operate, and so to fail to see that certain questions may sensibly be asked about some rules and not others. It is also to fail to appreciate that some social practices, or part of the 'framework', notably legal rules, may, unlike the social practice of promising, deliberately be created or changed through communal or political decisions. One logically possible way for those decisions to be taken democratically is directly, or with the consent of all (adult) citizens; i.e. for citizens to use their votes actually to make those decisions. If this were the case the *content* of political obligation would no longer appear as subordination to the judgement of others. At least, the individual citizen would no longer be subordinated to the judgement of *some* others (representatives) in the political sphere; rather he, together with all other citizens taken individually (as governed) would be subordinated to the decisions that he and they have themselves taken collectively (as government).[39] Thus it is possible to enlarge

[39] To avoid possible misunderstanding I should perhaps add that the remarks on the extended conceptual argument and on a directly participatory system are not meant to suggest that problems of consent and obligation are solved. The question of the composition of the decision making body is logically prior to the question of

the conceptual argument and retain the 'collectivist' emphasis necessary to a proper conceptual understanding of the idea of social life, but at the same time to encompass within this, in the spheres of both political and everyday life, the 'individualist' notion of obligation as self-assumed obligation, the notion of the individual explicitly taking upon himself *all* his obligations.

The enlargement of the conceptual argument can be taken further. Socialization is crucial to the conceptual argument about promising. But socialization includes political socialization and it is the socialization process that, as it were, knits together the two aspects of social life, the private and the public, into a complex totality. During the socialization process the individual learns what it is to assume an obligation—whether that obligation is 'private' (a promise) or political. He learns, that is, that individuals are both private individuals and public citizens who assume obligations in both capacities. If the narrower conceptual argument suggests that a 'private', individual act of promising cannot conceptually be abstracted from the social background of the practice of promise keeping, the wider argument suggests that neither can everyday, private life be conceptually abstracted from the framework provided by the social practice of political decision making (political obligation); nor can political life be properly understood if it is abstracted conceptually from the socialization process occurring in everyday life.[40]

The move made by some political philosophers from a simple conceptual point about social life and obligation to a dismissal of any need for the justification of political obligation to a particular form of government, implicitly

---

how the decisions are made (which is outside the scope of this paper) but if, e.g., they are taken by majority decision then the familiar problems of the position of the minority arise; the problem of obligation to specific decisions also remains, obligation is not unconditional.

[40] This third alternative depends on, and this a crucial point, the 'individual' being seen as a 'social' and not an 'abstract' individual; it is this latter conception which is at the root of the objections to the 'individualistic' model— recall, for example, Pitkin's comments on the individual as 'a self-contained unit'.

appeals to the extended conceptual argument which encom-
passes the different dimensions of social life, and also
implicitly assumes the answers to a wide range of vital,
empirical questions. It may well be that the arguments for the
legitimacy of the liberal democratic form of government are
convincing, but those arguments must be presented;
legitimacy and the justification of political obligation cannot
merely be assumed. Moreover, purely conceptual arguments,
by themselves, can solve no problems about the general
justification of political obligation in particular political
systems. Depending on an assessment of the arguments about
the empirical feasibility of realizing different forms of
democratic political institutions, it is possible to begin from
conceptual arguments and arrive at either of two conclusions;
that political obligation is only justified in a liberal democratic
system, or, alternatively, that it is only justified in a directly
participatory democratic system.

II

In this part of the chapter I shall discuss McPherson's
extension of the argument that there is no general problem
about political obligation, his claim in *Political Obligation*
that the concept of political obligation could be dispensed
with altogether.

1   The basis of McPherson's argument is his view that,
properly, the discussion of politics, the discussion of the
relationship between the citizen and the state, should not be
'moralized'. Or, put into more familiar language, he is
claiming that the discussion of the relationship between
citizen and state should be value-free. So far as political
obligation is concerned, the major job of the political
philosopher is that of explaining why citizens do in fact obey
the government. McPherson tells us that

> It is not the facts that I question—of governments requiring
> their subjects to do certain things and the subjects doing
> them—but the terminology of orders and obedience (and
> obligation) used to express those facts.[40]

[41] McPherson, pp. 15–16.

This kind of terminology, he argues, 'means looking at politics through the spectacles of ethics. It means what I am calling the moralising of politics.' Political philosophers should now realize that there is nothing to prevent them discussing politics and the relation of citizen and state in different terms, in 'neutral, non-morally-loaded' terms.[42]

Once it is assumed, on the basis of the conceptual argument, that general questions about political obligation are meaningless and absurd, it is easy to assume also that all that is left for the political philosopher to do is to *explain* the political obedience of citizens. On the other hand, the argument that the concept of political obligation could be dispensed with in this task is an odd one for a political philosopher who relies, as McPherson does, on the conceptual argument. If the political philosopher accepts the argument of the conceptual link between the idea of social life and the concept of obligation, between 'political society' and 'political obligation' as a necessary basis of any discussion of political obligation, then it is hardly possible for him to consider the relationship between citizen and state without using the concept of political obligation; the necessary price of trying to do without it must be conceptual incoherence.

The attempt to drop the terminology of 'obligation' certainly causes difficulties for the argument of *Political Obligation.* If the job of the political philosopher is to explain why the ordinary citizen obeys his liberal democratic government most of the time, then it is hard to see how this can be done without reference at some point to the belief of the citizen in the legitimacy of that government, to his belief that he ought to obey; McPherson makes the rather extraordinary claim that

> the moralising of politics is not on the whole true to the practice of governments themselves. 'Do this', or 'This is expedient', is the sense of government commands or pronouncements, rather than 'You ought to do this'.[43]

Is this really what the American (or other) government is saying as it conscripts young men? Governments, as well as students of politics, are well aware of the absolutely crucial role of legitimacy in ensuring the smooth running of the machinery of the state with the minimum of recourse to overt

[42] McPherson, p. 80.
[43] Ibid., p. 81.

coercion and force.[44] A government able only to say to its citizens 'do this, it is expedient' would not regard its position as a satisfactory one.

McPherson appeals to the attitude of the ordinary citizen to support his argument that to talk of obligation is improperly to moralize politics. He states that

> Many philosophical questions are of importance even though they might not seem so to people who are not philosophers. But that the moralising of political 'obligation' is untrue to the attitude of the man in the voting box can mean that the philosopher is distorting what he is trying to *explain*.

The man in the voting box does not, he says, 'naturally' think of his relationship to government in terms of obligation.[45] The ordinary citizen might perhaps wonder why we do obey the government but he is unlikely to wonder if we ought to. However, as McPherson himself shows, it is fairly easy to find answers to the question of why citizens do obey the government: I stop at red traffic lights because I don't want to be killed; I pay my income tax because it is difficult not to under the PAYE system; I don't object to conscription as it offers the prospect of excitement after my boring civilian job, and so on. What is a rather more interesting question is *why* the ordinary citizen does not usually consider whether he ought to do these things, why it is 'natural' for him not to. Presumably he does not have the sophisticated reasons that McPherson offers us. A recent study of the political socialization process suggests where one might look for an answer

> the young citizen first learns the lesson of obedience as submission and only later learns that authority is conventional; ... It is critical here that the *first* lesson is that of unquestioned obedience. ... (O)f all the mechanisms which might induce obligation, political socialization is the cheapest and most efficient. ... (M)ost nations really do not permit the citizen's sense of obligation to be contingent. Political socialization mechanisms replace fear or purchase as a way of maintaining citizenship loyalty. ... Citizens become

[44] Legitimacy has occupied a central place in discussion of the necessary conditions for stable democracy; see for example S. M. Lipset, *The First New Nation*, London, 1964; H. Eckstein, *Division and Cohesion in Democracy*, Princeton University Press, 1966.

[45] McPherson, p. 81 (McPherson's emphasis).

bound to the political community with such psychological
tenacity that the option of non-compliance is seldom raised.[46]

As Partridge has commented, with reference to Macdonald's
essay, the modern state is so long and so well established
today that 'to ask in general, Why should I obey the State?
seems as sensible as to ask why I should obey laws of gravity.'[47]

Such an explanation still leaves open the question whether
the 'natural' attitude of the citizen of the liberal democratic
state is justified. But this is the very question which political
philosophers like McPherson argue is meaningless. As I
suggested in Part One, the implication of their use of the
conceptual argument is that political obligation in the liberal
democratic state is a fact about the world, and a fact that it is
as meaningless to try to justify as it would be to try to justify
our 'obligation' to obey the laws of gravity. Ironically
enough, it is usually philosophers who, like McPherson,
reject the 'individualistic' model of social relations who
emphasize that the social world and its institutions should be
seen as the total pattern of interactions and relationships of
individuals; as unlike the natural world in that it is not
independent of individuals as are the laws of gravity (or our
optical perceptions). Specific forms of social and political
institutions are thus always open to justification and, if
necessary, to change, not withstanding the fact that patterns
of interactions may become so firmly established that they
appear to individual citizens (and political philosophers) as if
they were as unalterable as features of the natural world.

II   That McPherson can claim that the notion of political
obligation could be dispensed with, although his discussion is
based on the conceptual argument, paradoxically results from
the fact that his version of the conceptual argument is narrow
and condensed. That is, his own discussion in *Political
Obligation*, rests on an attempt to separate the conceptually
inseparable—namely, the two aspects, the private and the
public, of social life. It is this that underlies his discussion of
'morality' and 'the moralising of politics'. Furthermore, it

[46] R. E. Dawson, and K. Prewitt, *Political Socialization*,
Boston, 1969, pp. 210–12 (italics in the original).
[47] P. H. Partridge, 'Politics, Philosophy, Ideology' in
(ed.) A. Quinton, *Political Philosophy*, Oxford, 1967, p. 38
footnote.

leads McPherson, in his discussion of morals and politics, to treat political obligation in an 'individualistic' and so, on his own arguments, inapporpriate manner.

Morality, McPherson suggests, 'is a matter of personal relations and . . . relations of obligation, in what we may call the standard sense, hold between individual persons'.[48] In his discussion of specific instances of political obligation, McPherson argues that if government is seen in terms of its individual, and personally known agents, then our reason for obeying the law may be very different than if we see government in impersonal terms. Moreover, it might be considered 'perfectly properly, in my opinion—that the reasons why we *ought* to obey are different'. To use McPherson's example; because we know 'the kindly constable who lives down the road' and do not want to cause him extra work is not just an explanation of why we obey the 'No Parking' sign, it also

> may well provide an additional reason why we *ought* not to park by the local 'No Parking' sign. Perhaps this additional reason is a 'moral' reason. It does not matter much how it is labelled; the point is that it is a *relevant* reason.[49]

In this example it is precisely a 'personal relation', friendship, that provides the reason why one ought to obey the parking restriction. It is, therefore, according to McPherson himself, a moral reason. So despite his objection to the 'moralising' of politics, it now appears that where relations between a citizen and an agent of the state are concerned (when a specific instance of political obligation arises) moral reasons are in order, but in order if, and only if, a personal relation also obtains between the individual citizen and the agent of the state. It is the fact of the personal relationship and not matters relating to the governmental 'requirement' in question that justifies obedience.

To the objection that he is here confusing official and personal relations, McPherson replies that he is not confusing them but 'deliberately ignoring the distinction between them'. This distinction is not always relevant. It is only if political obligation is approached from a general, and not a specific, viewpoint that the distinction is important.[50] But to

[48] McPherson, p. 81.
[49] Ibid., pp. 55–6 (McPherson's emphasis).
[50] Ibid., p. 56.

insist with McPherson, that questions about political obligation are only meaningful if 'broken down' into specific cases where distinctions between personal and official relationships are *irrelevant* is to bring back in the 'individualistic' model of political relations, a model based on the personal relations of private, everyday life: the model that McPherson himself rejects. It is true that friendship, or other personal relationships, can be relevant to a specific decision about political obligation (consider Satre's would-be resistance fighter), but this is certainly not the same as saying that it is the extra work caused to a friend in his official capacity that is the relevant consideration. Because social actors are both private individuals and public citizens, decisions about what one ought to do when there is doubt about a specific instance of political obligation are doubly difficult. But this serves to highlight the (extended) conceptual argument that the public and private spheres are the two, inter-related, sides of the same coin of social life.

Only if it is assumed that these two spheres can be treated as conceptually separate and separable can it be held that 'morality' and moral terminology, such as 'obligation', are appropriate to one sphere, the private, alone. Only then could it be suggested that political relations could be discussed without recourse to terms like political obligation. The insistence that questions about political obligation, to be meaningful, must be 'broken down' into 'more limited and more personal terms', together with the linking of 'morality' with personal relationships, means that although politics is apparently 'de-moralised', this is at the price of the reintroduction of the 'individualistic' model of political relations; political obligation is reduced to a matter of discrete, individual, 'private', confrontations between citizens and agents of the state.

Yet at the same time, part of McPherson's argument explicitly denies the validity of this procedure. He objects (as he must, given his acceptance of the conceptual argument) to philosophers who 'take moral rules out of the total social situation, (and) interpret them basically in terms of individuals and their relationships'. This forces political philosophy into the position of a branch of ethics and thus leads to the 'moralising' of politics and political philosophy.[51]

[51] McPherson, pp. 82–3.

But since the 'total social situation' *includes* political relations why should these be regarded as 'non-moral', why should these alone be exempt from critical, moral evaluation and political obligation be regarded as, in general, unproblematical? Certainly the conceptual argument provides no good reason for treating political relations in this way. Just as we do not regard our personal relationships as social 'givens' nor need we our political relationships; to 'moralise' about political relations is not an illegitimate activity for either citizens or political philosophers.[52] Nor is such critical evaluation to 'subordinate political principles to moral' (or political philosophy to ethics); it only seems so if political and moral principles are seen as offering two separate and alternative sets of criteria, one of which must be 'superior', and which apply to two conceptually separable social spheres. To suggest an alternative view is not to say that exactly the same criteria are appropriate to both the private and public spheres, rather to indicate that the relationship between them is one of a complex, mutual inter-relationship; 'morality', as McPherson himself recognises, relates to the *whole* of social life.

Large claims have been made for conceptual analysis in philosophy, but in *political* philosophy at least such claims must be treated with caution. Invaluable as are the techniques of modern, analytical philosophy, in furthering our understanding of the problems in political philosophy, there is a limit to what such analysis alone can achieve. If our doubts and puzzles over, say, whether our perceptions are always delusory, are a result of linguistic bewitchment or conceptual confusion, our doubts about features of our social life, such as political obligation in the liberal democratic state, are not merely symptoms of conceptual disorder. Doubts and

---

[52] And, as I have already argued, it causes difficulties for philosophers who suggest that it is. McPherson (p. 61) argues that 'part of what is involved in choosing the present British political system is precisely that one accepts that the rightful government ... has authority', But, as he had just mentioned, the question can be asked of why 'choose' the British system. Strictly speaking, McPherson could not raise this at all because it involves general questions about political obligation and about the criteria for evaluating different forms of political system.

questions about aspects of political life are doubts and questions about actual patterns of human interaction, about actual relationships between citizens and their political representatives and political institutions. They are not purely conceptual problems but have a crucial empirical dimension. Social actors can critically evaluate their own interactions, relations and institutions, which are not 'givens', independent of the activities, purposes, expectations and concepts of those actors, but are always open, in principle at least, to development and change.

The argument is a familiar one that there is no need to 'question the facts' of political relationships, merely the terminology, the 'value' terminology, in which those facts are expressed. This approach ignores the significant question of the relationship between those facts and the terminology used to express them and seeks to enclose the philosopher in a world of reified concepts. Taken together with the related claim that general questions about political obligation are meaningless one has, to adopt McPherson's polemical words, an argument that is 'far from harmless, either to theory or practice'.[53] In this paper I have begun to look at some of the effects on theory. The effect on practice is to endorse the political status quo, including a certain conception of politics itself, and to give intellectual backing to the tendency towards a fatalistic attitude on the part of the ordinary citizen in the face of his political institutions.

[53]McPherson, p. 85.

11 Justice as Reversibility[1]

Lawrence Kohlberg

In previous work I have outlined: (a) the extensive research facts concerning culturally universal stages of moral judgement, (b) the psychological theory of development which I believe best fits those facts, and (c) a metaethical view which attempts to bridge the gap between naturalistic and nonnaturalistic, moral theories.[2] The present paper elaborates a conception suggested in this previous work—the moral decision procedures employed at a highest stage of moral development.

In this essay I would like to sketch the general notion of such a decision procedure and discuss its relation to one particular version of moral reasoning at the highest stage—namely Rawls's conception of the original position.

For Rawls principles of justice represent an equilibrium among competing claims. Justice, however, represents equilibrium only under certain assumptions—in particular the assumption that each player is choosing in an 'original position' prior to the establishment of a society or a practice and under a 'veil of ignorance' so that no one knows his position in society, nor even his place in the distribution of natural talents or abilities. The 'veil of ignorance' represents a statement of the fundamental formal conditions of the moral point of view, the conditions of impartiality and universalizability. Impartiality means a judgement made without any bias based on knowing that the judge or one of his friends is one of the players being judged. Universalizability is exemplified in Kant's maxim of the categorical imperative,

---

[1] I would like to acknowledge Jim Fishkin's friendship, help and advice at many points in working on this paper. A number of discussions led to clarifying the relation of Rawls' theory to my own, which Jim dubbed 'Moral Musical Chairs'.

[2] See Lawrence Kohlberg 'From Is to Ought: How to Commit the Naturalistic Fallacy and Get Away With It in the Study of Moral Development', in T. Mischel, ed., *Cognitive Development and Epistemology* (New York: Academic Press, 1971) pp. 151–235 and the references there to related work.

'So act that the outcome of your conduct could be the universal will,' or 'act as you would want all human beings to act in a similar situation.'

Kant wanted the form of universalizability to generate actual substantive principles of justice for a society or principles of moral decisions in concrete dilemmas. Rawls's effort to combine impartiality and universalizability in the idea of the original position works better. The veil of ignorance exemplifies not only the formalist idea of universalizability, but the formalist idea of Hare and others that a moral judgment must be *reversible,* that we must be willing to live with our judgement or decision when we trade places with others in the situation being judged. This, of course, is the formal criterion implied by the Golden Rule, 'it's right if it's still right when you put yourself in the other's place.' In Rawls's theory, a possible principle of justice is *the fair* principle of justice if it is the one which would be chosen under the original position: if one would choose it if one did not know who one would be in the society or situation after the principle was used. In this sense the choice is reversible; we choose it in such a way that we can live with the choice afterward, whoever we are.

Reversibility is similarly embodied by the fair procedure for cutting a cake which Rawls offers as an example of pure procedural justice. Fair division results when one person cuts the cake and a second person distributes it. If the first person cuts the cake to advantage himself, he must anticipate that he may receive the disadvantaged portion from the distribution. This practice would lead to equal shares except where there is an inequality surplus, where it would lead to the difference principle.

We can clarify the idea of reversibility implied by Rawls's original position by citing the use of reversibility in defining choice in the Heinz dilemma. The dilemma is presented, with Stage-typical responses in Table 11.1, reproduced from the 1971 article.

In the 1971 article I cited a 'Stage 6' response to this dilemma. 'Philosopher 3' started by saying "I believe that one has a moral duty to save a life whenever possible and the legal duty not to steal is outweighed by the moral duty to save a life. One can often 'see' or intuit that one 'ought' to break a law in order to fulfill a moral duty.'

Table 11.1

In Europe, a woman was near death from a very bad disease, a special kind of cancer. There was one drug that the doctors thought might save her. It was a form of radium for which a druggist was charging ten times what the drug cost him to make. The sick woman's husband, Heinz, went to everyone he knew to borrow the money, but he could only get together about half of what it cost. He told the druggist that his wife was dying, and asked him to sell it cheaper or let him pay later. But the druggist said, "No, I discovered the drug and I'm going to make money from it." So Heinz got desperate and broke into the man's store to steal the drug for his wife.
Should the husband have done that? Why?

SIX STAGES IN CONCEPTIONS OF THE MORAL WORTH OF HUMAN LIFE

Stage 1: No differentiation between moral value of life and its physical or social-status value.

> *Tommy, age ten* (III. Why should the druggist give the drug to the dying woman when her husband couldn't pay for it?): "If someone important is in a plane and is allergic to heights and the stewardess won't give him medicine because she's only got enough for one and she's got a sick one, a friend, in back, they'd probably put the stewardess in a lady's jail because she didn't help the important one."

> (Is it better to save the life of one important person or a lot of unimportant people?): "All the people that aren't important because one man just has one house, maybe a lot of furniture, but a whole bunch of people have an awful lot of furniture and some of these poor people might have a lot of money and it doesn't look it."

Stage 2: The value of a human life is seen as instrumental to the satisfaction of the needs of its possessor or of other persons. Decision to save life is relative to, or to be made by, its possessor. (Differentiation of physical and interest value of life, differentiation of its value to self and to other.)

> *Tommy, age thirteen* (IV. Should the doctor "mercy kill" a fatally ill woman requesting death because of her pain?): "Maybe it would be good to put her out of her pain, she'd be better off that way. But the husband wouldn't want it, it's not like an animal. If a pet dies you can get along without it—it isn't something you really need. Well, you can get a new wife, but it's not really the same."

Jim, age thirteen (same question): 'If she requests it, it's really up to her. She is in such terrible pain, just the same as people are always putting animals out of their pain."

Stage 3: The value of a human life is based on the empathy and affection of family members and others toward its possessor. (The value of human life, as based on social sharing, community, and love is differentiated from the instrumental and hedonistic value of life applicable also to animals.)

> *Tommy, age sixteen* (same question): "It might be best for her, but her husband—it's a human life—not like an animal, it just doesn't have the same relationship that a human being does to a family. You can become attached to a dog, but nothing like a human you know."

Stage 4: Life is conceived as sacred in terms of its place in a categorical moral or religious order of rights and duties. (The value of human life, as a categorical member of a moral order, is differentiated from its value to specific other people in the family, etc. Value of life is still partly dependent upon serving the group, the state, God, however.)

> *Jim, age sixteen* (same question): "I don't know. In one way, it's murder, it's not a right or privilege of man to decide who shall live and who should die. God put life into everybody on earth and you're taking away something from that person that came directly from God, and you're destroying something that is very sacred, it's in a way part of God and it's almost destroying a part of God when you kill a person. There's something of God in Everyone."

Stage 5: Life is valued both in terms of its relation to community welfare and in terms of being a universal human right. (Obligation to respect the basic right to life is differentiated from generalized respect for the socio-moral order. The general value of the independent human life is a primary autonomous value not dependent upon other values.)

> *Jim, age twenty* (same question): "Given the ethics of the doctor who has taken on responsibility to save human life—from that point of view he probably shouldn't but there is another side, there are more and more people in the medical profession who are thinking it is a hardship on everyone, the person, the family, when you know they are going to die. When a person is kept alive by an artificial lung or kidney it's more like being a vegetable than being a human who is alive. If it's her own choice I think there are certain rights and privileges that go along with being a human being. I am a human being and

have certain desires for life and I think everybody else
does, too. You have a world of which you are the center,
and everybody else does, too, and in that sense we're all
equal."

Stage 6: Belief in the sacredness of human life as
representing a universal human value of respect for the
individual. (The moral value of a human being, as an object
of moral principle, is differentiated from a formal recognition
of his rights.)

Jim, age twenty-four (III. Should the husband steal the
drug to save his wife? How about for someone he just
knows?): "Yes. A human life takes precedence over any
other moral or legal value, whoever it is. A human life
has inherent value whether or not it is valued by a
particular individual."
(Why is that?): "The inherent worth of the individual
human being is the central value in a set of values where
the principles of justice and love are normative for all
human relationships."

As stated, the intuition that one ought to break a law
because of a moral duty to save a life is one shared by 'Stage 6'
Philosopher 3 with the two other philosophers cited in the
1971 paper as thinking at Stage 5. Philosopher 3, however,
goes on to use 'a moral theory of Stage 6' to justify his
intuition. He says 'If intuition is not clear or convincing and if
someone claims not to recognize a duty to save life whenever
possible, then one can only point out that he is failing to make
his decisions both reversible and universalizable, i.e. he is not
seeing the situation from the role of the person whose life is
being saved as well as the person who can save the life
(reversibility) or from the point of view of the possibility of
anyone filling these roles (universalizability).'
The idea of reversibility in the Heinz dilemma invoked by
Philosopher 3 may be clarified in this way. Philosopher 3 is
saying 'start with the Golden Rule, change places with the
wife in deciding. Is your denying a duty to save the woman's
life consistent with the Golden Rule?' The wife, we may say,
holds that her right to life is higher or prior to the druggist's
right to property. She claims that the husband has a duty to
steal to protect this right, since she cannot. The druggist
denies that the husband has a duty to steal the drug and
asserts he has a right to property equal to or greater than the

wife's right to life. Is the druggist's denial of the husband's duty to steal reversible? No, this denial could not stand if he exchanged places with the wife. In the position of the druggist, he holds his right to property higher than the wife's right to life. Presumably, however, if it were his life at stake, not the wife's the druggist would be rational enough to prefer his right to life over his property and would sacrifice his property. If the druggist tried to make his conception of rights and duties reversible by imaginatively changing places with the wife, he would give up the idea that the husband had a duty to respect his property rights and would see that the husband had a duty towards his wife's life. In contrast, the wife's claim that her husband has a duty to life and that her right to life is prior to the druggist's right to property is reversible.[3]

Another word for reversibility is 'ideal role-taking' or 'moral musical chairs'. Moral musical chairs means going around the circle of perspectives involved in a moral dilemma to test one's claims of right or duty until only the equilibrated or reversible claims survive. In 'non-moral' or competitive musical chairs there is only one 'winning person'. In moral chairs there is only one 'winning' chair which all other players recognize if they play the game, the chair of the person with the prior claim of justice.

It is clear that Rawls has embodied the idea of reversibility as well as universalizability in the idea of 'the original position' or the 'veil of ignorance', although he does not develop the idea of equilibrium implicit in the reversibility criterion since he is bent on developing an equilibrium to be found in a bargaining game conception of the social contract.

An intuitively more appealing statement of reversibility as equilibrium comes from the conception of ideal role-taking as 'moral musical chairs' just elaborated.

[3] Suppose the husband, or the wife or the druggist were to try to choose a relevant principle of justice from behind the veil of ignorance, not knowing who they were to be. They would choose the principle that there is a natural duty to life, or that a human's right to life comes before another human's right to property. Rawls assumes such a natural duty to life as implied by his original position, prior to any contracts about rights and duties in particular roles in any society.

(1) This reversibility process of reaching fairness through ideal role-taking involves:
(a) The decider is to successively put himself imaginatively in the place of each other actor and consider the claims each would make from his point of view.
(b) Where claims in one party's shoes conflict with those in another's, imagine each party to trade places. If so, a party should drop his conflicting claim if it is based on non-recognition of the other's point of view.

We shall claim that such a process of equilibrated and complete use of Golden Rule role-taking is equivalent in its implications to Rawls's idea of decision in the original position.[4] The second reversibility process for reaching fairness then is stated by Rawls:

(2) The decider is to initially decide from a point of view which ignores his identity (veil of ignorance) under the assumption that decisions are governed by maximizing values from a point of view of rational egoism in considering each party's interests (Rawls's original position).

In the first procedure, the decider is assumed to start with an altruistic empathic or 'loving' orientation, in the second case, the decider is assumed to start with an 'egoistic' orientation to maximizing his own values, cancelled out by the veil of ignorance. To indicate that the two approaches to reversibility lead to the same solution, let us consider the Heinz dilemma from the original position as we did from the process of ideal role-taking.

In the Heinz dilemma, let us imagine someone making the decision under the veil of ignorance, i.e., not knowing whether he is to be assigned the role of husband, wife or druggist. Clearly, the rational solution is to steal the drug; i.e., this leads to the least loss (or the most gain) to an individual who could be in any role. This corresponds to our intuition of the primacy of the woman's right to life over the druggist's right to property and makes it a duty to act in terms

---

[4] It is equivalent so long as the original position is interpreted so as to rule out 'gambling' on the principle of average utility. Rawls introduces several features which would determine the argument in favour of the general maximin notion (See especially pp. 150–60). It is this version of the original position which is equivalent, in its implications, to 'moral musical chairs'.

of those rights. If the situation is that the dying person is a friend or acquaintance, the same holds true. In the Heinz dilemma, a solution achieved under the veil of ignorance is equivalent to one obtained by ideal role-taking, or 'moral musical chairs', of an altruistic person in the husband's position asking the wife and druggist to trade places.

Having considered reversibility in Rawls' philosophic theory, we can now relate it to its central meaning in Piaget's theory. In Piaget's equilibrium theory, the fundamental formal condition of equilibrium in logic as well as morality is reversibility.

> A logical train of thought is one in which one can move back and forth between premises and conclusions without distortion. Mathematical thinking is an example; $A + B$ is the same as $B + A$. Or again, the operation $A + B = C$ is reversible by the operation $C - B = A$.

Piaget defines a stage of logic as a group of logical operations, i.e., as a group of reversible transformations of ideas, classes or numbers which maintain certain relations invariant. Moral reasoning or justice in Piaget's theory represents decisions which are not 'distorted' or changed as one shifts from one person's point of view or perspective to anothers'. As I said in the 1971 paper morality is the 'logic' for co-ordinating the points of view of subjects with conflicting interests, as logic is the co-ordination of points of view on objects or symbols of objects. An example of a moral operation giving reversibility is reciprocity. There is a parallel to morality in logic in the idea of a reciprocal relationship. If I have a brother, my brother has a brother—me. The relationship of brother to brother is reciprocal. Logical reciprocity or reversibility is necessary but not sufficient for moral reciprocity or reversibility. All children who have some moral idea of reciprocity, as given by the Stage 2 notion of the obligation to return a favour, have some idea of logical reciprocity; i.e. they answer correctly the question 'Does your brother have a brother.' The reverse is not the case, however. Children may pass the logical item but fail to show reversible reciprocity in moral thought.

Piaget and I hold that the core structure of stages of moral reasoning consists of the set of operations or ideas which define justice or fairness. The two principal justice operations are the operation of equality and of reciprocity, both of which have logical parallels. Justice is a matter of distribution, involving the operations of equality and reciprocity. Distribution is by equality (equity, distributive equality proportionate to circumstance and need) or it is by reciprocity (merit or desert, reward in return for effort, virtue, or talent). Each stage defines and uses these operations differently and each higher stage uses them in a more reversible or equilibrated way. Both Rawls's theory and the theories of Piaget and myself, then, are theories of 'reflective equilibrium'. Both identify justice with equilibration in valuing. Piaget's theory is explanatory or psychological; it explains (a) why justice is a compelling, obligatory 'natural' norm and (b) why concepts of justice change, moving to greater equilibrium. Rawls's theory is justificatory; it undertakes to prove that certain principles of justice held at our sixth (and important at our fifth) stage are the ones which would be chosen in a condition of complete reflective equilibrium, i.e. the ones which would be chosen in the original position. In that case, Rawls claims, they are the right or true principles of justice. Our psychological claim, parallel to Rawls' claim, is that something like his principles of justice are chosen by those at our Stage 6, and they are chosen because they are reversible, or more reversible, or in better equilibrium than justice principles used at previous stages.

In the Piagetian framework, the core of a social judgement is a structure of justice, a structure including operations of reciprocity and equality. Each higher stage redefines these operations in a more reversible way. The operation of reciprocity is closely related to reversibility, but reciprocity can be used or defined with varying degrees of reversibility. A low degree of reversibility characterizes early stages of reciprocity.

In the earlier paper I noted the Stage 1 idea of reciprocity, justice as talion. My young son thought if Eskimos killed and ate seals, it was right to kill and eat Eskimos. Such an early notion of reciprocity is not reversible in the sense it does not meet the criterion of the Golden Rule. While Eskimos may not be doing to others (seals) as they would be done by, clearly killing Eskimos is not doing to others as one would wish to be done by. My son interpreted reciprocity not as reversibility (doing as you would wish to be done by) but as exchange (doing back what is done to you). This is generally the case for children at our first two stages. We have systematically asked children who 'know' or can repeat the Golden Rule the question, 'If someone comes up on the street and hits you, what would the Golden Rule say to do?' Children at the first and second moral stage say 'Hit him back. Do unto others as they do unto you.'

In contrast to Stage 1 and 2 concrete reciprocity, Stage 3 equates reciprocity with reversibility, with the Golden Rule. The Golden Rule (a) implies ideal role-taking or reversing perspectives ('trading places', 'putting yourself in his shoes') not exchanging acts and (b) reversing perspectives in terms of the *ideal* ('what you would like in his place') not the real ('what you would do in his place').

The meaning of Golden Rule reversibility is well expressed by a ten-year-old subject at our third moral stage who replied:

> Well, it's like your brain has to leave your head and go into the other guy's head and then come back into your head but you still see it like it was in the other guy's head and then you decide that way.

This Golden Rule ideal role-taking as reversibility entails differentiating the self's perspective from the other's and co-ordinating the two so that the perspective from the other's view influences one's own perspective in a reciprocal fashion. At Stage 3, then, reversibility is reciprocity of perspectives, not of actions.

Let us now consider how the increased reversibility of moral stages from Stage 1 to Stage 3 leads to a more adequate valuing of human life in one moral dilemma. This increased reversibility of the valuing of life is illustrated by Tommy's response to life dilemmas, reported in Table 11.1.

At Stage 1, Tommy's thinking fails to pass the test of the Golden Rule reversibility even at the level of Stage 2 egoistic exchange. Whether to save the life of another person depends not only upon rigid rules (Don't steal, don't kill) but upon the wealth of the person to be saved. This is a failure to take the point of view of the dying person even at the level of egoism, in which the dying person would egoistically value his life regardless of its relation to furniture.

At Stage 2 Tommy's 'instrumental egoism and exchange view' of the value of a friend or a wife's life, ignoring rigid rules, does not pass the test of Golden Rule reversibility. In a dilemma involving euthanasia he has the doctor take the 'selfish' point of view of the husband, who cannot replace his wife, rather than the 'selfish' point of view of the wife, who would be better off out of her pain. He does not have either the doctor or the husband look at the situation from the wife's shoes.

At Stage 3, Tommy engages in ideal role-taking but the role-taking is not complete. There is a conflict between the wife's point of view and the husband's. According to Tommy, the husband does not want to allow mercy-killing because he loves his wife and will grieve for her. This lack of reversibility between the perspective of husband and wife leads us to feel Tommy's view of the husband's love is still 'selfish' or 'non-moral', the husband will let his wife suffer pain to avoid grief to himself. If the husband really loves his wife, we would say, he would put himself in her place, and then would want her death if that were what was best for her. We sense that a 'more loving' or 'more moral' attitude would lead to a solution to this dilemma. But we can only define a more moral solution in terms of fairness or reversibility. Why is the implied perspective of the husband in Tommy's response selfish? If the husband should consider the wife's pain, the wife (if she loves her husband) must also consider the husband's grief at her death. If the wife puts herself in the husband's place, the grief she anticipates about her own death is more than matched by the grief a husband should feel at her pain.

We are here applying to the mercy-killing dilemma the idea of reversibility as 'moral musical chairs' which earlier we said Philosopher 3 used in the Heinz dilemma and which we said would require the druggist to trade places with the wife and the wife with the druggist before making claims on the husband. In the mercy-killing dilemma, we also imagine the husband and wife trading places before making claims on the doctor. This Stage 6 process of ideal role-taking or 'moral musical chairs' is a 'second order' use of the Golden Rule. Before the doctor (in IV) or the husband (in III) are to base action on Golden Rule empathy with any one actor, they must imaginatively have that actor trade places with any other interested party in the situation. Intuitively, we feel that the 'second order' interpretation of the Golden Rule leads to a solution to the two dilemmas (if we allow the wife with cancer to be the best judge of her rights and interests.)[5]

If we interpret reversibility as Rawls's original position, we get the same solution for the mercy-killing dilemma as we get using 'moral musical chairs'. The doctor, not knowing who he would be, would choose the solution he could live with in the position of the least advantaged, the dying woman in pain.

A more difficult case yields the same results. This is the case of an individual drowning in the river. A passerby can save him, but at a 25% risk of death (and a 75% chance that both will be saved). Should the passerby jump in with a 25% chance both would drown? From the point of view of simple Golden Rule empathy, with the drowning person, the passerby should. But is such empathy fair or reasonable or is it ultimate sacrifice? To see, we ask, 'If the drowning person put himself in the bystander's shoes and returned to his own position, could he still make the claim?' Here moral musical chairs is clarified by a Rawls-type calculation. Stated in terms of the 'veil of ignorance' (if an individual did not know whether he was the bystander or the drowning person) the right decision is that of jumping in as long as the risk of death for jumping was definitely less than 50%. Egoistic maximization behind the veil of ignorance (or maximin) leads to the choice of jumping in if the actor does not know the probabilities of which party he will end up being, but does know the minimum probability of being alive is greater than 50% if the bystander jumps in, less than 50% if he does not.

We have enunciated a criterion of fairness as reversibility and have applied it to three dilemmas. In light of this criterion, the Stage 2, 3, and 4 solutions to the Heinz and mercy-killing dilemmas, reported in Table 11.1, are judged to be unbalanced.

[5] In other situations, like the Talmudic dilemma of two parties in the desert and only one having a water bottle with just enough water to save one, the 'second order' interpretation of the Golden Rule leaves one difficulty as the first order one does. The first order Golden Rule interpretation leaves each party passing the bottle back and forth to the others like Alphonse and Gaston. An equilibrium at the second order level requires something like a precedence or fairness principle under the veil of ignorance, e.g. drawing shares or recognizing ownership rights even in a life or death situation.

What about Stage 5? Stage 5 solutions in terms of human rights usually generate reversible solutions to the dilemmas (III steal the drug, IV permit mercy-killing, and save the drowning person). Stage 5 solutions in terms of rational act-utilitarianism (integrated with some concepts of rule-utilitarianism) also usually generate reversible solutions. For instance, the 'fair' solution to the river dilemma under the veil of ignorance is also the fair solution as utility, maximizing numbers of lives, each to count as one. Because the utilitarian maximization principle has built into it the justice principle, each life or person to count as one, it usually leads to reversible solutions. Rawls, however, stresses that in issues of justice dealing with the distribution of goods or income 'justice as aggregate utility' differs from his maximin notion (the difference principle) and that by the criterion of reversibility or of the original position justice as the difference principle should be preferred.

Table 11.2

THE CAPTAIN'S DILEMMA

In Korea, a company of ten marines was outnumbered and was retreating before the enemy. The company had crossed a bridge over a river, but the enemy were still on the other side. If someone went back to the bridge and blew it up, the company could then escape. However, the man who stayed back to blow up the bridge would not be able to escape alive. The captain asked for a volunteer, but no one offered to go. If no one went back it was virtually certain that all would die. The captain was the only person who could lead the retreat.

The captain finally decided that he had two alternatives. The first was to order the demolition man to stay behind. If this man was sent, the probability that the mission would be accomplished successfully was .8. The second alternative was to select someone to go by drawing a name out of a hat with everyone's name on it. If anyone other than the demolition man was selected the probability that the mission would be accomplished successfully was .7.

	Expert Goes	Draw straws
outcome for expert	00%	70%
outcome for anyone else	80%	70%

Which of the two alternatives should the captain choose and why?

*   *   *   *   *

Two Responses to the Captain's Dilemma

Philosopher 2 (Stage 5)

He should order the expert, and himself do his own job of captain in the hope of preserving the company. He should not draw lots because this would not yield as skilled and reliable a man. The expert has no right to refuse since he has undertaken to serve in the war and to be trained as a demolition man. The main consideration is: who is most likely to perform the job and preserve the most lives. The captain might consider, in addition, the factor that the death of one man with a family might be a greater loss than the death of another. An important consideration would be the effect on the other men. Whatever the captain's own views about justice, he would have to regard his men's views because an act thought by them as unjust would be harmful to morale.

Philosopher 3 (Stage 6)

The lottery. If you choose the expert you are denying him the same chance to pull through. I think that he would want to live as much as anyone else and would claim the same chance as everyone else. It would be nice to maximize the chances of saving lives but that should be secondary to the justice considerations at hand. Justice means treating the people in the situation as having the same intrinsic value or claim to life without distinctions that are utilitarian or are subjective on the part of the captain. The expert has an equal claim to life. He wants to preserve his life, he expects the others to have the same claim. He feels he ought to exert his own claim to the extent that it is no greater than anyone else's. He just doesn't want it subordinated to the others. Sending the expert is using the demolition man for other people's welfare, to maximize the probability of saving all lives. I think that utilitarianism, trying to maximize life so the most people should survive is a consideration that should be taken into account after the justice one.

In Table 11.2 we present a difficult dilemma pitting aggregate utility against the difference principle not in regard to income, but in regard to life. Philosopher 2, cited in the 1971 article as having a rule-utilitarian Stage 5 normative ethic opts for aggregate utility. Considering justice in the eyes of the other man is not a direct basis of choice, it is one utilitarian consequence with others to be weighed by the captain. In contrast Philosopher 3, classified as Stage 6 feels a utilitarian solution by the captain is not reversible, and opts for the lottery.

Let us clarify why we agree with Philosopher 3 that the lottery is better because it is the fair solution by the test of reversibility.

The dilemma (in either form) poses a choice by the captain between (a) ordering a man to his death by a utilitarian criterion which would maximize the probability of saving the remaining lives or (b) leaving the choice to a lottery. It presupposes a prior choice, that the captain should order someone to go, at gunpoint if necessary, rather than having everyone die. Such a choice assumes that the captain (or anyone else) has an obligation to preserve each person's life, and that the obligation to the rights of each to life are not exhausted by respecting any particular individual's wish not to be ordered. Whether the utilitarian or 'equal-chance' version of justice is accepted, justice would be taken to involve respecting the lives of each, counting each person as one. Because a person refuses to risk his life so that all may be saved does not mean his life can be treated as of greater value than the others. Why do we say this? Why not argue that respect for persons implies allowing all to go down. The right to life is not so different from the druggist's property rights in the Heinz dilemma, if we interpret rights in terms of moral musical chairs. We said the druggist's claim to property rights could only be upheld if he could be imagined to maintain them after trading places with the wife, or to maintain them choosing under a veil of ignorance as to his position, including ending in the least favoured position, the wife's. In the captain's dilemma, does the expert have a right to refuse to go, or at least to draw straws? He could not maintain the right to refuse if he were to change places with the others. If he did not know who he was in the situation, the old and weak man or the strong man, a rational man would still want someone to go.

Given that the captain should order someone to go, should he select the person who would maximize the probability of survival or should he use a lottery? We can secure an answer by asking 'Does the expert have the right to insist on a lottery? Could he insist on the claim if he were to consider the claim in the strong man's (or the captain's) shoes?' In making the claim, he is saying he has the right to a probability of living equal to the probability the other man has, even if this lowers the average probability for all.

He claims that this is implied by the assumption that he has a right to equal treatment of his life to that of others. This claim seems to hold up even if he trades places imaginatively with the captain or the strong man. In terms of the Rawlsian original position, we ask 'What would be chosen by the captain (or the strong man or the weak man) in an original position, with an equal probability of being the weak man or the strong man (or the captain)? If a lottery is used the expert's probability of living is 70%; if he is ordered, the probability of living is 0%. From the standpoint of the least advantaged position—the expert's—the lottery increases his life chances 70%.

How does the lottery affect the other positions? The other man's chances of life decrease only 10% by the use of the lottery, compared to the 70% decrease in life chances of the weak man if he is ordered to go, instead of using a lottery. Both the strong man and the weak man, then, choose the lottery in an original position. Alternatively stated, they would choose to apply the difference principle, stating that no inequalities in life chances are justified unless they are of benefit from the point of view of the least advantaged, here the weak man.

In this dilemma, then, justice as reversible role-taking agrees with utility in denying an absolutist concept of the right to life which would allow all to die in order to avoid coercion. It disagrees with utility in what it means to count each person's life as one. This cannot be arrived at by aggregating lives to find a solution, but requires taking the point of view of each individual claiming his right to life as equal to that of others.

This conclusion follows not only from Rawls's original position but also from the general notion of ideal role-taking I have named 'moral musical chairs'.

12 Relativism and Tolerance[1]

Geoffrey Harrison

I

In this essay I shall first set out a schema for moral systems. No originality is claimed for this structure, and while I believe that there are good reasons for accepting it I shall make little attempt to argue for it here. I shall describe it in order to discuss certain implications which are often held to follow from it.

The schema is concerned with the deductive justification of moral obligation judgements made on particular occasions. The paradigm case of such judgements would take the form 'A ought to do X' or 'X is the right course of action for A'. These two I take to be strictly equivalent. There are other forms which more or less approximate to this model, but for my purpose, and simplicity, they may be ignored. If such judgements, made on particular occasions about individual actions, are to be justified by a deductive argument, then that argument must contain another obligation judgement, presumably a universal, among its premises. If this second judgement is also to be justified, to be the conclusion of a valid argument, then one of its justifying premises must also be an obligation judgement, probably of a more general nature, and so on ad infinitum. Well, not quite ad infinitum. In practice all moral arguments, like all explanations, must stop somewhere. At some point our logical moralist will refuse to answer the question 'Why ought one to behave like this?' He will refuse since for him there is no answer. We have reached his ultimate moral principle. By definition no moral justification of this principle is possible. If A can justify P_1, then principle P_1 is not ultimate in the required sense and we must regard P_2, from which P_1 is derived, as being the ultimate for A. I can see nothing especially sinister in this. At the purely commonsense level it seems nonsensical to ask a utilitarian why we ought to maximize happiness or a believer why we ought to obey God's commands.

If these ultimate principles are to be justified at all, there are two possibilities. Either they are to be justified by

[1] Reprinted from *Ethics* 86, 2 (Jan. 1976): pp. 122–35.

274   *Geoffrey Harrison*

something beyond themselves or they are in some way self-justifying. And if they are justified by something 'beyond', then that something must be nonmoral, since moral justifications are ruled out by definition. I said in my opening paragraph that I was going to describe my metaethical position rather than argue for it, and now I am going to be what may be regarded as dogmatic in the extreme. I shall simply reject these alternatives out of hand. I would reject the self-justifying view since I would claim that any principle which was self-justifying must be analytic and that no analytic proposition could function as a substantive moral principle. I accept the well-known view that moral principles do not simply record our determination to use symbols in a certain fashion. Equally, I am not impressed with the chances of a nonmoral justification—the repeal of Hume's law. In recent years numerous attempts have been made to bridge the logical stream between 'is' and 'ought.' I cannot recall a would-be bridge builder who did not get his feet wet.

These possible forms of justification would appear to be exhaustive. If, as I think, none is acceptable, then ultimate principles have no justification. In this they may be contrasted with particular obligation judgements or the more specific rules which are classifiable as right or wrong in terms of some ultimate principle, or set of principles, and the system which it generates. The phrase 'some ultimate principle' brings us toward our central problem. Clearly there will be more than one possible candidate for the role of first principle. Indeed I see no reason to doubt that logically there could be an infinite number of candidates or at least as many as language could make meaningful.

Faced with the daunting prospect of this massive proliferation of principles and their attendant systems, moral philosophers will attempt to cut down the problem to manageable proportions by introducing criteria by which to decide what is acceptable as a moral system. It goes without saying that the assessment made at this point is a nonmoral one. While it is no part of this article to establish and defend any given set of criteria—a task which would occupy many conscientious moral philosophers for several decades—I shall present a specimen group by way of illustration.

1. As already mentioned, no ultimate moral principle shall be analytic, since such a principle could not yield substantive

moral judgements without the introduction of another, nonanalytic moral premise.

2. A moral system should be internally consistent. That is, it should be impossible to prove that, for example, A ought to do X and A ought not to do X by using the same system on the same occasion. This is likely to occur in those systems which have more than one ultimate principle.

3. The system should be applicable to all men, or with Kant, to all rational beings.

4. Given two rival moral systems, the one which is applicable to a greater area of human choice and action is to be preferred. If the purpose of having a moral system is to make it possible for us to take decisions on a consistent and rational basis, then the wider the field of application the better.

5. As moralities are for human purposes, it should be the case either that it is physically and psychologically possible for men to live up to their demands or, if an ideal is set up, that it would be possible for men to approach that ideal to a greater or lesser degree, and that any step toward it, however small, would be of value. It is in this last condition that the most severe pruning of logically possible systems would take place.

Let us suppose that a test like the above in spirit, if not in actual content, can be applied to any moral system anyone cares to propose. While many will fail, it is too much to hope that only one candidate will pass the test. Any system which does pass may be called a 'well-established moral system.' We may then find ourselves with a number of these well-established systems on our hands. Due to the ruling about psychological possibility, it is likely that these systems will have a great deal in common, for they will tend to recommend and prohibit the same sort of thing. But equally, despite the overlap, one could not reasonably expect that all well-established moral systems would turn out to be extensionally equivalent. There will almost certainly be times at which system A proves X to be obligatory and system B does the same for not-X and both A and B are well established.

The above is a metaethical schema of a possible world. I shall now make a claim that will strike some readers as wildly implausible. I shall claim that, allowing for the fact that it is schematic, it is not too distorted a reflection of the world that we have actually got. It is inaccurate in that no one could seriously believe that any individual ever had such clear-cut moral views logically deducible from one all-embracing first principle (plus some descriptive propositions), as I have suggested. Most moral perspectives are riddled with inconsistencies and irrelevancies. They have never been subject to critical examination. But if they were, and if the faults could be ironed out without totally destroying the agent's moral attitudes, then one of my well-established systems would emerge. In this way my picture bears a similar sort of relationship to reality as does Kant's idea of the Kingdom of Ends. It is inaccurate, too simple, but, I hope, illuminating. And it shares another prominent feature with the Kantian ideal. It pictures the moral scene as it would be if men were completely rational. But here the similarity ends. In the Kantian Kingdom all would be harmony. Men would all recognize the same Good and pursue it. My state, on the other hand, would always be on the verge of a moral civil war.

The methaethical theory I have described I will call 'relativism', and those who, like myself, accept it I will call 'relativists'. We can now discuss a moral attitude commonly believed to follow from the acceptance of relativism. Suppose A and B are disputing what action ought to be taken on a given occasion. Being both fair-minded and rational they listen attentively to each other's arguments and discover that their disagreement does not rest on any factual dispute and that neither has produced an invalid argument. Their dispute can be traced directly to differing moral premises and eventually to differing ultimate principles. They then nonmorally assess their respective systems on the basis of mutually accepted criteria. Both have well-established moral systems. *Ex hypothesi* all rational argument has come to an end. (I realize that there are those following R. M. Hare who will say that a compelling argument can still take place between those who have no moral principles in common. I am disinclined to accept this, but for those who do we have a dispute between what Hare would term 'fanatics'.) The alternatives are now to settle the dispute by some nonrational means—persuasive appeals à la Stevenson, threats, bribery, violence—or to agree to differ. For quite good reasons philosophers dislike nonrational solutions. Such settlements do not prove anything about what is right. They merely provide evidence that one party in the dispute is physically or psychologically or economically stronger than the other.

Given a relativist metaethic, must one then always agree to differ? It would seem so. No one, of course, would suggest that relativism entails, in a strict logical sense, that one should agree to differ. Such crude exceptions to Hume's law are not envisaged. But some would say that if you accept relativism, agreeing to differ is the only sensible and fair course. Sensible, since the alternative suggests a Hobbes-like state of moral nature, with moral interest taking over the role traditionally filled by self-interest. Fair, because neither side can conclusively prove his case, or refute the other, and he has no right to impose his own views. Looked at objectively, one moral system is as good as another.

If this argument does not seem sufficient to establish that the only rational course for a relativist is to agree to differ, it may be supported by a second—the argument from determining factors. One of the problems of relativism is to find an answer to the charge that the choice of one ultimate principle rather than another is necessarily an arbitrary one. The natural answer to the question 'Why do you accept A?' will be 'I prefer it to the others.' But at most this is a holding operation. If one is asked for the grounds of this preference, there can be no answer. So to the parody of relativism—'Heads I'll be a utilitarian, tails I'll be an egoist, and if it stands on its edge I'll be a Kantian.' To avoid the charge of the arbitrary and irrelevant choice, some relativists will defend themselves by virtually denying that we make any choice at all. The adoption of a moral system is the un-critical acceptance of standards already held by others. The moral stance we adopt is a function of our general personality and circumstances and, like our personality, is the result of certain causal factors. Certain characters will tend toward certain values and moral perspectives. While there are no reasons for choosing one system against another, there will be causes for our choosing the way we do. Some empirical evidence can be produced for this. In the case of moralities it is difficult, due to the problem of establishing just what morality a given person accepts, but in the allied cases of religion and politics where a man's allegiances are more clearly visible one can produce significant correlations between, say, occupation and voting habits or the faith of parents and the faith of their children. There seems no theoretical reason why this kind of investigation should not reveal something of interest in the moral field also. One could accept this type of explanation without being committed to a full-blooded determinism.

Thus we can no longer even afford the luxury of considering our moral opponents as willfully wicked. We are all in similar boats. They, like us, have been unable to make a rational choice between alternative moral systems. Those who do not realize this have been swept along by circumstances into the blind and uncritical acceptance of one morality as objectively correct. The relativists, who do realize this, so it is argued, have liberated themselves, but only at the price of being unable to take any moral decision seriously. In the face of this, agreeing to differ—tolerance of those who by one's own standards are morally wrong, a kind of moral passiveness—is the only answer. To insist on backing your own moral belief, ultimately unfounded, is to be insensitive, self-righteous, and arrogant.

These two arguments are in combination superficially quite persuasive. They are also, I think, quite mistaken.

I I

In the last section we looked at the moral dispute between two irreconcilable parties through the eyes of an outside observer, who was assumed to see more of the game. Let us now look at similar disputes through the eyes of one of those taking part.

Suppose that a man claims to believe that a state of affairs X would be undesirable in a nonmoral sense and that anyone who would allow X to occur when he could prevent it would be morally wrong. If this situation does arise for him and he fails to prevent X, what explanation could we give? Four answers would cover the possibilities. (1) When he claimed that anyone who allowed X would be morally wrong, he was not sincere. He is a hypocrite. He had some ulterior motive for making the claim. (2) Although he still disapproves of letting X take place, he was tempted by some attractive nonmoral reason not to interfere with the course of events. He feels guilty. There is a difficult question here about whether such a man is really to be regarded as being psychologically capable of preventing X or not. In that argument I take no sides here. Those who would label all such cases as 'psychological impossibility' can ignore this type of explanation. I shall call it 'weakness of will.' (3) Since he made the claim he has changed his mind. (4) He has a reasonable excuse. By that I mean, while he admits X is a bad thing, he believed that the only means of combating X successfully was via Y, and that would have been even worse. He opted for the lesser of the two evils. Although, other things being equal, to permit X would be morally wrong, it is justified in this instance.

As this concept of a 'reasonable excuse' will figure a good deal in what follows. I shall try here and now to deal with two possible objections to the above account.

1. Although this paper purports to be neutral between various moral systems, my description of a reasonable excuse reveals my act-utilitarian bias for all the world to see. It is only plausible if one assumes that on any occasion a man ought to produce as much nonmoral good as possible. In reply to this I will plead guilty to the charge of being pro-utilitarian but argue that this concept can be expressed in deontological nonutilitarian terms if anyone so desires. To borrow the terminology of W. D. Ross, the prevention of X may be regarded as a *prima facie* duty. If the agent has no other *prima facie* duties, then the prevention of X will be an absolute duty. If he has a *prima facie* duty to prevent Y also, if not-X plus not-Y is impossible, if his duty to prevent Y is more stringent than his duty to prevent X, and if he has no other *prima facie* duties apart from preventing X and Y, then it is his absolute duty to prevent Y. And he has a 'reasonable excuse' for not preventing X.

2. I have talked as though what was to count as a reasonable excuse was a fixed and objective feature of any situation. Subjectivists will point out that what one man considers to be acceptable another will not. From my own relativist standpoint I must see this. 'Who is to judge that an excuse is reasonable?' is the important question. Again I accept the basic charge and claim that the concept is convertible into subjectivist-relativist terms. An excuse in this sense is reasonable if it is acceptable in terms of the agent's own moral system. Here at least a man is his own judge.

Now we can apply this to tolerance. There are two necessary conditions for calling A's attitude 'tolerant.' (1) Another party, B, must behave in a manner which A sincerely regards as wrong, and A must be aware of this. (2) A must be capable of preventing or at least hindering B in this activity. To accept the inevitable may be realistic, but it is not tolerant. This second condition is perhaps oversimplified. We might talk of A only thinking that he could prevent B, or even of knowing that he could not but considering being critical after the event, and so on. However, as such refinements do not touch the central issues, I shall ignore them, concentrating only on the case where A could prevent B and knows it. In this situation, If A makes no effort to prevent B we might call him tolerant, or we might not. Why we might withold the judgement I hope to make clear later.

The class of tolerant actions then is a subspecies of the more general class of actions where one permits an event to occur which one could have prevented and which one regards as a bad thing. Earlier I listed four types of explanations of this class of action which I considered to be exhaustive. Of these the first three do not apply to tolerance. The tolerant man is not a hypocrite or weak willed, though some apparent cases of tolerance may disguise a genuine weakness of will, and he has not changed his mind. He must therefore have a reasonable excuse. What sort of excuse could this be? We may imagine this kind of situation. B is going to bring about X or let X happen. A regards X as nonmorally undesirable and B's behaviour in allowing X or in actively pursuing it as morally wrong. If X were a natural event not connected with any other person, A would not hesitate to prevent it. And yet because B, who regards the bringing about of X as either obligatory or at least permissible, is the instigator of X, A allows X. Why? Setting out A's attitudes, we have this picture. A thinks that, other things being equal, there is a possible state of affairs, Y, which is better than X. But other things are not equal since A knows that B approves of X rather than Y. If A has a reasonable excuse for letting X occur, he must say this: (1) X is worse than Y, but (2) X plus B's approval is better than Y plus B's disapproval. The new factor, B's attitude, is enough to tip the scales in favour of X. Let it be.

I have already conceded that what is to count as a reasonable excuse will vary from person to person, but the above presents some special problems which should be taken into account.

1. Above the level of what to have for lunch, almost all our

actions, choices, and decisions will be disliked or disapproved of by someone. If we were to accept the rule 'No action without unanimous approval' we would never do anything. And many others would disaprove of that.

2. It is B's favourable attitude to X which makes A decide to allow X to occur. But what about his own unfavourable attitude? That must be weighed in the balance also. What he now says is: (1) X is worse than Y, but (2) X plus B's favourable attitude plus my unfavourable attitude is better than Y plus B's unfavourable attitude plus my favourable attitude. From this it follows that he finds B's attitude as being of more importance than his own. On occasion this might indeed be a correct interpretation of A's thoughts. But one must notice what it implies. It implies that at least on this occasion A thinks B is more knowledgeable or sensitive or morally aware than he, A, is. He thinks the odds are that B is actually right. But if so, this is not at all an example of tolerance. It is not for A to 'tolerate' B's 'immorality.' At the very least he has agreed to suspend his judgement on B, at the most to be converted.

3. We have talked about A giving way to B in these circumstances. We could equally have talked of B allowing A to overrule him. If the argument in favour of tolerance works for one it should work for the other. They should both try to allow the other to do what they consider to be wrong. One is reminded of two men ushering each other through a doorway. Neither can be so impolite as to go through first. They both starve to death. It is impossible for all to be morally self-effacing all the time.

It will be claimed with some justice that in the above I have produced a travesty of of our normal concept of tolerance. I have rather oversimplified the position and consequently distorted it. That is neither how the world is nor how it ought to be. The root cause of the trouble is this. I have naively assumed that the moral community is a collection of individuals desperately struggling against one another to ensure that their own views prevail—a moral free-for-all with no rules governing members' behaviour. Fortunately, in practice this is not so. A society will have a complex system of rules, rights, and obligations laying down not what ought to be done in a given circumstance but who has the legal/moral right to decide what ought to be done. These rules I shall call 'decision-assigning rules,' or 'DA rules' for short. In common coin our unofficial acceptance of some tacit and ill-defined network of DA rules is manifested in the concept of 'minding your own business.' Without the network of DA rules, that concept could have no meaning. That we also often agree on the content of particular DA rules is witnessed by normal reactions to reading Mill's *On Liberty*. There may be criticism of the soundness of Mill's arguments or the vagueness of his formulation, but his fundamental point that in certain areas a man has a right to make his own mistakes is disputed by no one.

If one accepts DA rules one may regard them as separate from and logically prior to other moral rules. That is, the first question in any moral situation would be 'Who has the right to make the choice here?' Only if the answer is 'I' or perhaps 'I among others' does the central moral question 'What ought I to do?' arise at all. The recognition of this logical priority of DA rules would be sufficient to extricate tolerant A from the difficulty in which we left him. He does not need to resort to the incredible excuse of claiming that B's moral beliefs are somehow more important than his own. He simply says B has the right to make this particular choice, and while he, A, totally deplores it he is obliged not to intervene. Tolerance is the acceptance of a DA procedure and of the unpalatable but inevitable truth that others are going to make decisions which we may regard as foolish, disgusting, or wicked, and that we have no right to stop them. It may be added that this leaves relativism still in a strong position. Within the moral community there may be many different perspectives but behind them considerable agreement on the content of the DA rules.

Despite a certain attraction, I find this analysis too neat and tidy to be true. I would now like to introduce a concrete instance of a clash of two moralities which I hope will clarify the part played by DA rules. The case is becoming something of a cliché, but I am unrepentant since I find it so illuminating. Smith is a doctor, and Jones is a Jehovah's Witness. Jones's daughter is badly injured in a car accident, and it is Smith's considered medical opinion that without a blood transfusion she will die. Jones, however, has convictions which prohibit blood transfusions, and Smith is well aware of this. We shall assume that both Smith and Jones can argue their case from well-established moral systems differing in their ultimate moral principles. Smith has time to order and complete the transfusion before Jones arrives. Should he do so?

If my first simplified analysis of moral disputes had been correct, it would be hard to see what excuse Smith could have for holding back. His own moral attitude is at least as well founded as that of Jones, and that there exists a man, Jones, who does not approve of transfusions and who stands in no special moral relation to the girl (without DA rules there are no special relations) cannot be a reason for not saving her life. To withdraw in such circumstances would show a deplorable lack of moral self-confidence.

But we have already rejected the first simplified account. If we apply a DA rule to this situation the scene will change considerably. Smith can say he is not using the excuse 'On balance the girl's death and Jones's approval is better than the girl alive and Jones's disapproval.' He has asked the question in the right order. First, 'Who is to make the decision?' He accepts the DA rule that below a certain age all the major decisions for children are made by their parents or legally appointed guardians. This is a major decision; Jones is the girl's father and therefore stands in a morally special relation to her. So he is to make the choice. For Smith the question 'Should I give this girl a blood transfusion?' does not even arise. It is not that he has been tried and found not guilty. On the contrary, there was never any charge to answer.

The most appropriate among the possible polite replies to this defence would come naturally from a Sartrean as being *mauvaise foi*. The doctor is surely ducking the issue. The *de facto* decision about the transfusion was his, and given that he takes seriously his responsibility to save life, he cannot claim that this was none of his business. If we look at Smith's case again I think we may find that his excuse rests on two implausible assumptions (1) Too much weight is being put on the DA procedure. There is an assumption that for every choice which has to be made there is either one person uniquely fitted by the DA procedure to make it or, if this is not so, there is some agreed means of allocating the right to choose to a group of people, for example, a vote of all present. It is possible that one might design a moral system in which this were so, but it is unlikely that such a system would gain wide acceptance. In this case there is some argument that the father is uniquely fitted to make a decision about his daughter's life. As presented it is a relatively simple situation. Suppose we add a complication. Mrs. Jones, improbably perhaps, is not a Witness and is convinced that her child should have a transfusion. Who is now to say which parent stands in the more important moral relation to the girl? Again, one could devise a system where the father always has the right to decide, but in most circumstances to opt for either parent against the other seems purely arbitrary. Nor can other means of settling disputes like this be easily envisaged. The usual means do not work. They cannot take a vote, as it would be an even split; they cannot call on a third party, since no third party would be acceptable to both; and in so serious a matter they cannot draw lots. Nor can they agree to differ, since one must get his or her way.

Smith may deny that he believes there is one unambiguous rational answer to all DA questions but still hold that in some cases, including this one, there will be a generally acceptable verdict. He survives the first objection, but it is more difficult to see how he can resist the second. (2) This objection is to an assumption already mentioned. This is the assumption that the question 'What ought I to do?' is separate from the question 'Who is to make the decision?' and that the latter is logically prior to the former. This assumption is quite mistaken and rests on the belief that 'It is Jones who makes the decision in this case' is a statement of fact like 'It is Jones who is the father of this child.' But it is not. It is in itself a moral position like 'This parent has a right to educate his child as he sees fit.' Once we see that, we also see that 'Who is to make the decision?' is not separate from 'What ought I to do?' but part of it. It is as if Dr. Smith is asking himself, 'I have the power and the opportunity to make this decision myself; ought I to allow it to pass to someone else?' This is why Smith cannot claim that the child's death would not be his responsibility. He is responsible for holding two moral rules to be binding. (*a*) Parents have the right to make decisions which concern their children. (*b*) Doctors have the duty to save the lives of their patients. To have a reasonable excuse Smith has to be able to explain to himself why on this occasion he allowed the former to override the latter. Whether he can satisfy his conscience will depend on the circumstances and on his own moral system.

III

So far we have two arguments with opposed conclusions. In Part I it was claimed that anyone who took a relativist view of morality would be committed to tolerance as the one virtue he must accept. In Part II I argued that tolerance had no special place among the virtues, whether or not one was a relativist, and indeed that it raised some awkward conceptual problems of its own. As the latter argument represents the position I actually wish to adopt, I shall have to attempt to expose the weakness of the former.

Before confronting this problem directly, let us fill in some of the relevant background. In any activity it is always logically possible to separate the participants in that pursuit from the observers of it. Or since they may be the same person at different times, it is always possible to separate the role of observer from the role of particpant. We can differentiate between doing your job and talking about it, between living your life and writing your memoirs. The feature of the participant is that he acts, talks, and thinks within the conventions of that activity, while the observer is essentially playing by rules which are external to the behaviour observed. This is as true of morality as anything else. The participants in this case are the moral agents, making decisions, adopting attitudes, following principles, and so on. But it should be noted that we can also include a second group—the moral critics, propagandists, preachers, etc.—in the class of participants. This may seem odd in that moral criticism, for example, is clearly a second-order activity, dependent on the first-order activity of moral and immoral behaviour. Therefore the critic looks like an observer rather than a participant. However, the critic when he denounces or the preacher when he exhorts is still acting within the conventions of morality, and therefore, within the meaning of the act, they are participants. To get the genuine observer role, we need to introduce the psychologist or anthropologist or, in some circumstances, the moral philosopher. I hesitate over the last case in that while what is commonly called 'metaethics' would certainly count as external-observer country, I am inclined to think that normative ethics is a form of participation.

Applying this to the argument from relativism to tolerance, I arrive at the following conclusion. Relativism is a metaethical theory, and its truth or falsity is a question for an outside observer. Advocating tolerance or being tolerant are activities which are internal to particular moral systems— the activities of participants. There is nothing that the relativist, qua relativist, can say either for or against tolerance from a moral point of view. The moment he does this he ceases to be an observer of morality and becomes a user of a moral system. And on a relativist analysis of morality, this is exactly what one would expect. If tolerance is to be defended, or, come to that, attacked, it may be from a Christian or Kantian or utilitarian point of view, but it must be from *some* point of view. There is no such thing as a moral judgement made from a morally neutral or 'extramoral' position. One may, of course, conceive of morally noncontroversial judgements agreed on by all parties, but that is a different thing altogether.

Much of what is wrong with the first argument can be traced back to the view which I previously expressed in the highly ambiguous remark that 'looked at objectively, one moral system is as good as another.' As this essentially confused idea is often popularly regarded as the central tenet of relativism, it is necessary to unpack the proposition here and now. The key phrase in the ambiguity is 'as good as,' which can be taken in either a moral or a nonmoral sense. In the nonmoral sense it is a conclusion which it is quite in order for a relativist to reach, although it is, as a matter of fact, an unlikely one. What he would mean is that, for example, all moral systems were equally consistent and coherent or that all were equally incapable of being deduced from factual premises. While this is legitimate enough, it seems far removed from any argument for tolerance. For example, how do we get from (1) 'B's moral system is equally as consistent and coherent as A's moral system' to (2) 'A has no right to prevent B doing anything which accords with B's own moral system'? (1) certainly does not entail (2). To do that, we must combine it with the premise (3), 'No one has the right to prevent another person from acting in accord with that person's own moral system, where that system is as logically consistent and coherent as his own.' One can always adopt any moral principle if one chooses, but I find it difficult to see what reason anyone could have for adopting that one. Apart from (1) entailing (2), what other relation could there be between them? Some might see (1) as a reason for (2) without bringing in strict entailment, but 'being a reason for' is such a cloudy notion that it would be an unilluminating reply unless spelled out in some detail. And even then it would require the acceptance of some belief similar to (3).

If we put a moral interpretation on 'as good as,' then we would have a reason for being tolerant. For if morality A is as good from a moral point of view as morality B, then there could be no moral reason for preferring either A or B and hence no reason for preventing anyone from acting in accord with either A or B. But we cannot put such an interpretation on 'as good as.' If we do, it becomes a moral judgement, and as I have already noted, no relativist, being an outside observer, can make a moral judgement. Once he does so he becomes a participant, making his judgement from a particular moral standpoint. And what we may further notice is that this is one moral judgement with no participant could ever actually make. It is true that we could understand a man who said, 'All moralities apart from mine are equally good' (this is perhaps more correctly interpreted as 'equally *bad*'). But if he said, 'All moralities including mine are equally good,' we should be at a loss. Could, for example, a Christian who admitted that other religious/moral positions were just as good as Christianity still be regarded as a Christian? I think not, in that adopting a morality will necessarily involve rejecting at least some aspects of any rival doctrine which is not compatible with one's own. One variant on the moral interpretation might be thought to be this. For the relativist's purposes, all moral systems can be treated *as if* they were morally equal. This does not mean that they have all been tested against some moral standard and come out with equal scores, but that no such test is relevant. For the purposes of the Inland Revenue, all men are of equal height. However, while this does fairly represent what a relativist wants to say it does not solve the problem, since it is really only the negative version of the view that 'as good as' must be regarded nonmorally, and it reintroduces the difficulties involved in that interpretation. You cannot get from 'All moralities may be *treated* as morally equal' to any proposition about appropriate levels of tolerance.

Given that morality can be viewed in these two ways, internally and externally, someone might raise the question 'Which is the correct standpoint?' And this might be something of a rhetorical question, carrying with it the suggestion of an obvious reply that, as the outside observer is both impartial and more aware of alternatives, he is the better judge. But anyone who raises this question, whether rhetorically or not, has missed the whole point of the distinction. To ask which is the better position would be like asking which is the better means of transport—a bicycle or an ocean liner. Well, it all depends on where you want to go. The two standpoints do not represent rival positions. If you want to answer moral questions or solve moral problems, then you must be a participant. If you want to answer nonmoral questions or solve nonmoral problems about morality, then you must be an outside observer. The two do not overlàp. Only two closely related points of asymmetry may be noted. First, the observer role is logically dependent on the participant role. That is, there can be particpants without observers but not observers without participants. Second, while one cannot avoid being a participant—everyone who lives in a society and is sane has some moral point of view—one can easily avoid being an observer. No one is compelled to be a moral philosopher.

Before we leave this point, there is one final objection to my view which deserves a reply. A critic may accept the distinction between acting within morality and studying it from without but still raise the question 'May not the discoveries made as an observer dictate or modify the decisions taken as a participant?' Or more specifically, 'Why should an acceptance of relativism as a true account of moral reasoning not lead to the acceptance of tolerance as a virtue?' This could possibly be regarded as a factual question, for example, 'Do relativists tend to be more liberal or more tolerant than non-relativists?' I must confess that I do not know the answer to that, but it is clearly a question for the psychologists rather than the philosophers. From the philosophical point of view, the question would be 'Is a belief in relativism a reason for being tolerant?' If this is the question, then I claim to to have already answered it.

IV

In order to clear some possible misunderstandings from the scene, I shall close with three explanatory notes.

1. Despite the contrary appearance of much that has gone before in this paper, I am not in general against tolerance but, rather, in favour of it. All I hoped to show is that it has no necessary connection with relativism. If I were defending tolerance I would do so from a utilitarian point of view, as Mill did in *On Liberty*. While I do not regard Mill's actual arguments as too impressive, his general strategy is quite correct. The real problem in explaining the link between utility and tolerance is that if you hold a moral theory which advocates treating each case on its merits there is a difficulty about laying down general reasons for any style of behaviour. Bearing that in mind, I offer the following considerations as points in favour of tolerance.

(a) The utilitarian wishes to promote happiness. As people are happier if they can do what they want without outside interference, there is a *prima facie* utilitarian presumption in favour of tolerance. The onus of proof is always on those who wish to intervene.

(b) Many cases are too trivial to warrant intervention. For example, although we may be able to modify someone's behaviour for what we consider the better, this benefit may well be outweighed by the ill will our interference would engender. This is a case of the cure being worse than the disease.

(c) Many cases will involve (typical utilitarian problem) doubt about the facts. This may occur in two quite distinct ways. We may believe that our solution to a problem is better than another person's and that we could stop him acting in the wrong way but, due to lack of evidence, feel that we are not really entitled to force our answer on him. He may, conceivably, be right. This must be one of the more common reasons for tolerance. The alternative way in which the facts might give us pause would be the case where, although we have enough evidence to convince us we are right, we are not sure that we have the means to alter the other party's behaviour—a case of some frustration.

(d) The last class of cases is the most interesting and the

most difficult. I am thinking of cases of reciprocal arrangements. The utilitarian permits nonutilitarian behaviour
which he could prevent on the assumption that non-
utilitarians will acord him a similar right to follow his own
beliefs. This is the basis for any 'decision-assigning
procedure,' and the case of the doctor and the Jehovah's
Witness proves how difficult this may be in practice.

2. I have talked as though all cases of tolerance were cases of
allowing X to happen although one disapproved of X and
could prevent it. Some people may feel this is a somewhat
restricted usage and include in the term a rather different sort
of picture. An individual might be properly called 'tolerant'
not if he believed that many of the acts of his neighbours were
wrong but refused to interfere, but rather if he realized that
others had different ideals from his but that these ideals were
not necessarily wrong. In other words, he thinks many
different views of life are equally good. I would really prefer
to call such a person broad-minded, but I am not really
interested in a dispute over correct English usage. All I would
point out is that this type of tolerance has little to do with this
paper.

3. I said earlier that not all cases of allowing something to
happen where one disapproved of it and could prevent it
would typically be called tolerant. The reason for this is that
in common parlance 'tolerance' is a partially evaluative term
with a favourable meaning. Just as we would not usually
apply 'courage' to a criminal act of daring, or 'freedom' to a
situation where everyone followed his immediate desires, we
should not be happy about describing behaviour of which we
disapprove as 'tolerant.' For instance, the policies of the
British and French governments toward Nazi Germany
before 1939 were not 'tolerant' but 'appeasing.' However, I
have tried in this essay to use 'tolerance' in a more neutral and
perhaps technical sense in which it does only mean 'allowing
to happen what you believe to be wrong' without any
favourable or unfavourable overtones.

13 The Problematic Rationality of Political Participation[1]

Stanley I Benn

'... *Do you really believe that the ballot will become the law of the land any sooner because you incur this danger and inconvenience?*'

'*Look here, Mr. Finn; I don't believe the sea will become any fuller because the Piddle runs into it out of the Dorsetshire fields; but I do believe that the waters from all the countries is what makes the ocean. I shall help; and it's my duty to help*'.

'*It's your duty as a respectable citizen, with a wife and family, to stay at home*'.

'*If everybody with a wife and family was to say so, there'd be none there but roughs, and then where should we be?... If every man with a wife and family was to show hisself in the streets to-night, we should have the ballot before Parliament breaks up, and if none of 'em don't do it, we shall never have the ballot. If that's so, a man's duty's clear enough. He ought to go, though he'd two wives and families*'. And he went.

A. TROLLOPE, *Phineas Finn.*

[1] An earlier version of this paper was presented as the lead paper in a symposium, to which Richard Wollheim, Alan Ryan and Brian Barry contributed prepared comments, presented to the Fifth Bristol Conference on Philosophy 1975—'Reason in Politics'—sponsored by the Society of Critical Philosophy, at the University of Bristol. The whole symposium, with additional comments contributed by Martin Hollis and Carole Pateman and a Rejoinder by the present author, has now been published as: Stanley Benn and others: *Political Participation*, Australian National University Press, Canberra, 1978. The author and editors thank the A.N.U. Press for permission to reprint this paper in the present collection.

I

Philosophers and political theorists from Aristotle and Rousseau to J. S. Mill have taught us to believe that a person attains his full stature as a rational, responsible moral being through political participation, and that not to have an active interest in politics is not merely to fall short of one's duty as a citizen but to show oneself defective as a free man or woman. Democratic theorists in particular have given us to believe that a democracy can function—or function well—only if a substantial part of its electorate exercises the right to vote, and maintains a political vigilance that expresses itself, for instance, in party activism, telegrams to ministers, and letters to the newspapers; moreover, this is the way people would behave who valued reason above authority, and put public before private interest.

All this has been put in doubt, however, by the discovery, by certain moral philosophers on the one hand, and certain political theorists on the other, that where goals are at stake that require the participation of large numbers of people, any given individual's participation is going to make no perceptible difference to the outcome. Indeed, in matters to be decided by a majority of a mass electorate, where the difference between total success and total failure depends on whether a critical threshold (for instance, 50% of valid votes cast) is crossed, to vote is almost always a waste of time, energy, and resources.[2] Anyone would have a better chance of making positive gains in utility by pursuing some private end, where his action *would* make a difference. Consequently, for anyone to participate in mass political action will generally be irrational. Whatever other people may do, his own performance, so far from yielding the best result possible, generally yields no result at all. And though, if everyone argued like that, the system he wants to see preserved would break down, that is no reason for any particular person's participating: if no one else participated, nothing *he* did would save the system; if, however, the number of people participating was

[2] See David Lyons, *Forms and Limits of Utilitarianism,* Oxford, 1965, for a discussion of threshold problems, including voting, and the ways in which utilitarians have tried to cope with them.

enough to have a chance of keeping it going, to add his mite to so many would still make no perceptible difference.

This is clearly an awkward conclusion for democrats, especially for those who place high value on both rationality and participation. The claim is often made for democracy that, being government by discussion, in which criticism is encouraged and consensus sought by reasoned argument, it is a more rational form of government than any other. Democratic theory would be seriously weakened, should it turn out that democracy would work only if a large number of people exerted themselves to form rational beliefs about politics, and to act on them, while for almost anyone to do so who hadn't the special motivation of, say, a member of parliament, would be an irrational waste of effort.

Providing one recognizes a distinction between epistemic and practical rationality, there is nothing logically incoherent in the notion of irrationally striving to form rational beliefs.[3] A person's beliefs are held with *epistemic* rationality if, unlike superstitions, they are held for reasons satisfying the relevant criteria for forming true beliefs. An action is *practically* rational if, given whatever beliefs the agent has, it is done for reasons that relate to optimising in terms of his ends or values. For a utilitarian, acting with practical rationality amounts to acting to maximise utility; so, unless one happened to get satisfaction from holding true beliefs, striving to form rational beliefs in politics would be practically irrational if the actions based on them made no perceptible difference to outcomes.

Much depends, of course, on the considerations for rational acting that are postulated in the theory. My starting point in this essay is a form of democratic theory that employs the standard decision theory rationality models found in microeconomics and game theory. It is a model also accepted by most act-utilitarians and some rule-utilitarians. I argue that the dilemma of participatory theory arises only if one accepts the consequentialist presuppositions of the model, i.e. that the rationality of an action depends on its

---

[3] For discussion of this distinction, and of the different distinction between rational beliefs and rational action, see the Introduction, and Chapters 1, 4, and 7 of S. I. Benn and G. W. Mortimore (eds.), *Rationality and the Social Sciences,* London, 1976.

appropriateness as a means to some valued outcome or end-state, which it is selected to bring about. In my view, this is a special case of a more general consideration for rationality in action. My thesis is that action is rational if it manifests attitudes, values, or principles that it would be inconsistent in a person, under appropriate conditions, not to give expression to, given the character that he is generally content to acknowledge as his own. Selecting a course of action that can reasonably be expected to produce a valued outcome is one way of being consistent in action. This is expressed in the maxim that 'to will the end is to will the means'. I claim, however, that there are other ways, too, of being consistent which in mass politics may be more important than this one.

In the course of arguing this case I shall sketch a schema for the analysis of preference-structures that takes account of the fact that someone may act not only in accordance with his personal preferences but also in accordance with preferences appropriate to his roles, and with the kind of person he takes himself to be, and that consistency has a good deal to do with the ranking of such preference-rankings. A merit of my theory is, I suggest, that the forms of argument deriving from it will embrace rational explanations and justifications not only for participatory acts, but, under different conditions, for abstentions too. A significant, if subsidiary, advantage of the theory is that it can find a place in a framework of rational action, for some wholly ineffectual but heroic acts of martyrdom and self-sacrifice, which may be undertaken with the kind of sober consideration that belies any description of them as non-rational or irrational. At the same time, it leaves open the possibility that other self-sacrificial acts may be irrational. It is important, as I argue later, that explanatory and justificatory schemata do not become so all-embracing that nothing could conceivably be left out.

II

Anthony Downs has developed a theory of democratic politics based on the postulates 'that democratic governments act rationally to maximize political support',[4] and that since

[4] *An Economic Theory of Democracy*, New York, 1957, p. 20.

voters act rationally too, they will give their governments support under specified conditions. This is a strong explanatory hypothesis: Downs claims for the theory that it yields determinate predictions, is falsifiable, but is in fact generally though not completely corroborated by the facts; and in so far as it is not corroborated, it raises useful questions about the area of irrationality in political behaviour. The concept of rational action employed includes not merely the formal requirements usual in theories of rational choice subject to constraint, viz.: the disposition to optimise according to a preference ordering of available options that is transitive and connected; it includes certain substantive requirements. These can best be explained by distinguishing several conditions for rationality that Downs builds into the theory, not all of which are clearly differentiated by Downs himself, and some of which may turn out, on occasion, to preclude others.

There is, in the first place, what Downs calls 'personal rationality'—the rationality of the optimiser (or utility-maximiser) in terms of any set of ends that would count for him as being to his advantage (benefiting him, or as in his interests). If it is difficult to formulate this restriction it is because, though such rationality is termed 'selfish', these ends may yet be other-regarding, even altruistic, provided that achieving them would represent, in the agent's opinion, an increase in his 'utility-income'. So personally rational action could be of advantage not directly to oneself, but, say, to one's children, provided one cared about them enough to make their well-being one's objective.

Secondly, an action would be 'politically rational' if it were 'efficiently designed to achieve the consciously selected political or economic ends of the actor'.[5] Action can be personally rational but politically irrational if it employs political means for non-political ends, such as voting Tory to placate one's Tory wife. Because 'ends' is understood strictly consequentially, politically rational action is always understood in terms of outcomes altogether distinguishable from the act itself. One votes rationally if one votes not for parties, persons, or principles as such, but in the way most likely to promote the adoption of policies favouring one's interests. This might require voting for a party one liked less if the

[5] Ibid., p. 20.

party whose policies one liked more had no chance of being returned to power or of influencing policies implemented later on.

Political rationality can be manifested in different ways according to one's political role (or roles) within the system. So the conditions for rational action for voters and party leaders will be correspondingly different. I shall call this notion 'role-rationality'[6]—acting in ways calculated to produce the kind of outcomes for the agent that might be regarded as standard benefits for someone occupying that role in the particular game. So a chess-player would exhibit role-rationality in sacrificing a piece in order to capture his opponent's queen, but not because he wanted a favour from him outside the game. This is a gloss on Downs, but not, I think, inconsistent with his general approach.

Downs's theory of democratic government depends crucially on voters' acting with political rationality—voting to maximise the benefits they expect from the policies governments adopt. But it depends equally on another implied condition of voters' role-rationality, that they act so as to play their part in selecting a government efficiently. I call this *functional* rationality, since it makes it a condition for rational action in a given role, that the act shall contribute in the appropriate way to the maintenance of the system as a going concern. Again, this is exegetical gloss; Downs doesn't put it quite in this way.

Downs wants to show that a democratic system works because:

> (1) people in general act with personal rationality;
> (2) in political situations, personal rationality is manifested as political rationality;
> (3) seeking to act with political rationality in their respective roles, people will exhibit role-rationality;
> (4) in exhibiting role-rationality, people will do what is necessary for the continuing operation of the system, i.e. they will exhibit functional rationality.

Unfortunately, as Downs himself recognises, there is a dangerous weakness in this structure. If personal rationality requires that people act to maximise their utility-income, or

---

[6] I borrow this term from N. Frohlich, J. A. Oppenheimer, and O. R. Young, *Political Leadership and Collective Goods,* Princeton, 1971, p. 29. Downs does not use it.

more precisely their expected utility, a rational elector will perceive that the chance of his own vote making a crucial difference to the policies adopted, and so to his utility-income, is so small that voting would rarely be worth the effort. *A fortiori* it would be practically irrational for him to take much trouble to inform himself on the issues of the election, canvass for the parties, and so on. Downs is content with the conclusion that the level of political activism in a democracy would be generally low, for that accords with practical experience, and the theory is designed in part to account for this, and explain the system's continuous operation in spite of it. But if voting itself turns out to be an irrational act, the theory has clearly gone much too far, for a democracy of rational choosers could then never survive. So Downs has a supplementary hypothesis to supply the motivation that the model seems to lack: living in a democracy being itself part of the utility-income of many voters, they will recognise this as an additional benefit, outweighing the short-term cost of voting, and making the effort worthwhile after all.

Downs's saving hypothesis will not do, at least in this rather crude form.[7] For the abstentianist consequences follow not from any sefishness, whether long- or short-term, but from a much more far-reaching consequence of the rationality postulates employed. The maintenance of democratic institutions would be, on Downs's account, what Olson calls a collective good[8] (a public park is another example), a good which cannot feasibly be witheld from any individual in the group if it is supplied to any other. Consequently, unless the group is very small, there is only a tiny chance that the contribution of the single individual X to the cost of providing the good would make all the difference between the good's being provided and not being provided. So for any particular elector, to participate in politics would be a waste of effort, whether there were enough irrational citizens to keep the benefits of democratic government flowing to him, or whether there weren't. The chance that his

[7] For an elaboration of the argument of this paragraph, see Mancur Olson Jr., *Logic of Collective Action*, Cambridge, Mass., 1965, and Brian Barry, *Sociologists, Economists, and Democracy*, London, 1970.
[8] Ibid., p. 14.

effort would make a crucial difference is microscopic. Even a thorough-going altruist would do better to devote his time to good works, rather than to politics. And the same argument will apply to participation in any mass political or industrial action, unless there are selective incentives offered to members individually on condition that they help to bear the costs. (Australian democracy, with its penalties for not voting, may thus survive where others fail.)

The hypotheses proposed by Downs and Olson are relatively strong and open to falsification, precisely because their requirements for rational action are not so weak as to be consistent with any intentional action whatsoever.[9] Though the concept of 'selfishness' or 'self-interest' may be looser than one would wish, rational action is specifically said by both authors to exclude any acts save those done for the expected advantage of the individual himself, or of those in whom he has particular interest, and, more particularly, to exclude any done solely with reference to some intrinsic valued property of the act itself. By contrast, a recent work by W. H. Riker and P. C. Ordeshook[10] adopts far weaker requirements, extending the range of conditions that could count as costs and benefits to include any consideration whatsoever that someone could have as his reason for action. In this way the act of voting is rationally accounted for, despite the low expected utility of the consequent policy outcomes, by adding to its utility 'the satisfaction of complying with the ethic of voting', that of 'affirming allegiance to the political system', 'affirming one's partisan preference', and so on. The only substantive restriction on rational action is that any expected benefit that can count to offset the costs must be stateable in terms of satisfactions *resulting* from acting, rather than from something inherent in the act itself. But this amounts not to an explanatory hypothesis, but to a methodological prescription or procedural requirement that every consideration claimed as affecting a decision must be expressed in terms of a calculus of

[9] In Chapter 10 'Rationality and political behaviour', of Benn and Mortimore (eds.), op. cit., I have examined the Downs-Olson method in political science in rather more detail. The present essay draws on material included in that chapter, but for quite different purposes.

[10] *Introduction to Positive Political Theory*, Englewood Cliffs, 1973.

utilities and probabilities. The explanatory force of the theory is reduced to the research recipe: If the net costs seem too heavy to make an act plausible that has nonetheless been done, find some compensatory benefit to account for it; conversely, if the expected net benefits should have been large enough to excite action that nevertheless did not take place, look for some countervailing costs.

Riker and Ordeshook aim to provide a single explanatory and predictive schema, to be expressed formally in symbolic functions, into which all the intentional considerations affecting political action can be fed, and from which determinate predictions and retrodictions can then be derived. Unhappily, we are not told how to assign determinate and commensurable values to the variables, and without that, the equations are empty. If the voter's actually going to vote is both *explicandum* and the only available evidence that the satisfaction of affirming his allegiance to the political system exceeds his dissatisfaction in getting wet on his way to the poll, no progress will have been made towards a genuinely explanatory hypothesis, despite all the formulae.[11]

A disadvantage of such theories is that, by lumping together as satisfactions all the considerations that someone might entertain as reasons for action, they obscure the distinction between acting for the sake of some expected advantage to which the action is believed to be a means, and acting for the sake of a principle or from duty—between what Max Weber called *Zweckrationalität* and *Wertrationalität*.[12] The point of a *zweckrational* action— that for the sake of which it is done—lies in the value attached to some consequence of doing it (which may, of course, be a state of mind subsequent to the act); the point of a *wertrational* act, if not immediately evident, can be explained only by exhibiting it as an instance of some principle or ideal of conduct. In that sense, it is true, something done for its own sake may be done for the sake of something else: but it would be a caricature to

[11] For a more extensive critique of the theoretical model proposed by Riker and Ordeshook, see my paper 'Rationality and political behaviour' cited above.

[12] See Max Weber, *Economy and Society,* ed. G. Roth and C. Wittlich, New York, 1968, pp. 22-6. Whether Weber meant precisely what I mean by *Wertrationalität* is open to argument. But since my purpose is theory analysis, not exegesis, it is not important for this essay.

say that it is done for the sake of the satisfaction of having done it. For there would often be no satisfaction either in doing or having done it had the agent no prior belief that it was worth doing apart from the satisfaction. But leaving aside the psychological and moral importance of Weber's distinction, one would expect that, since both styles of political behaviour can doubtless be found, something useful could be discovered about the differences between systems that foster and accommodate them in different degrees. So one might reasonably doubt the heuristic value of a model that deliberately obscured the distinction, making the taxonomy necessary for such inquiry difficult to formulate.

III

In Chapter Six of *Democracy and Illusion,* John Plamenatz makes a number of points against what he calls 'neo-utilitarian theories of democracy'. Among them is the criticism that these theories pay very little attention to the so-called ultimate ends such as the satisfaction of wants, to which they point to explain or justify the practices or principles that interest them.[13] Plamenatz makes a distinction between a person's private ends and those which he has as an official in an organisation. He questions the value of an interpretation of action couched wholly in terms of private ends, taking no account of the way in which a person's ends are shaped by his social roles.

> Though everyone [he says] has both personal and social aims, the theorist who wants to explain social rules and practices as means to satisfying wants or achieving goals seems always to have personal aims in mind. And yet... people not only have both social and personal aims; they also quite often choose between them, sometimes preferring social to personal aims, and sometimes the other way about. (p. 165)

For Downs's 'self-interest axiom' Plamenatz suggests substituting a 'minding one's own business axiom', viz.:

[13] John Plamenatz, *Democracy and Illusion,* London, 1973, p. 159.

that men do often set greater store by their private aims
(which may or may not be egoistic) than by the official aims of
the organizations or communities they belong to, when the
two kinds of aims conflict, *except when they are themselves
acting in an official capacity.* (p. 157)

There is at least an inkling of this in Downs. For though he
never expressly distinguishes what I have called 'role-
rationality'— acting to optimise in terms of aims appropriate
to one's role— this does seem to be one component of his
'political rationality'. His difficulties arise from his failure to
show how acting in this way could ever be a rational agent's
preferred course, given that the expected utility of promoting
private, family, or business interests would generally be
greater and require a different course.

Revising Downs in the light of Plamenatz, we might
develop a social schema along the following lines. Everyone
has not one but a multiplicity of first order rankings. One of
these ranks his plain likes and dislikes—his preference for
apples rather than oranges or for being at liberty rather than
in gaol. This I shall call his personal preference ranking. But
besides this one, there is a ranking of states corresponding to
each of the roles he acknowledges as his own; and this ranking
too is his. For instance, if he believes that some particular kind
of schooling would benefit his children more than any
ordinarily available, he may as a parent prefer a situation in
which they get it to one in which all children have equal
opportunities. But as a citizen, or even more perhaps as
Minister of Education, he may reverse this ordering. So
though he sends his children to a favoured private school, he
votes for a party with egalitarian educational policies, and as
Minister initiates policies penalising private schools. This
may not mean that his preferences are shifting or unstable—a
condition excluded by the standard rational decision models.
On the contrary, his seemingly discordant preferences may
be asserted quite consistently over the years. It is rather that
in situations of different types he acts in different roles; and
each role has its own appropriate preference ranking.

A person may be said to have rational or consistent
preferences, even though he acts sometimes in accordance
with a role-ranking A to procure *a* rather than *b*, sometimes in
accordance with role-ranking B to procure *b* rather than *a*,
providing there is some second-order ranking of roles such

that he can be said consistently to prefer under conditions p to act in accordance with his role A rather than B, and under q in accordance with B rather A.[14] If this second-order ranking satisfies the formal rationality condition of completeness, it would amount to a total way of life, a principle or a complex but coherent set of principles, determing for each kind of choice situation the priority (or preference-ranking) to be given to the various roles in which the individual figures in that situation. Such second-order rankings could be treated, perhaps, as setting out cues, switching the individual from one socially-defined role to another, as different social situations confront him. If regularities could be established to account for such role-recognition structures, the socially-defined requirements of different roles might still figure as preference orderings, in a decision-theory model capable in principle of accounting for social phenomena like those of democratic politics.

But such an account of role-performances might be much too rigid, leaving too little room for individual rationality in the acknowledgment and interpretation of roles. We cannot assume, for instance, that someone necessarily acknowledges all the social roles that society at large assigns to him. If he can get away with it, a conscript soldier may refuse to act on the ranking of options socially appropriate to that role; that is to say, in his way of life (his ranking of his role-rankings), fulfilling his military duties ranks high only when that is a necessary means of avoiding outcomes, like detention, low on his personal preference ranking. So his military role-ranking figures in his total preference scheme not as an independent first-order ranking that could on occasion take precedence over his personal preferences, cued in at appropriate points by his second-order ranking; instead, it appears only instrumentally, as a means of optimising in terms of his personal preferences. Indeed, there may be some other role-ranking which dominates his personal ranking and on that

[14] See Stephan Körner, 'On the coherence of factual beliefs and practical attitudes', *Amer. Phil. Q.*, Vol. 9, 1972, pp. 1-17, for a discussion of the coherence of preference orderings, which, though not associating attitudes with roles, goes far more deeply and more carefully than I have here into the relations of attitudes of different levels. See also Chapter 7 of the same author's *Experience and Conduct*, Cambridge, 1976.

account dominates too the subordinate preference for doing his military duty. Membership of a subversive political party might be a role of this kind.

Just as a person need not acknowledge all the roles society assigns to him, so his role-rankings, even in respect of roles he does acknowledge, need not be strictly what others expect of someone in that role. We may disapprove of someone's decisions in the exercise of a role not only because we have different factual beliefs from his about the probable outcomes, but also because we differ in the ranking of ends that we deem appropriate to someone bearing that role; for instance, we may disagree about the propriety of a university teacher's propagating some ideological view in his courses, while agreeing that he may properly do so in a public meeting. Such differences arise commonly from disagreements about the point of an institution.

The heuristic attraction of role-theory in social science lies in the promise that it will dispense with the need to investigate the motivations of individuals, once the roles constituted by a social system and the bearers of those roles have been identified. But if the plain decision-theory model, sketched in this section, turned out to require very extensive modification to accommodate vagaries of individual selection and interpretation of roles, this advantage would disappear unless some equivalent regularities in the assumption of second-order rankings could be established. A theory like Downs's does seem to have to recognise that political choices may sometimes reflect personal preferences and sometimes role-preferences other than political ones. It certainly needs some hypothesis about the kind of second-order ranking that would explain why a number of electors sufficient to keep the system going should choose to act in accordance with their civic role on polling day despite the minuscule probability for any particular individual that his contribution would be decisive. But, at the same time, it has to account for the reluctance of more than a relative handful to become more deeply involved, even though the abstainers might recognise that their civic role requires it of them. On reflection, this may not be so difficult after all. Leaving aside a person's personal preferences, for staying home on a rainy night and so on, he has other calls on time and energy arising from his other roles in the social groupings and activities in which he is caught up, whether as family man or as member of the darts team at the local. Voting, of course, is a ritual act with strong symbolic significance; so his ranking of role-rankings may assign to the performance of his civic role *on polling day* a high priority over other preferences, whether private or role-dependent. But the sustained interest, inquiry, and activity traditionally thought necessary to give point to voting is likely to be far more costly in terms of his other ends. If the probability of a policy payoff from political participation is very low, a second-order principle would have to rank acting in one's civic role very highly indeed, if these more exacting and everyday performances are preferred to the competing demands of other more immediate roles, let alone to personal enjoyments. Unless, of course, one just enjoys politics.

The Downsian kind of theory is meant to explain democratic institutions using the standard formal conditions of rational choice, supplemented by only a few general substantive conditions. But to account for the actual social mix of electoral participation and apathy, more elaborate substantive conditions may be needed. It may depend on the distribution in a society of different substantive second-order preference rankings, which only particular descriptions of socialization and culture patterns could explain. The more diverse the preference rankings in terms of which rational agents optimize, the less illuminating the decision-theory models become.

But that, of course, does not close discussion of the rationality of participation: it simply casts doubt on the adequacy of the standard rational decision-theory models to capture all the reasons that there might be for participating. I try, in the rest of this paper, to broaden that model, to accommodate, as rational, some participatory acts, undertaken for non-consequentialist reasons, without, however, abandoning the essentials of the social action schema that has been sketched above.

IV

People who favour general participation in politics often claim that political cultures that provide plenty of opportunities for participation at low political levels, foster ways of life that rank participation highly at all levels. For even though the issues at low levels commonly seem less weighty, the chances of one's intervention being effective are much higher than in national politics; so one's belief in the importance of politics, cultivated by the more encouraging experience, spills over into the area where the payoffs of individual action are far less evident. Supposing this to be true, the motivation lacking in the Downs-Olson model would be supplied by the socialisation patterns engendered by the system itself. This is rather like saying that the market economy works (so far as it does) because socialisation into it involves coming to value making profits, maximising one's income, and so on; thus it provides the motivation necessary to keep it going. Still, there are many critics of the market economy—among them participationists—who could claim that this is an instance of a formally rational system sustaining itself only by perpetuating the irrational or alienated attitudes or goals necessary to it. Is there any reason for seeing the participationists' own claim differently? What reason can there be for favouring social arrangements that tend to produce people who care about acting in their political roles? Is there any reason to prefer, among all the possible rankings of role-preferences, some member of the sub-set that rates political participation highly? And would such a reason necessarily presuppose a third-order ranking, itself only one of a set, preferred in the light of a fourth, and so in an infinite regression? Or could something else count as a reason for the participationist preference?

Participationists' reasons generally fall into two broad classes, one instrumental, the other educational or developmental.[15] The form of the first type is that other values,

---

[15] For summary expositions of participationist arguments, see Geraint Parry, 'The idea of political participation' in G. Parry (ed.), *Participation in Politics*, Manchester, 1972, pp. 3–38, and C. Pateman, *Participation and Democratic*

such as justice, freedom, the interests or the rights of the governed, will be protected or promoted only if citizens are vigilant and active. But while this is an argument for valuing the cultivation of participationist preferences in others, it is not an argument for having them for oneself. Unless there is some intrinsic payoff like comradeship to be had, why not benefit from having second-order preference rankings different from those of most other people, so that one can get on with the things one simply likes doing and does well, or attend to the demands of other roles where action may have a more immediate point?

The second kind of reason is that people participating in collective decision-making develop certain morally desirable properties, notably a sense of responsibility both for themselves and for others. Whether or not this is true, it would still have to be shown that a disposition to participate was either a casually or a logically necessary condition for being a morally responsible person. Certainly, one might legitimately doubt whether a person was morally responsible in the required sense if he refused to do his share when that put extra burdens on other people or significantly weakened the collective effort. But failure to join in mass politics is clearly not such a case. Consider someone who is already mature and responsible, who does not shirk in small group politics, where shirking would clearly matter, but who has no special skills that might give him unusual influence in national politics; what reason has he for continuing to be active as member of the rank and file? Perhaps, like Candide, the rational man would learn from his youthful experience of political action the wisdom of cultivating his garden, and like *Candide's* author retire to his Ferney to do humble good works among his neighbours.

Participation in national politics can be rational, then, for anyone who simply enjoys it, or who sets great store by fulfilling his political role. Someone else who cares about certain values like freedom and justice may have a reason, given certain empirical assumptions, for favouring conditions tending to generate such preferences in others. But

Theory, Cambridge, 1970. See also J. S. Mill, *Representative Government,* Chpater III, where most of the standard arguments appear at least in embryo.

would he be irrational or in some other respect defective if, having other interests of his own, he put them very much before performance of his own responsibilities as a citizen?

V

There is something distasteful in the picture of the man who sits comfortably at home applauding the readiness of others to bear the heat and burden of the day, recognising how necessary they are, and how fortunate he is that so many of his fellow citizens are more politically inclined than he is. One feels his attitude to be pusillanimous in part no doubt because one accepts the implied paradigm of epic and dangerous struggles against injustice. Someone taking a more indulgent and less dramatic view of politics, who described it, perhaps, as 'attending to the general arrangements of a set of people'[16] or who, like the pluralist political scientists of a few years back, viewed the political scene as a field of manoeuvre in which competing interests arrived at more or less reasonable accomodations by consent, would be less censorious towards the bystander. There are political battles to be fought, and it is well that there are those ready to fight them; but there are other important things to be done too, and it wouldn't do (some would say) if we all neglected them for the sake of politics.

Suppose, however, one is less complacent; suppose one is very conscious of injustice and oppression all around; can one still claim that because anything one did oneself to put it right would make little difference, there can be no reason for voting, joining protest demonstrations, writing letters to the press, contributing funds or whatever, unless one happens to care for that sort of thing? My intuitive response to such a claim is to reject it, to say that for any morally responsible person there can be a reason, under some conditions at least, for caring for that sort of thing whether it ranks high among

---

[16] Michael Oakeshott's phrase; see his 'Political education' in his *Rationalism in Politics*, London, 1962, p. 112.

his personal preferences or not. But I confess that I find no
form of utilitarian argument that would adequately support
this.[17] I am inclined to think, however, that there may be a
kind of action the rationality of which, having to do with
consistency conditions for having attitudes and expressing
them, is not easily captured by utilitarian or preferential-
optimisation models. A good deal of political activity that
may properly be called unprofitable by a utilitarian may be
rational enough in this sense.

Imagine that the participationist's educational process has
achieved Mill's aim of making someone a morally responsible
person. Though politics ranks low among his personal
preferences, he does care a great deal about the freedom and
justice and the rights and welfare of others. I cannot go into
the question whether having such attitudes can be rational, or
whether rationality can be attributed to attitudes at all except
in a relational way. I must limit myself to asking whether,
having the attitudes he does, he can be rationally committed
by that alone to participate in politics even, say, for the sake of
a lost cause.

Now the notion of a morally responsible person is not as
clear as one would like. The following characterisation seems
to me, however, not particularly eccentric. In the first place,
he is someone with a conception of himself as agent rather
than process, as a subject with a capacity not only for making a
difference to the way the world goes, but for choosing for
reasons that it should go this way rather than that. He is
conscious, that is, that it matters which course he chooses.
Such a person will have—and know he has—enterprises
which he will judge successes or failures by certain standards.
He will learn to assess not only his enterprises but also himself
as their author. Indeed, he will be inclined to think of himself
as a success or a failure as a person to the extent that he
respects his own enterprises and achievements, appraising
them by standards he acknowledges as his own.

[17] Besides the critical discussion of utilitarian ways of
dealing with 'threshold' problems, in David Lyons, op.
cit., see Sec. 5 'Integrity', of Bernard Williams's essay 'A
critique of utilitarianism' in J. J. C. Smart and B.
Williams, *Utilitarianism*, Cambridge, 1973, for a
characterisation of a non-utilitarian reason for action with
which I am broadly in agreement.

Of course, the kinds of enterprises he cares about, and the standards by which he makes his assessments, will be in large measure the products of a socialization process. But as a rational chooser, he has the capacity to examine these standards critically, to test them for coherence with one another and with his experience, and by various analogical, extrapolatory, or re-combinatory operations to extend the range of his sympathies and of his creative enterprises. In such ways he makes himself a person of some particular kind, defined by the things he cares about. And he can be held responsible for what he is. For to the extent that he actually goes through the developmental process I have described, he is his own author, the object of an over-arching enterprise, the making of himself. And he will have certain beliefs about what he is that will entitle him to expect certain kinds of action from himself in appropriate situations. Given the structure of attitudes that he identifies as his own personality, there will be some things that to contemplate them with indifference would be to give the lie to what he believes himself to be, and to have made. To be indifferent would not be true to his nature, as we say.

My characterization of the morally responsible person has been pretty formal, concerned principally with the categorial framework of his self-perception. But I have attributed to him, too, certain substantive attitudes—concerns for justice, freedom, and the rights of others. Now there can be injustice and oppression around the parish pump, no less than in Whitehall and Westminster. Where the collective decision-making process is virtually face-to-face, an individual's intervention may well be decisive, so that these high-order concerns can generate instrumental reasons for participating in that process. But can they provide reasons for involvement in national politics?

Now there may be fortunate times and places in which deep indignation is not excited by political issues, when a person need find in them no challenge to his good faith. At such times one would not expect every morally responsible person's way of life to assign a high ranking position to his role as a citizen. It may well be open to someone whose natural inclinations are non-political, even for someone who, as I have postulated, cares deeply for justice and freedom, but who finds plenty that is worth-while doing in his other activities, to take the detached view I attributed earlier to the political pluralist. But repression, cruelty, and injustice can exist on a greater scale perhaps in the field of national politics than in any other area of human activity; and when they do, a person who makes the claim to himself that he cannot condone them surely has reason enough for demonstrating where he stands. For what would it mean to care deeply for freedom and justice if one did not express one's concern in any of the standard ways on those occasions when its objects were abused? To remain passive and silent then would seem inconsistent with being the sort of moral agent one claims to be, with the moral concerns one claims to have. For political activity is the standard way in which concerns of this sort are expressed. Short of some very powerful countervailing concern, one could not be a morally responsible person in the sense I have outlined, with a concern for the principal moral ideas, yet select for oneself a way of life that assigned a low ranking to one's political roles even in conditions such as these.

I am suggesting, in short, that political activity may be a form of moral self-expression, necessary not for achieving any objective beyond itself (for the cause may be lost), nor yet for the satisfaction of knowing that one had let everyone else know that one was on the side of the right, but because one could not seriously claim, even to oneself, to be on that side without expressing the attitude by the action most appropriate to it in the paradigm situation.

Someone will ask, no doubt, why the expression must be in one of the standard ways. If it makes no appreciable difference to the outcomes how or whether a given individual expresses his attitudes, why should he not choose some private or less exacting mode of expression, like singing political songs in the bath, or some mode that he chooses quite at random to count as expressing his attitude— slowing down, say, as he drives past the Post Office?

Now it may well be that attitudes closely linked to emotions, such as anger, can express themselves in a variety of ways, some highly idiosyncratic, like grimacing or cracking one's knuckles. But principled attitudes seem not to be like that. The smaller the possibility that the relevant states of affairs will be significantly altered by the individual's decision, the more strictly the expressive act must conform to some socially understood pattern for expressing that attitude.[18] Blowing up a tailor's shop[19] can be an act of political participation when it is part of a concerted terrorist strategy, each incident of which can reasonably be expected to make a significant contribution to the outcome. But an isolated explosion would be no more an act of political participation than would a mugging in the park. To be understood as political, a participatory act must either be calculated to effect a political outcome, such as a change of policy, or it must be more or less ritualistic, an act conventionally understood to betoken a concern for some principle or ideal characteristically and importantly at issue in governmental decision-making. There is no property of an act as such that is either necessary or sufficient to characterise it political. Sitting down at a bar and tooting a Morse V have both counted as political at different times. But in all such cases the act is symbolic and ritualistic in its context, where no actual change can be brought about by doing it. Still, the necessity that obliges the man of political principles to adopt such expressive modes is not that he wants others to understand the nature of his protest (though he very likely will want that too.) In a highly efficient police state he may know that his dissident vote will be known to scarcely anyone, and even if he breaks the windows of the Ministry they will be repaired before daylight. It is rather that only by using such standard modes can the protester claim, even to himself, to have made his protest, to have expressed his attitude, and so to have been true to himself.

It is no accident, of course, that an attitude like a concern for freedom, justice, or respect for rights should be most aptly expressed by acts in the political mode. For the rule utilitarian answer to this kind of problem is right thus far: if all the people who felt deeply about an ideal expressed their

[18] I arrived at the formulation of this paragraph only after a fruitful discussion of these points with Mr W. L. Weinstein, whose helpful criticism and suggestions I gratefully acknowledge.

[19] Gieves, a fashionable tailoring establishment in Mayfair, was bombed by Irish terrrorists in 1975. Other bombings, mainly of restaurants in the same district, followed in rapid succession. A cumulative effect was clearly hoped for, and the selection of resorts of wealthy and supposedly influential people was evidently part of the strategy.

attitude in the standard ways, the ideal would have a better chance of being realised than if they sang songs in the bath about it. So if freedom and justice are important, there is a reason for approving of our mode of conceptualisation, of our making a conceptual connection between having such attitudes and expressing them in political ways. This is to see in our making this connection a kind of functional rationality, akin to the functional rationality of voting that I referred to earlier—the rationality of a practice necessary to the survival of the approved system, but instrumentally irrational for each voter in particular, since his action is hardly ever indispensable. In the same way it may be claimed that participationist attitudes are functionally rational for a just and free society; a demiurge contriving such a society would have fixed us up with such a set of concepts. But that is quite different from saying either that it is the utility of the individual's participatory act as promoting freedom and justice that makes it rational—for this does so only to a microscopic degree; or that it is the utility of the rule that people fulfil their civic responsibilities that provides the individual with a reason for conforming to it—for his own conforming will have little to do with the efficacy of the rule. His only good reason for action may be that he is committed to participation by his claim to care about the principle which is its *telos*.